AN INTRODUCTION

TO

ASTROLOGY

BY

WILLIAM LILLY

*WITH NUMEROUS EMENDATIONS, ADAPTED TO THE
IMPROVED STATE OF THE SCIENCE*

Newcastle Publishing Company, Inc.
Hollywood, California
1972

A Newcastle Book
ISBN 0-87877-014-3
First Printing August 1972
Printed in the United States

PREFACE.

AFTER a lapse of 205 years since the first publication, in 1647, of *Lilly's Introduction to Astrology*, there would be no necessity for an apology for its re-appearance, were it not for the prevailing fashion of the day, which is to rail at and vituperate that science, and all who dare to say a word, not in its favour, but in favour of examining into its merits, with a view to ascertain what were the grounds on which our honest ancestors believed, and strictly followed, that which we conceive only fit for ridicule. As I have long outlived the days when I, like many others, thought myself at liberty to laugh at, and condemn, what I did not understand ; the world will forgive me if I be bold enough to advise those who value truth, to spend a few days (and but a few days will be necessary) in examining the principles laid down in this work, and applying them to their own individual cases, before they join the herd of learned and unlearned in pledging their words to a false assertion, viz. that Astrology is an unfounded science. If any man will take the trouble to examine for himself, and should find that the prejudices of his education against the science of foreseeing the future, and many other matters which it teaches, are in reality well-founded, and that it has no claims to truth, then will he have the proud satisfaction of knowing, that his opinions on a matter of some consequence are based on experiment, and are the result of his own conviction, not of another person's assertion.   On the other hand, if he find truth flash with lightning force upon his mind, and convince him that Astrology, notwithstanding prejudice and abuse, is founded in nature, and is indeed a noble science, given by a benevolent Creator to enlighten man in his wanderings, and enable him to shun the vice and folly which his passions throw in his path; then will he, if a spark of piety exist within his breast, offer thanks to that Creator for the blessing he has discovered.   In either case, he must admit that I do him a service in putting forth this plain and simple means of discovering the truth.

This is " the age of enquiry;" and yet prejudice continues to press down her leaden foot upon the neck of examination in this matter.   I can only attribute the pitiable fact to the circumstance of there being no recent publications on those parts of Astrology which are the most easily acquired. The art of *Nativities* requires many years of patient experimenting before it can be well understood, and practised with certainty and satis- faction. The art of *Atmospherical Astrology*, and also that of *Mundane Astrology*, alike demand much time to penetrate their arcana, and a good education to follow their practice. Hence we may account for their com- paratively confined study : few have either the abilities or the opportunity to wrestle with their difficulties.

But *Horary Astrology*, the chief subject in this work, may be speedily learned by any person of even moderate abilities ; and may, as far as regards its elementary difficulties, be mastered in a few days' study. It may be well understood, and reduced to constant practice in less than a quarter of a year, and no one will find him- self at a loss for occasions to test its reality or its utility ; for his own avocations, and the affairs of his friends, will offer these almost daily. If a proposition of *any nature* be made to any individual, about the result of which he is anxious, and therefore uncertain whether to accede to it or not, let him but note the hour and minute when it was *first* made, and erect a figure of the heavens, as herein taught, and his doubts will be instantly re-

solved. He may thus, in five minutes, learn infallibly
whether the affair will succeed or not; and, consequently, whether it is prudent to adopt the offer made
or not. If he examine the sign on the 1st house of the
figure, the planet therein, or the planet ruling the sign,
will exactly describe the party making the offer, both in
person and character; and this may at once convince
the inquirer for truth of the reality of the principles of
the science.

Moreover, the descending sign, &c. will *describe his
own person and character*; a farther proof of the truth
of the science, if he require it. Here, then, is a ready
test of the *truth* of Astrology. Will its adversaries dare
to make its application? It would, methinks, be better
than relaxing the broad muscles, which ever denote
ignorance and surprise, the feelings which, combined
are the undoubted source of laughter; the only argument
of the idiot, the ready resource of the ignorant.

In editing this work, my chief object has been to
render it useful to the student in Astrology and so, by
forwarding the science, to promote the general interests
of humanity.

With this view I have re-written those parts of the
work which modern discoveries in Astronomy and
Astrology have rendered obsolete. *Tables for calcu-*

lating Nativities and a *Grammar of Astrology* are adjoined, and every ingredient of the science given which the student is likely to require.

As regards the deviations I have made from the rules of the author, they are few, and founded on much experience. I have omitted his chapters on nativities, as in that part of the science he was less perfect than in any other; the reason being that he relied on essential dignities, which are, by my experience, of little, if any, avail. The rules for calculating arcs of direction will be found in the *Grammar*.

In conclusion, I have no desire to offend any class of men by putting forth this work: I do not know whether I should not respect even prejudice, for the sake of peace, were it not that I cannot conscientiously consent to abandon truth in the effort. I am callous to the puny efforts of critics who may desire to pour on me the waters of vituperation or ridicule, having already passed through a flood. After many years' experience, I have found the laws of Astrology unfailing; and as I can discover no prohibition of its practice in the Word of God, I am prepared to defend it against all the foolish attacks of those who falsely declare that it upholds fatality, or is opposed to the providence or the revelation of the Deity. And I am contented, with God's blessing, to give up the ghost in the firm persuasion, that, in maintaining what I believe is the truth in this respect, I shall meet, hereafter, through the goodness of God and the merits of my Saviour, with a merciful judg ment.

I am, reader, your devoted friend and well-wisher in all science which may honour God and benefit man kind

ZADKIEL.

TABLE OF CONTENTS

OF THE INTRODUCTION TO ASTROLOGY.

LIFE OF WILLIAM LILLY.

In offering an abstract of the most valuable of this clever astrologer's works to the notice of the public, I consider myself called upon to make some mention of his personal history. And it fortunately happens that this is not made up of imaginary ideas, founded on a few known facts, and a multiplicity of suppositions; for what we know of this man of extraordinary talent rests on the best evidence. He undertook, in his sixty-sixth year, to write a history of his own life to his "worthy friend," Elias Ashmole, Esq., afterwards *Sir* Elias Ashmole, the founder of the celebrated museum which bears his name. Mr. Ashmole made marginal notes therein, which testify his high opinion of our Author; and, fortunately for the cause of Astrology, this gentleman verified the correctness of the Figures of Heaven, which are given in the subsequent pages; for we find the following note at the foot of page 131 :—" *I devised the forms and fashions of the several schemes, E. A.*" This note was made after these observations of Lilly. "The desire I had to benefit posterity and my country, at last overcame all difficulties; so that what I could not do in one year, I perfected early the next year, 1647; and then in that year, viz. 1647, I finished the third book of nativities; during the composing whereof, for seven whole weeks, I was shut up of the plague, burying in that time two maid-servants thereof; yet, towards November that

b

vear, the Introduction, called by the name of *Christian Astrology*, was made publick."

The fact of this work having been chiefly composed under
such awful circumstances, with a dreadful death immediately
before his eyes, with the pestilence ravaging his own household, might, with unprejudiced men, have been taken as a
proof that the writer was sincere in what he wrote ; and
really believed in the truth of that which he taught to others
as truth under the solemn appeal to Almighty God, which is
so beautifully worded in his introductory epistle.   Modern
critics, however, can see no force in this argument, but un-
hesitatingly condemn *William Lilly* "as an accomplished
impostor, and a knavish fortune-teller."*   Such, reader, is
the force of prejudice.   It will not allow men to examine before they condemn ; for if it did, then would the literary
world speedily acknowledge the reality of those doctrines
which our Author has so ably set forth in the following pages.

William Lilly was born of an honest yeoman family, in the
town of " Diseworth, seven miles south of the town of Derby,
on the first day of May, 1602."   At eleven years old he was
sent to Ashby de la Zouch, to be instructed by one Mr. John
Brindley.   Here he says he learned the following authors,
viz., *Sententiæ Pueriles, Cato, Corderius, Æsop's Fables,
Tully's Offices, Ovid de Tristibus ;* lastly, *Virgil*, then *Horace;*
as also *Camden's Greek Grammar, Theognis*, and *Homer's
Iliads;* and entered *Udall's Hebrew Grammar*.   In the
eighteenth year of his age his master "was enforced from
keeping school, being persecuted by the Bishop's officers ;"
and our Author was "enforced to leave school."   He then
kept school himself for " one quarter of a year."   On Monday,
April 3rd, 1620, he left Diseworth and came to London,
where he was compelled to accept the humble situation of a

* Retrospective Review, vol. ii. p. 51.

footboy, nis father being then "in Leicester gaol for debt," and, of course, incapable of doing much for his son. He had only seven shillings and sixpence left when he arrived at London, having "footed it all along" with the carrier. In 1624 his mistress died, having given him "five pounds in old gold." After which he lived "most comfortably," his master having a great affection for him. In 1626 his master married again, having first settled on our Author twenty pounds a year, which he enjoyed all through life. In October, 1627, he was made free of the Salters' Company. And on the "eighth day of September, 1627," married his master's widow, this same lady; and they "lived very lovingly" until her death, October, 1633.

In the year 1632 he began to study Astrology, being instructed in the rudiments by one Evans, a Welshman, of indifferent abilities. Lilly tells us that he applied himself to these interesting studies "many times, twelve, or fifteen, or eighteen hours, day and night;" adding, "I was curious to discover whether there was any verity in the art or not." By this his first wife he acquired a fortune of "very near to one thousand pounds." In the year 1634 he purchased the moiety of thirteen houses in the Strand, for which he gave £530. The figure of the heavens, erected on this occasion, will be found in the following pages. November the 18th, 1634, he married again, and had £500 portion with that wife. "She was of the nature of Mars," and he lived not very lovingly with her, as seems by his observations at her death. He appears to have now practised horary astrology with success, and to have instructed numerous individuals in the art; among others he taught John Humphreys, in the year 1640, for which service he received forty pounds. He also wrote, in the year 1639, a Treatise on the Eclipse of the Sun, May 22d, 1639; and appears, about that period, to have turned his attention much to Mundane Astrology.   He says,* "I did carefully, in 1642 and 1643, take notice of every grand action which happened betwixt king and parliament; and did first then incline to believe, that, as all sublunary affairs did depend upon superior causes, so there was a possibility of discovering them by the configurations of the superior bodies; in which way making some essays in those two years, I found encouragement to proceed further, which I did: I perused the writings of the ancients, but therein they were silent, or gave no satisfaction; at last, I framed unto myself that method which then and since I follow, which I hope, in time, may be more perfected by a more penetrating person than myself."

He appears to have dabbled a little in magic also, but he soon "grew weary of such employment," and burned his books.   Lilly's better sense led him to perceive which of these studies was worthy of an honest and intelligent man's pursuit, and which not.

About April, 1644, he first published *Merlinus Anglicus Junior*.   This work contained some of his most remarkable predictions, and was continued for many years.   It attracted much attention, and was the means of adding greatly to the fame of our Author as an Astrologer.   In that year he printed the *White King's Prophecy*, "of which were sold, in three days, eighteen hundred;" and some other works of like nature, the *Prophetical Merlin*, &c.

In 1645 he was twice had before a Committee of the Parliament, for some observations in his *Starry Messenger;* but he escaped, partly by means of his numerous friends, and partly by his own ingenuity.

In 1647, when he published the present work, he was introduced to General Fairfax, who paid him and his art some

* See p. 101 of Lilly's History of his Life and Times.

compliments. In this year he was consulted by King Charles I., as to a safe place to conceal his royal person ; but the King, unfortunately for himself, neglected Lilly's advice, and was accordingly ruined. Again, in 1648, the King consulted Lilly ; but though he promised to take the Astrologer's advice, and come up to London with the Commissioners, he did not, however, keep his word, and again lost a good opportunity of escaping from his evil destiny.

" In this year," says Lilly, " for very great considerations, the council of state gave me in money fifty pounds, and a pension of one hundred pounds *per annum*, which for two years I received, but no more." In January 1649 he was present at the trial of King Charles, " who spoke," says he, " excellently well."

In 1651 he published *Monarchy or No Monarchy*, which contained several hieroglyphics ; among others those of the great plague and fire of London, which the reader will find a copy of in this work.

These celebrated predictions were made by means of the motions of the fixed stars, as is evident by the words of Lilly ; who says, " the asterisms and signs and constellations give greatest light thereunto." The *Bull's North Horn*, a star which, Ptolemy says, is " like Mars," was, in the year 1666, when the fire occurred, in ♊ 17° 54', which is the exact ascendant of London. It was, no doubt, by this means Lilly judged the city would suffer by fire ; for in his Almanac for 1666 he states, that the 19th degree of ♊ is London's horoscope. Our Author was not very nice in his calculations ; and it may be observed, that though it may be called the 19th degree, being within 6 minutes of it, yet, in reality, ♊ 17° 54' is the true ascendant of London. It was that which ascended at the moment of *driving the first pile of the new London Bridge*.

The longitude of the *Bull's North Horn*, 1st January, 1834 . . . .   Ⅱ 20° 15'

Longitude of London's ascendant . . .   Ⅱ 17 54

———

Difference 2 21

This difference of 2° 21' is equal to 8460 seconds of longitude, which, divided by 50⅓" (the rate at which the fixed stars proceed yearly), gives 168.

From the year 1834

Take away 168

———

1666

it gives the year when that evil star was crossing the ascending sign of London.   And as it is of the *fiery* nature of Mars, we need not be surprised that it produced such terrific results.   The celebrated *Nostradamus* had predicted the same event in that year, about 111 years previously, as follows :—

> " Le sang du juste à Londres fera faute
> Bruslez par feu, de vingt et trois, les six."

The blood of the just, which has been spilt in London, requires it to be burned with fire in sixty-six.   He states that he made this prediction by " Astronomical Affections."

In 1651 Lilly was again had before the Parliament, on account of his predictions, and was thirteen days in the custody of the Serjeant-at-Arms.   But the prediction which gave offence, viz. that the " Parliament stood upon a tottering foundation, and that the commonalty and soldiery would join together against them," was amply fulfilled by the members being turned out of doors by Oliver Cromwell.

In February, 1654, his second wife died ; and in October following he married a third, signified, in his nativity, " by *Jupiter in Libra ;* and," says he, " she is so totally in her conditions. to my great comfort."

In 1655 he was indicted at Hicks's Hall by a half-witted young woman. The cause of the indictment was, that he had given judgment upon stolen goods, and received two shillings and sixpence; contrary to an act made in King James's time.

"I owned," says he, "the taking of half-a-crown for my judgment of the theft, but said, that I gave no other judgment but that the goods would not be recovered, being that was all which was required of me. I spoke for myself, and introduced my own *Introduction* into court, saying, that I had some years before emitted that book for the benefit of this and other nations; that it was allowed by authority, and had found good acceptance in both Universities; that the study of Astrology was lawful, and not contradicted by any scripture; that I neither had, or ever did, use any charms, sorceries, or enchantments, related in the bill of indictment,' &c. The jury, who went not from the bar, brought in, No true Bill."

"In 1666 happened," says our Author, "that miraculous conflagration in the city of London, whereby, in four days, the most part thereof was consumed by fire." He then gives an account of his being brought before the House of Commons by the following summons :—

MONDAY, 22nd OCTOBER, 1666.

"At the Committee appointed to enquire after the causes of the late fires :—

"ORDERED,

"That Mr. Lilly do attend this Committee on Friday next, being the 25th of October, 1666, at two of the clock in the afternoon, in the Speaker's chamber, to answer such questions as shall be then and there asked him.

"ROBERT BROOKE."

In remarking on the circumstance, he says, "I conceive there was never more civility used unto any than unto myself; and you know there was no small number of parliament men appeared, when they heard I was to be there."

"Sir Robert Brooke spoke to this purpose:—

"'Mr. Lilly, this Committee thought fit to summon you to appear before them this day, to know, if you can say anything as to the cause of the late fire, or whether there might be any design therein. You are called the rather hither, because, in a book of your's long since printed, you hinted some such thing by one of your hieroglyphics.' Unto which I replied,

"May it please your honours,

"After the beheading of the late King, considering that in the three subsequent years the parliament acted nothing which concerned the settlement of the nation's peace, and seeing the generality of the people dissatisfied, the citizens of London discontented, the soldiery prone to mutiny, I was desirous, according to the best knowledge God had given me, to make enquiry by the art I studied, what might, from that time, happen unto the parliament and nation in general. At last, having satisfied myself as well as I could, and perfected my judgment therein, I thought it most convenient to signify my intentions and conceptions thereof in forms, shapes, types, hieroglyphicks, &c., without any commentary, that so my judgment might be concealed from the vulgar, and made manifest only unto the wise; I herein imitating the examples of many wise philosophers who had done the like. Having found, Sir, that the city of London should be sadly afflicted with a great plague, and not long after with an exhorbitant fire, I framed these two hieroglyphicks, as represented in the book, which, in effect, have proved very true."

"Did you foresee the year?" said one.—"I did not," said

I, " or was desirous ; of that I made no scrutiny." " I pro-
ceeded :—'Now, Sir, whether there was any design of burning the city, or any employed to that purpose, I must deal
ingenuously with you ; that, since the fire, I have taken much
pains in the search thereof, but cannot, or could not, give
myself any the least satisfaction therein. I conclude that it
was the finger of God only ; but what instruments he used
thereunto I am ignorant.'

" The Committee seemed well pleased with what I spoke,
and dismissed me with great civility."

After this, nothing very remarkable happened to our Author.
He left London, having acquired an independence, and settled at Hersham, in the year of the great plague, 1665. He
then applied himself diligently to the study of physic, and on
the 11th October, 1670, he received a licence to practise as a
physician. He continued to practise with much success, no
doubt by applying his astrological science thereto ; and he
gave his advice and prescriptions freely, without money. His
skill and his charity gained him extraordinary credit and estimation.

He continued generally in good health till August, 1674 ;
but his health and his eyesight remained very weak afterwards. He still continued to write his monthly observations
and astrological judgments, though latterly by aid of an
amanuensis (Mr. Henry Colley, who succeeded him as an
astrologer), even until the year 1682.

In the beginning of 1681 he was seized with a flux, which
he recovered from, but then became totally blind. The 30th
of May of that year he was seized with a dead palsy ; and,
after some days of severe suffering, he died about three o'clock
on the morning of the 9th of June, 1681, "without any shew
of trouble or pangs."

He was buried in the chancel of Walton Church, his friend,

Sir Elias Ashmole, assisting at the laying him in his grave, which was "on the left side of the communion table."

A black marble stone was afterwards placed thereon by his friend, with the following inscription :—

Ne Oblivione Conteretur Urna

GULIELMI LILLII

ASTROLOGI PERITISSIMI

QUI FATIS CESSIT

Quinto Idus Junii Anno Christo Juliano

MDCLXXXI

Hoc Illi posuit amoris Monumentum

ELIAS ASHMOLE

ARMIGER.

"*An Epistle to the Student in Astrology.*

"My Friend, whoever thou art, that with so much ease shalt receive the benefit of my hard studies, and doest intend to proceed in this heavenly knowledge of the starres; In the first place, consider and admire thy Creator, be thankfull unto him, and be humble, and let no naturall knowledge, how profound or transcendant soever it be, elate thy mind to neglect that Divine Providence, by whose al-seeing order and appointment all things heavenly and earthly have their constant motion: the more thy knowledge is enlarged, the more doe thou magnify the power and wisdome of Almighty God: strive to preserve thyself in his favour; for the more holy thou art, and more neer to God, the purer judgment thou shalt give.

"Beware of pride and self-conceit: remember how that long agoe no irrationall creature durst offend man the Macrocosme, but did faithfully serve and obey him; so long as he

was master of his own reason and passions, or until he sub-
jected his will to the unreasonable part. But, alas! when
iniquity abounded, and man gave the reins to his own affection, and deserted reason, then every beast, creature, and
outward harmfull thing, became rebellious to his command.
Stand fast (oh, man) to thy God: then consider thy own
nobleness; how all created things, both present and to come,
were for thy sake created; nay, for thy sake God became
man: thou art that creature, who, being conversant with
Christ, livest and reignest above the heavens, and sits above
all power and authority. How many pre-eminences, privi-
leges, advantages, hath God bestowed on thee: thou rangest
above the heavens by contemplation, conceivest the motion
and magnitude of the stars: thou talkest with angels, yea,
with God himself: thou hast all creatures within thy dominion, and keepest the devils in subjection. Doe not, then,
ior shame deface thy nature, or make thyself unworthy of
such gifts, or deprive thyself of that great power, glory, and
blessednesse, God hath allotted thee, by casting from thee his
favour for possession of a few imperfect pleasures.

"Having considered thy God, and what thyself art, during
thy being God's servant, now receive instruction how in thy
practice I would have thee carry thyself. As thou daily con-
versest with the heavens, so instruct and form thy mind according to the image of Divinity: learn all the ornaments of
virtue, be sufficiently instructed therein: be humane, curtius,
familiar to all, easie of accesse: afflict not the miserable with
terrour of a harsh judgment; direct such to call on God to
divert his judgments impending over them: be civil, sober,
covet not an estate; give freely to the poor, both money and
judgment: let no worldly wealth procure an erronious judgment from thee, or such as may dishonour the art. Be sparing
in delivering judgment against the common-wealth thou livest

in ; avoyd law and controversie : in thy study be *totus in illus*, that thou mayest be *singulus in arte*. Be not extravagant, or desirous to learn every science ; be not *aliquid in omnibus;* be faithfull, tenacious, betray no ones secrets. Instruct all men to live well : be a good example thyselfe ; love thy own native country ; be not dismaid if ill spoken of, *conscientia mille testes*. God suffers no sin unpunished, no lye unrevenged. Pray for the nobility, honour the gentry and yeomanry of England ; stand firme to the commands of this parliament ; have a reverent opinion of our worthy lawyers, for without their learned paines, and the mutual assistance of some true spirited gentlemen, we might yet be made slaves, but we will not ; we now see light as well as many of the clergy. Pray, if it stand with God's will, that monarchy in this kingdom may continue, his Majesty and posterity reigne : forget not the Scottish nation, their mutual assistance in our necessity, their honourable departure. God preserve the illustrious *Fairfax*, and his whole armye, and let the famous city of London be ever blessed, and all her worthy citizens.*

"WILLIAM LILLY."

* I have retained the exact orthography of this epistle, which is a curious and interesting remnant of our author's day. It was penned in 1647.—ED.

INTRODUCTION TO ASTROLOGY.

CHAPTER I.

THERE are in the heavens several bodies which appear to shed their light directly on this Earth; and also some others which, having no light of themselves, serve to reflect that of the Sun, and thereby become visible to our organs of sight. The former are termed *Fixed Stars*, because they appear to retain the same situation, or to be fixed in the same place; but the latter, being observed to wander, are termed Planets. The number and distance of the former are so extensive, that I shall take no further notice of them here, than to observe, that they are not much used in that portion of Astrology which is denominated *Horary*, and that those persons who desire to make use of them in nativities, will find their right ascensions and declinations given with great accuracy in the Nautical Almanack for each year. In the Appendix to this work, I shall give rules, to ascertain their latitude and longitude by trigonometry, for the benefit of such persons as may be curious to make experiments as to their influence; though I do not, in general, pay much attention to them when judging a nativity.

Of the Planets.

These are ♅ Herschel, ♄ Saturn, ♃ Jupiter, ♂ Mars.

⊙ So., the Sun,* ♀ Venus, ☿ Mercury, and ☽ Luna,
Moon.   These characters have been always in use, and may,
(with the exception of ♅,) be traced to the remotest antiquity, and their origin found among the hieroglyphics of
Egypt.   But as the object of this work is practical utility,
no more need be said on the subject.

The Signs of the Zodiac.

They are twelve, each containing 30 degrees, thus making
360 degrees, into which every great circle is divided.   The
first six are,

Northern Signs.

♈ Aries, ♉ Taurus, ♊ Gemini, ♋ Cancer, ♌ Leo, ♍ Virgo.

Southern Signs.

♎ Libra, ♏ Scorpio, ♐ Sagittary, ♑ Capricorn, ♒ Aquarius, ♓ Pisces.

The first sign, ♈, commences the zodiac, its beginning
being that spot in the heavens where the Sun is when crossing the equator in spring ; and the latter sign, ♓, finishes
the circle of the zodiac, the latter end of it being that spot
in the heavens where the Sun is when he has gone his round,
and is again about to enter ♈.

By referring to the annexed diagram, the student will perceive, that when the Sun enters ♈ (about the 21st of March)
he proceeds northward, and *increases in declination* until he
reaches the tropic of ♋ Cancer (about the 21st of June),
when he speedily begins to return to the south; and when
he reaches ♎, he again crosses the equator (about the 23d or
September), where, having no declination, he causes equal

* The Sun and Moon are considered as planets in all astrological
matters.

day and night all over the world.   He then *declines away to the south ;* shortening our days in the northern hemisphere, until he reaches the southern tropic ♑, Capricorn ; at length he returns towards the equator, and crosses it by entering the sign ♈ (about the 21st of March), where again he has no declination, and gives equal days and nights.

Diagram of the Sun's Motion in the Zodiac.

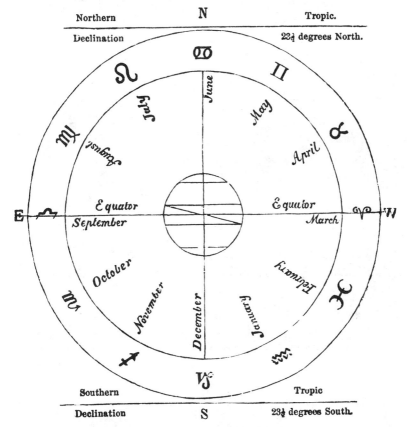

EXPLANATION.—The space between the two outer circles may be considered as the line of the Sun's motion ; and then

the sign opposite the name of each month will shew where
the Sun is about the 21st of each month. The globe in the
centre may be taken for the Earth, the northern parts of
which receive the greater portion of the Sun's light in summer, and the southern parts in winter.

These signs are divided into,

Northern Signs . . . . ♈, ♉, ♊, ♋, ♌, ♍.
Southern Signs . . . . ♎, ♏, ♐, ♑, ♒, ♓.
Tropical Signs . . . . ♋, and ♑.
Equinoctial Signs . . . . ♈, and ♎.
Double-bodied Signs . . . ♊, ♍, ♐, ♓.

They are again divided into

Moveable. . . . . . . ♈, ♋, ♎, ♑.
Common . . . . ♊, ♍, ♐, ♓.
Fixed . . . . ♉, ♌, ♏, ♒.

Also into

Fiery . . . . ♈, ♌, ♐.
Earthy . . . . ♉, ♍, ♑.
Airy . . . . ♊, ♎, ♒.
Watery . . . . ♋, ♏, ♓.

The student must become well acquainted with the above
particulars ; but especially so with the northern and southern
signs, the former being *opposite* to the latter. By attending
to this, he will readily come to understand the figure of the
heavens, and the relative situations of the planets.

N.B. The moveable, common, and fixed signs are always
in *square* aspect to each other, three signs apart ; and the
fiery, earthy, airy, and watery signs are always in *trine* aspect
to each other, four signs apart.

THE DRAGON'S HEAD AND TAIL

The Moon's north node is known by the character ☊,

termed the Dragon's Head; and her south node by this ☋, termed the Dragon's Tail. The former of these in horary questions denotes good, and is considered of the character of ♃, and increases the good qualities of a benefic, with which it may be found; and diminishes the evil of a malefic planet. The latter is of the nature of ♄, and does the reverse. In nativities these characters have no avail, and are not to be considered, except with regard to the Moon, who is found to produce good or evil when she reaches them by direction.*

The Part of Fortune.

This is that spot in the heavens which is equally distant from the degree ascending that the Moon is from the Sun. It is found by the following rule :—

To find the (⊕) Part of Fortune in a Nativity.

Add 90° to the right ascension of the meridian, and it will give the oblique ascension of the ascendant. From the oblique ascension of the ascendant subtract the oblique ascension of the Sun (having first added 360° to the former, if necessary); to the remainder add the right ascension of the Moon: the sum will be the right ascension of ⊕.

The ⊕ is always *under* the horizon *before* the full Moon, and *above* the horizon *after* the full Moon. Having found its right ascension, take it from that of the meridian above or below the earth, according as it may be situated; or, take that of the meridian from it, and the sum or difference will shew the distance of ⊕ from the cusp of the 10th or 4th house.

---

* These nodes are the points in the ecliptic where the Moon crosses from north into south latitude, or the reverse, which occurs twice each month.

C

Example :—A. R. of midheaven . . .   221° 5′

Add thereto 90 0
_____

Oblique asc. of the ascendant .   311 5

Subtract oblique asc. of ☉ . .   17 34
_____

293 31

Add right ascension of the ☽ .   345 34
_____

639 5

Take away. 360 0
_____

It leaves right ascension of ⊕ .   279 5

Then, as the birth took place after full Moon, and the ⊕ will be above the Earth, find the difference of right ascension between it and the meridian above the Earth.

Thus :   Right ascension of ⊕ . . . .   279° 5′

Right ascension of the midheaven.   221 5
_____

Distance of ⊕ from the 10th house   58 0

If the ⊕ be in the same hemisphere as the ☽ ; that is, if both be above or below the Earth, it will have the semi-arc of the ☽ ; but if otherwise, it will have the opposite semi-arc ; which may be found by taking the ☽'s from 180°. In this nativity (which is that of the Duke of Wellington) the semi-arc of the Moon is 90° 57′, which taken from 180° leaves the semi-arc of ⊕ 89° 3′, two-thirds of which are 59° 22′ ; and it appears that ⊕ is just 1° 22′ outside the cusp of the 12th house.*

The ⊕ has no influence on the *health or life* of the native ;

* This is found by taking its distance from the 10th 58° 0′ from ⅔ of its semi-arc 59° 22 .

but it influences the pecuniary affairs very powerfully, and also, in some degree, the profession or employment.*

To find the Place of ⊕ in the Figure of a Horary Question.

In horary astrology ⊕ is merely a symbol, and has much to do with all questions regarding property, loss or gain, &c. In this case it is found by a more simple rule, as follows :—

Add together the longitude of the ascendant and longitude of the ☽, from which subtract the longitude of the ☉: the remainder will be the longitude of ⊕.

Example :—Where was the ⊕ at 3h. 20m. P.M. 28th of December, 1644 ?†

	Signs	deg.	min.
The Ascendant was ♋ 11° 33, or	3	11	33
The ☽ was in ♉, 16° 49′, or	1	16	49
	4	28	22
For subtraction add	12	0	0
	16	28	22
The ☉ in ♑, 17° 54, or	9	17	54
Place of ⊕ in the figure	7	10	28

or ♏ 10° 28′.

* In proof of this, it is evident that in the Duke's nativity ☽ came to ♂ of ⊕ in November 1834, when he was appointed to the ministry. Thus ⊕ is 58° from the meridian, and ☽ 124° 29,; the difference is 66° 29′; which arc of direction, added to the right ascension of ☉ at his birth 39° 21′, gives 105° 50′, the right asc. of ♋ 14° 34′. The ☉ arrived at this point at 1 P.M. 6th July 1769, or 65 days 13 hours after birth, which, the Placidian measure of a year for a day, gives 65 years 6½ months, the Duke's age when the event occurred.—N.B. The ascendant came to ♂ of ☉ at the same time, which, by referring to our author's rules for the effects of directions, will be seen to cause such eminent preferment. The semi-arc of ☉ is 68° 13′, ☉ dist. from 4th house 1° 44′; the difference is 66° 29′, the arc of direction.

† See the figure.—Question. " A ship at sea, if lost ?"

CHAPTER II.

Fig. 1.

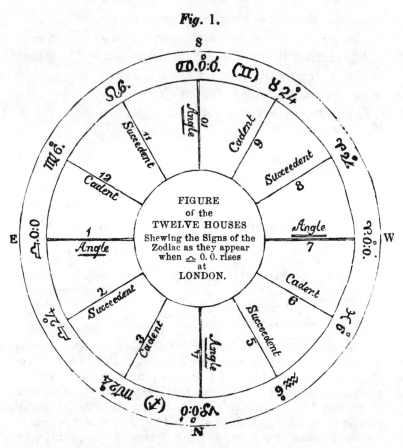

EXPLANATION.—In the above figure the ANGLES and the succeedent and cadent houses appear at one view. The 1st house embraces 24° of longitude in the zodiac, viz. from ♎ 0° 0′ to ♎ 24°; the 2nd house contains 30°, viz. from ♎ 24° to ♏ 24°; the 3d house contains 36°, viz. from ♏ 24° to

♑ 0° 0', being 6° of ♏ and the whole of ♐ ; the 4th house contains 36°, viz. the whole of ♑ and 6° of ♒ ; the 5th house
contains 30°, viz. from ♒ 6° to ♓ 6° ; and the 6th house
contains 24°, viz. from ♓ 6° to the end of that sign, or ♈
0° 0'.—N.B. The other *six* houses will be found to embrace
exactly the same number of degrees of the opposite signs of
the zodiac ; the 7th being opposite to the 1st, the 8th to the
2d, &c. If the student look for ♋ 0° 0' on the 10th house
in the table of houses for London, he will find the longitude
of the six *eastern* houses, as here noted ; and, of course, the
six opposite or *western* houses have the same degrees of the
opposite signs on their cusps.

OF ERECTING A FIGURE OF THE HEAVENS.

THIS is merely a map to represent the heavens at any particular moment, such as when a child is born, or a question
asked, &c. In the first place, draw three circles, as in *figure*
1 ; and then draw lines to represent the horizon, and others,
at right angles with them, to represent the meridian : thus
will be shewn, the natural divisions formed by the rising and
setting of the Sun, and by his passing the meridian at noon
and midnight. Each of these quarters or quadrants is to be
again divided into three equal parts, forming

The Twelve Houses.

These are marked from No. 1 to No. 12 ; and it will be observed, that the double lines 1 and 7, which represent the
eastern and western horizons, and those marked 4 and 10,
which represent the meridians below and above the Earth,
are the cusps or commencement of the *angles*. Those lines
numbered 2, 5, 8, and 11, are the cusps of the *succeedents*,
so called because they follow or *succeed* to the angles. These
houses are next in power to the angles. Those lines marked
3, 6, 9, and 12, are the cusps or beginnings of the *cadent*

houses ; so called because they are *cadent*, that is, *falling* from the angles : these are the weakest of all the houses.

Thus the student will perceive, that if a planet, &c. be in one of the *angles*, it is powerful ; if in a *succeedent* house, it is less powerful ; and if in a *cadent* house, it is weak and in· capable of effecting much either good or evil.

Rule to erect the Figure of the Heavens at any Time.

1. Learn in an ephemeris* for the year what was the right ascension of ⊙ at the noon previous to the required time, in hours, minutes, and seconds. To this right ascension add the number of hours and minutes which have elapsed since that noon :† the sum will be the right ascension in time of the meridian above the Earth (the mid-heaven) at the required time.

2. Find the longitude answering to this right ascension, in the column marked 10th house in the Table of Houses, which longitude is to be marked over the line which denotes the mid-heaven or 10th house.

3. In a line with this will be found the longitude on the cusps of the 11th, 12th, 1st, 2d, and 3d houses ; which copy out from the table, and enter over the lines which denote those respective houses.

4. Having thus completed the *six eastern* houses, find the signs and degrees exactly opposite to each of them, and enter it over the cusps of the opposite or western houses, in the following order :—

| 10th house | opposite | 4th house |
| 11th | do. | 5th |

* Ephemeris signifies a journal or Almanac, in which the places of the planets, &c. for each day are registered. For all years before 1834. *White's* is the best.

† This time must first be corrected for the error of the clock, by, add-ing what the clock is too slow, or subtracting what it is too fast.

12th	opposite	6th house
1st or ascendant	do.	7th
2d	do.	8th
3d	do.	9th

5. Having thus completed the figure, as far as regards the signs of the zodiac, it now remains to place in the planets as they may be situated. The most distant from the ☉ is ♅, whose longitude is generally given in the ephemeris for each ten days, and if the time of the figure fall between it, it must be found by proportion. When his longitude is found, write it in the figure, thus, ♅ 13° 19′, just by the cusp of the house, which falls in the same sign in which ♅ is found. If the cusp be farther on than the planet in the sign, place the planet *outside* the cusp ; but if the planet be the farthest advanced in the sign, place it *inside* the cusp. After having entered ♅, enter in the same way ♄, then ♃, ♂, ☉, ♀ ☿ and the ☽. To find the exact longitude of these seven, which is usually given for the noon of each day, find the distance they travel in longitude between the two noons preceding and succeeding the time of erecting the figure; and then take the proportional part for the time after the previous noon, and add it to, (or if the planet be retrograde subtract it from), the planet's longitude for the previous noon.

6. Find the longitude of ☊ in the same manner, and enter it accordingly, and place ☋ in the sign and degree and minute exactly opposite thereto.

7. If it be a horary question, calculate the place of ⊕, and enter it accordingly ; when the figure of heaven will be complete. But if it be a nativity, you must calculate the ⊕ according to the rule given, first having prepared a Speculum, or Table of Data, as taught in *Chap.* 9 of the *Grammar of Astrology.*

CHAPTER III.

OF THE ASPECTS.

THE figure of the heavens being erected, it now remains to observe how the planets are situated as regards each other; or, in other words, how they are aspected.   And, first,

Of Zodiacal Aspects.

These are as follow :—

Semi ⚹, a Semi-sextile, or 30 degrees.

Semi ◻, a Semi-square, or 45 degrees.

⚹, a sextile, or 60 degrees.

A Quintile, or distance of 72 degrees.

◻, a Square, or quartile, 90 degrees.

△, a Trine, or distance of 120 degrees.

A Sesquiquadrate, or square and a half, 135 degrees.

A Biquintile, or double quintile, 144 degrees.

☍ an Opposition, 180 degrees.

Good aspects are the semi-sextile, sextile, quintile, trine, and biquintile.

Evil aspects are the semi-square, square, sesquiquadrate, and opposition.—N.B. The conjunction, marked thus ☌, s when two planets are in the same degree and minute of the zodiac: when it is exact, it is very powerful, and is called a *partile* ☌; but if within the planets' orbs, it is called a *platic* conjunction, and is less powerful.   To know whether it should be considered at all, the orbs of the two planets should be added together, and one-half the sum taken; if the planets be beyond that distance, they are not even in platic ☌.   The same holds good with regard to other aspects.

The orbs of the cusps of the houses are 5°, so that if a

planet be one-half its orb and 5° more distant from a house, it is not in aspect to that house; the same if the *aspect* of the planet fall beyond that distance from the cusp of any other house.

Orbs of the Planets.

♄, 9°; ♃, 9°; ♂, 7°; ☉, 15°; ♀, 7°; ☿, 7°; ☽, 12°. —N.B. ♅ has had no orb of operation discovered; but I think it may safely be considered as 7° in all horary figures, &c.

Of Mundane Aspects.

These are formed by the houses in horary astrology, and by the semi-arcs of the planets in nativities. Thus, a semi ⚹ is 1 house; a semi ▢, 1½; a ⚹, 2 houses; a ▢, 3 houses; a △, 4 houses; a sesqui ▢, 4½ houses; and an ☍, 6 houses.

The ⅓ of a semi arc is a semi ⚹; the ½ of a semi-arc is a semi ▢; the ⅔ of a semi-arc is a ⚹; the whole semi-arc is a ▢; and 1-5th less than the semi-arc is a quintile; the whole semi-arc and ⅓ more is a △; the whole semi-arc and ½ more is a sesqui ▢; the one-tenth part of a semi-arc added to a sesqui ▢, is a biquintile.—N.B. The entire arc of a planet, or double the semi-arc, will not give the measure of its distance from the opposite point of its place; but if the two semi-arcs of a planet, both diurnal and nocturnal, be added together, they make 180°, an opposition aspect.

Of Parallels.

The Zodiacal Parallel is when two planets have the same amount of declination from the equator. It is the most powerful of all aspects, but is not generally used in horary astrology.

The Mundane Parallel is an equal distance from the meridian. It is used by some horary astrologers. When any of the above aspects are formed between the planets, they are found to have a mutual influence or action on each other, according to the nature of the aspect. For example : if the ⊙ be 60 degrees (a ✳) from ♃ in any figure, it *denotes* that the person signified by the Sun is under the benefic influence of the benevolent ♃; and *shews* success according to the nature of the question. In nativities it *causes* good health and good fortune in life. But if ⊙ be 90 degrees (a □) from ♄, it *shews* discredit, a failure of hopes, &c. in a question; and in a nativity it produces much sickness to the native, and also misfortunes to his father. This was verified in the nativity of Napoleon Bonaparte's son, who was born at 9h. 15m. A.M. 20th March, 1811, when ⊙ was in 28° 53'°of ♓, and ♄ was in 26° 28' of ♐; just 92° 25 distant from each other. This very close □ aspect of ⊙ and ♄ caused great trouble to the native, through his father's misfortunes; and, as ⊙ was the hyleg, produced a consumptive disease, and early death. It is remarkable, that his father's troubles began immediately after his birth; and it will always be found in the nativity of a child, that the fortune of its parents may be ascertained thereby until the birth of another child. If, for example, the child have evil planets in the fourth house, its father will be more or less unfortunate until the birth of another child; when, if that other have ♃ and ♀ in the fourth house, the father's affairs will become more fortunate : so very beautifully do the nativities of parents and their children sympathise together.

CHAPTER IV.

OF THE TWELVE HOUSES, THEIR NATURE AND SIGNIFI-CATION.

As before we have said there are twelve signs, and also twelve houses of heaven ; so now we are come to relate the nature of these twelve houses, the exact knowledge of which is so requisite, that he who learns the nature of the planets and signs without exact judgment of the houses, is like an improvident man, that furnishes himself with a variety of household stuff, having no place wherein to bestow them. There is nothing appertaining to the life of man in this world which, in one way or other, hath no relation to one of the twelve houses of heaven ; and as the twelve signs are appropriate to the particular members of man's body, so also do the twelve houses represent, not only the several parts of man, but his actions, quality of life, and living. And the curiosity and judgment of our forefathers in astrology was such, that they have allotted to every house a particular signification ; and so distinguished human accidents* throughout the whole twelve houses. He that understands the questions appertaining to each of them, shall not want sufficient grounds whereon to judge or give a rational answer upon any contingent accident, and success thereof.

Of the FIRST House, and its Signification.†

The first house contains all that part of heaven from the line where the figure 1 stands unto the figure 2, where the second house begins : it is *one-third* of the distance between the horizon and meridian below the earth. It has significa-

---

* The term *accidents* here signifies the events of life generally.

† See *Fig* 1

tion of the *life* of man, of the stature, colour, complexion, form, and shape of him that propounds the question, or is born; in eclipses and great conjunctions, and upon the Sun his annual ingress into ♈; it signifies the common people, or general state of that kingdom where the figure is erected. And as it is the first house, it represents the head and face of man; so that if either ♄ or ♂ be in this house, either at the time of a question or at the time of birth, you may observe some blemish in the face,* or in that member appropriated to the sign that is then upon the cusp of the house; as, if ♈ be in the ascendant, the mark, mole, or scar is, without fail, in the head or face; and if few degrees of the sign ascend, the mark is in the upper part of the head; if the middle of the sign be on the cusp, the mole, mark, or scar is in the middle of the face, or near it; if the latter degrees ascend, the face is blemished near the chin, towards the neck; this I have found true in hundreds of examples. Of colours, it hath the white; that is, if a planet be in this house that has signification of white, the complexion of the party is more pale or wan; or, if you inquire after the colour of the clothes of any man, if his significator be in the first house, and in a sign corresponding, the party's apparel is white or grey, or somewhat near that colour: so also if the question be regarding cattle, when their significators are found in this house, it denotes them to be of that colour, or near it: the house is masculine. The consignificators of this house are ♈ and ♄: for as this house is the first house, so is ♈ the first sign, and ♄ the first of the planets; and therefore, when ♄ is but moderately well fortified in this house, and in any benevolent aspect of ♃, ♀, ☉, or ☽, it promises a good sober constitution of body, and usually long life; ☿ doth also joy in this

---

* This is verified in the nativity of Lord Brougham, who was born with ♄ ascending in ♏: he has a very great natural defect in the face, a nervous catching of the muscles of the mouth, &c.

house, because it represents the head, and he the tongue, fancy, and memory; when he is well dignified and posited in this house, he produces good orators;* it is called the Ascendant, because when the ☉ and planets come to the cusp of this house, they *ascend*, or then arise, and are visible in our horizon.

Questions concerning the SECOND House.

From this house is required judgment concerning the estate or fortune of him that asks the question, of his wealth of property, of all moveable goods, money lent, of profit or gain, loss or damage; in suits of law, it signifies a man's friends or assistants; in private duels, the querent's second; in an eclipse or great conjunction, the poverty or wealth of the people: in the Sun his entrance into ♈, it represents the ammunition, allies, and support the commonwealth shall have; it imports their magazines. It represents, in man, the neck and hinder part of it towards the shoulders; of colours, the green. It is a feminine house, and succeedent.

It has consignificators, ♃ and ♉; for if ♃ be placed in this house, or be lord hereof, it is an argument of an estate or fortune; ☉ and ♂ are never well placed in this house: either of them shew dispersion of substance, according to the capacity and quality of him that is either born or asks the question.†

The THIRD House

Has signification of brethren, sisters, cousins, or kindred, neighbours, small journeys, or inland journeys, often removing from one place to another; epistles, letters, rumours, messengers: it rules the shoulders, arms, hands, and fingers.

* Lord Brougham, who is one of the best orators of the age, was born with ☿ just rising.

† ☽ in this house, if in good aspect to ♃, gives the native wealth The Duke of Wellington had ☽ in this house in △ to ♃ in the 10th.

Of colours, it governs the red and yellow, or sorrel colour: it has consignificators, ♊ and ♂, which is one reason why ♂ in this house, unless joined with ♄, is not very unfortunate: it is a cadent house, and is the joy of the ☽; for if she be posited therein, especially in a moveable sign, it is an argument of much travel, trotting, and trudging, or of being seldom quiet: the house is masculine.

The FOURTH *House*

Gives judgment of fathers in general, or ever of his father that inquires, or that is born; of lands, houses, tenements, inheritance, tillage of the earth, treasures hidden; the determination or *end* of any thing; towns, cities, or castles besieged or not besieged; all ancient dwellings, gardens, fields, pastures, orchards; the quality and nature of the grounds one purchases, whether vineyards, cornfields, &c., and shews whether the ground be woody, stony, or barren.

The sign of the fourth denotes the town, the lord thereof, the governor;* it rules the breast and lungs; and of colours, the red: its consignificators are ♋ and the ☉: we call it the angle of the Earth, or *Imum Cœli :* it is feminine, and the north angle. In nativities or questions this fourth house represents fathers; so does the ☉ by day, and ♄ by night; yet if the ☉ be here placed, he is not ill, but rather shows the father to be of a noble disposition, &c.

The FIFTH *House.*

By this house we judge of children, of ambassadors, of the state of a woman with child, of banquets, of ale-houses, taverns, plays, messengers or agents for republics, of the wealth of the father, the ammunition of a town besieged; if

---

* This alludes to questions of sieges, which were too frequent in the land in the author's time

the woman with child shall bring forth male or female; or
the health or sickness of his son or daughter that asks the
question. It rules the stomach, liver, heart, sides, and back,
and is masculine. Of colours, black and white, or honey
colour; and is a succeedent house; its consignificators are
♌ and ♀, who does joy in this house, in regard it is the house
of pleasure, delight and merriment; it is wholly unfortunate
by ♂ or ♄, and they therein shew disobedient children, and
untoward.

The SIXTH House.

It concerns men and maid servants, galley slaves, hogs,
sheep, goats, hares, conies, all manner of lesser cattle, and
profit or loss got thereby; *sickness*, its quality and cause; the
principal humour offending, curable or not curable; whether
the disease be short or long; day-labourers, tenants, farmers.
shepherds, hogherds, neatherds, warreners, and it signifies
uncles, or the father's brothers and sisters. It rules the inferior part of the belly and intestines, even to the *rectum*.
The house is a feminine and cadent house, unfortunate as
having no aspect to the ascendant. Of colours, *black*; ♂
rejoices in this house, but its consignificators are the sign ♍
and planet ☿ : we usually find that ♂ and ♀ in conjunction
in this house are arguments of a good physician.*

The SEVENTH House.

It gives judgment of marriage; and describes the person
inquired after, whether it be a man or woman; all manner of
love questions; or public enemies, the defendant in a lawsuit,
in war, the opposing party; all quarrels, duels, lawsuits; in
astrology, the artist himself; in physic, the physician; thieves
and thefts, the person stealing, whether man or woman; wives,

* This alludes to questions regarding sickness, and by no means to
nativities

sweethearts, their shape, description, condition, nobly or ig
nobly born; in an annual ingress, whether war or peace may
be expected; of victory, who overcomes and who is worsted
fugitives or runaways, banished or outlawed men.   It has
consignificators ♎ and ☽ ; ♄ or ♂ unfortunate herein, shew
ill in marriage. *   Of colour, a dark black.   It rules the
haunches, and the navel, to the buttocks, is called the angle
of the west, and is masculine.

The EIGHTH *House.*

The estate of men deceased ; death, its quality and nature;
the wills, legacies, and testaments of men deceased ; dowry
of the wife, portion of the maid, whether much or little, easy
to be obtained or with difficulty.   In duels, it represents the
adversary's second ; in lawsuits, the defendant's friends;
what kind of death a man shall die; it signifies fear and an-
guish of mind;† also who shall be heir to the deceased.   It
rules the privy parts.   Of colours, the green and black.   Of
signs, it has ♏ for consignificator and ♄ .   The hemorrhoids,
the stone, stranguary, and bladder, are ruled by this house,
also poisons ; it is a succeedent house, and feminine.

The NINTH *House.*

By this house we give judgment of voyages or long jour-
nies beyond seas, of religious men, or clergy of any kind,
whether bishops or inferior ministers ; dreams, visions, foreign
countries, books, learning, church livings or benefices, and of
the kindred of one's wife or husband.   Of colours, it has the

---

* We always find that ♄, ♂, or ♅, in this house are *causes* of ill-fortune in marriage, or the married state, in nativities, let them be aspected
how they will ; and in questions, we have no opinion of them, though
ever so strongly dignified.   The Duke of Wellington had both ♄ and ♂
in the 7th, and was unfortunate in marriage.

† This alludes to the significator of the querent being placed in the
8th house.

green and white ; of man's body, it rules the fundament, the hips, and thighs ; ♃ and ♂ are consignificators of this house; for if ♃ be herein placed, it naturally signifies a devout man in his religion, or one modestly given. I have often observed when the Dragon's tail, ♄, or ♂ have been unfortunately placed in this house, the querent has either been little better than an atheist or a desperate sectarian.* ☉ rejoices to be in this house, which is masculine and cadent.

The Tenth House.

Commonly it personates kings, princes, dukes, earls, judges, prime officers, commanders-in-chief, whether in armies or towns ; all sorts of magistracy and officers in authority, also mothers ; honour, preferment, dignity, office, lawyers, professions or trade ; it also signifies kingdoms, empires, dukedoms, counties ; it has of colours red or white, and rules the knees and thighs. It is called the *medium cœli*, or midheaven, and is feminine. Its consignificators are ♑ and ♂ . Either ♃ or the ☉ are very fortunate in this house, especially when they are placed together ; ♄ or ☋ usually deny honour as to persons of quality, and to the vulgar little prosperity in profession or trade.

---

* This merely alludes to horary questions, and can have no kind of *influence* this way, these things being at the most *symbols* of a good or bad man ; for in nativities the mind is influenced by the Moon and Mercury only. The error of confounding these two branches of the science, nativities, in which the planets are *causes* (under God) of events, and horary questions, in which they are only *signs* of the events, has been the chief means of bringing this sublime science into disrepute. This error appears to have arisen from the low state and condition of astronomy in the middle ages, when, even as late as the days of Charles II., Dr. Goad, his physician, assures us that the astronomers could not calculate an opposition of the planets ♃ and ♄ nearer than a week. How, then, can it be expected that the judgments of astrologers should have always been correct, when the very data on which they depended were often erroneous?

The ELEVENTH *House.*

It does naturally represent friends and friendship, hope, trust, confidence, the praise or dispraise of any one ; the fidelity or falseness of friends. As to kings, it personates their favourites, counsellors, servants, their associates or allies ; their money, exchequer or treasure ; in war, ammunition and soldiery, it represents courtiers, &c. In a commonwealth, governed by a few of the nobles and commons, it personates their assistance in council ; as, in London, the tenth house represents the lord mayor ; the eleventh, the common council, the ascendant the generality of the commoners of the said city. Of members, it rules the legs to the ancles ; of colours, saffron or yellow. It has ☉ and ♒ for consignificators : ♃ especially rejoices in this house. It is a succeedent house, and masculine, and in virtue is nearly equivalent either to the seventh or fourth house.

The TWELFTH *House.*

It has signification of private enemies, great cattle, or horses, oxen, elephants, &c. ; sorrow, tribulation, imprisonment, all manner of affliction, self-undoing, &c. ; and of such men as maliciously undermine their neighbours, or inform secretly against them. It has consignificators ♓ and ♀. Saturn does much delight in that house, for he is naturally the author of mischief. It rules, in man's body, the feet. In colour it represents the green. It is a cadent house, and feminine.

This is the true character of the several houses, according to the Ptolomeian doctrine, and the experience I have had myself for many years. I must confess the Arabians have made several other divisions of the houses ; but I could never, in my practice, find any verity in them ; therefore I will say nothing of them.

CHAPTER V.

OF SATURN, AND HIS SIGNIFICATION.

HE is the supremest or highest of all the planets,* **and is** placed between Jupiter and the firmament; he is not **very** bright or glorious, nor does he twinkle or sparkle, but is **of a** pale or wan ashy colour; slow in motion, finishing his **course** through the twelve signs of the zodiac in 29 years, 167 **days,** and 5 hours, or thereabouts. His mean motion is two **minutes** and one second; his diurnal motion sometimes is three, four, five, or six minutes, seldom more; his greatest north latitude from the ecliptic is 2 degrees 48 minutes; his greatest south latitude is 2 degrees 49 minutes.

In the zodiac he has two of the twelve signs for his houses; viz. Capricorn ♑, his night house; Aquarius ♒, his day house. He is exalted in ♎, receives his fall in ♈, and rejoices in the sign Aquarius, ♒. He governs the airy triplicity by day, which is composed of ♊, ♎, ♒.

If in any question he be in any degree wherein he has a term, he cannot be said to be peregrine, or void of essential dignities; or if he be in any of those degrees allotted him for his face or decanate, he cannot then be said to be peregrine : understand this in all the other planets.†

He continues retrograde 140 days; is five days in his first stage before retrogradation, and so many in his second station before becoming direct. He is cold and dry (being far removed from the Sun); melancholy, earthy, masculine; and the greater infortune, author of solitariness, malevolent, &c.

When well dignified, he is profound in imagination, in his

* This was true, as far as the author knew; the planet Herschel not having been then discovered.

† For the terms, &c., see the table of Essential Dignities

acts severe, in words reserved, in speaking and giving very
spare ; in labour patient, in arguing or disputing grave, in obtaining the goods of this life studious and solicitous, in all
manner of actions austere.*

When ill dignified, he is envious, covetous, jealous, and
mistrustful; timorous, sordid, outwardly dissembling, sluggish,
suspicious, stubborn ; a contemner of women, a liar, malicious, murmuring ; never contented, and ever repining.

Corporature.—Most part of his body cold and dry ; of a
middle stature, his complexion pale, swarthy or muddy ; his
eyes little and black, looking downward ; a broad forehead,
black or sad hair, and it hard or rugged ; great ears, hanging,
lowering eyebrows, thick lips and nose ; a rare or thin beard,
a lumpish, unpleasant countenance, either holding his head
forward or stooping ; his shoulders broad and large, and many
times crooked ; his belly somewhat short and lank ; his thighs
spare, lean, and not long ; his knees and feet ill made ; and
frequently striking against each other, with a shuffling gait.

Saturn *Oriental.*—You must observe, if Saturn be oriental
of the Sun, the stature is more short, but decent and well
composed.

Saturn *Occidental.*—The man is more black and lean, and
fewer hairs ; and again, if he wants latitude, the body is more
lean ; if he have great latitude, the body is more fat or fleshy ;
if the latitude be south, more fleshy, but quick in motion. If
north, hairy and much flesh.

♄ in his first station, a little fat ; in his second station, fat,
ill-favoured bodies, and weak ; and this observe constantly in
all the other planets.

Quality of Men.—In general ♄ signifies husbandmen,

* By these descriptions is meant, that persons signified in horary questions by this planet are of such a character; and if he influence the
native by being in the ascendant at the time of birth, it applies also in
nativities.

clowns, beggars, day labourers, old men, fathers, grandfather, monks, jesuits, sectarians.

Employment. — Curriers, night-farmers, miners under ground, tinners, potters, broom men, plumbers, brickmakers, maltsters, chimney-sweepers, sextons of churches, bearers of corpses, scavengers, hostlers, colliers, carters, gardeners, ditchers, chandlers, dyers of black cloth, and herdsmen, shepherds, or cow-keepers.

Sicknesses.—All impediments in the right ear, or teeth; all quartan agues proceeding from cold, dry and melancholy distempers, leprosies, consumptions, black jaundice, palsies, tremblings, vain fears, fantasies, dropsy, the hand and foot gout, apoplexies, too much flux of the hemorrhoids; and *ruptures,* if in Scorpio or Leo, in any ill aspect with Venus.

Orb.—His orb is nine degrees before and after; that is, his influence begins to work when either he applies or any planet applies to him, and is within the half of nine degrees added to the half of that planet's orb, and continues in force until he is separate an equal distance.

Years.—The greatest years he signifies is 465. His greater 57; his medium years 43½; his least 30. The meaning whereof is this: admit we frame a new building, erect a town or city, or a family, or principality is begun when Saturn is essentially and occidentally strong, the astrologer may probably conjecture the family, principality, &c. may continue 465 years in honour, &c. without any sensible alteration. As to age, he relates to decrepit old men, fathers, grandfathers; the like in plants, trees, and all living creatures.

Places.—He delights in deserts, woods, obscure vallies, caves, dens, holes, mountains, or where men have been buried, churchyards, &c.; ruinous buildings, coal-mines, sinks, dirty and stinking places, houses of office, &c.

Countries.—Late authors say he rules over Bavaria, Saxony, Stiria, Romandiola, Ravenna. Constantia. Ingoldstadt.

CHAPTER VI.

OF THE PLANET JUPITER, AND HIS SIGNIFICATION.

JUPITER is placed next to Saturn. He is the greatest in appearance to our eyes, of all the planets (the ⊙, ☽, and ♀ excepted): in his colour he is bright, clear, and of an azure hue. In his motion he exceeds Saturn, finishing his course through the twelve signs, in 14 years, 314 days, and 12 hours; his middle motion is 4 minutes 52 seconds. His greatest north latitude is 1° 38′. His greatest south latitude is 1° 40′. He is retrograde about 120 days, is five days in his first station before retrogradation, and four days stationary before direction.

Nature.—He is a masculine planet, temperately hot and moist, and the *greater fortune;* author of temperance, modesty, sobriety, justice.

Manners and Actions when well placed.—Then he is magnanimous, faithful, bashful, aspiring in an honourable way at high matters; in all his actions a lover of fair dealing, desiring to benefit all men; doing glorious actions; honourable and religious, of sweet and affable conversation, wonderfully indulgent to his wife and children, reverencing aged men, a great reliever of the poor, full of charity and godliness; liberal, hating all sordid actions; just, wise, prudent, grateful and virtuous; so that when you find ♃ the significator of any man in question, and well dignified, you may judge him well qualified as aforesaid.

When ill dignified.—When ♃ is unfortunate, then he wastes his patrimony, suffers every one to cozen him, is hypocritically religious, tenacious, and obstinate in maintaining false tenets in religion; he is ignorant, careless, nothing caring for the love of his friends; of a gross. dull capacity;

systematical, abasing himself in all companies, insinuating and stooping where no necessity is.

Corporature.—He signifies an upright, straight, and tall stature; brown, ruddy, and lovely complexion; of an oval or long visage, and full or fleshy; high forehead; large grey eyes; hair soft, and a kind of auburn brown; much beard; a large deep belly; strong proportioned thighs and legs, his feet long, being the most uncomely parts of his body; in his speech he is sober, and of grave discourse.

Oriental.—The skin more clear, his complexion honey colour, or between a white and red, sanguine, ruddy colour; great eyes, the body more fleshy; generally some mole or scar on the right foot.

Occidental.—A pure and lovely complexion, the stature more short, the hair a light brown, or near a dark flaxen, and smooth; bald about the temple or forehead.

Quality in general.—He signifies judges, senators, counsellors, ecclesiastical men, bishops, priests, ministers, cardinals, chancellors, doctors of the civil law, young scholars and students in an university or college, lawyers, clothiers, woollen drapers.

Diseases.—Pleurisies, all infirmities in the liver, apoplexies, inflammation of the lungs, palpitation and trembling of the heart, cramps, pain in the back bone, all diseases lying in the veins or ribs, and proceeding from corruption of blood; quinzies, flatulence; all putrefaction in the blood, or fevers proceeding from too great abundance thereof.

Places.—He delights in being near altars of churches, in public conventions, synods, convocations; in places neat and sweet; in wardrobes, courts of justice, and oratories.* His greatest years are 428; his greater, 79; his mean, 45; least, 12.

---

* This implies, that the person inquired about in a horary question, if signified by ♃, frequents such places.

Men of middle age, or of a full judgment and discretion, are described by him. Babylon, Persia, Hungaria, Spain, Cullen, are ruled by him. *

CHAPTER VII.

OF THE PLANET MARS, AND HIS SEVERAL SIGNIFICATIONS.

MARS does in order succeed Jupiter, is less in body, and appears to our sight of a shining, fiery, sparkling colour : he finishes his course in the zodiac in 1 year, 321 days, and 22 hours : his greatest latitude north is about 4° 31′; his south, 6° 47′; and is retrograde 80 days; stationary two or three. He governs wholly the watery triplicity, viz. ♋, ♏, and ♓.

Nature.—He is a masculine, nocturnal planet, in nature hot and dry, choleric and fiery ; the lesser infortune, author of quarrels, strifes, and contentions.

Manners when well dignified.—In feats of war and courage invincible, scorning that any should exceed him ; subject to no reason, bold, confident, immoveable, contentious, challenging all honour to themselves ; valiant, lovers of war and things pertaining thereto, hazarding himself in all perils, unwilling to obey or submit to anybody ; a boaster of his own acts ; one that slights all things in comparison of victory, and yet of prudent behaviour in his own affairs.

When ill dignified.—Then he is a prattler, without modesty or honesty; a lover of slaughter and quarrels, murder, thievery, a promoter of sedition, frays, and commotions ; an highway thief, as wavering as the wind, a traitor, of turbulent spirit, perjured, obscene, rash, inhuman, neither fearing God nor

---

* We have no opinion of the rule of the planets over different countries : but in mundane astrology the signs which rule them must be observed.

caring for man; unthankful, treacherous; oppressors, **ravenous,** cheaters, furious, and violent.*

Corporature.—Generally martialists have this form; they are but of middle stature, their bodies strong, and their bones large, rather lean than fat; their complexion of a brown, ruddy colour, their visage round, their hair red or sandy, and many times crisping or curling; sharp, hazel, piercing eyes; a bold confident countenance; and they are active and fearless.

Oriental.—He signifies valiant men; some white mixed with their redness, inclined to be tall, and of a hairy body.

Occidental.—Very ruddy complexion, but low stature, little head, smooth body, and not hairy; yellow hair, stiff, and the natural humours generally more dry.

Qualities of Men and their Professions. — Generals of armies, colonels, captains, or any soldiers having command in armies; all manner of soldiers, physicians, apothecaries, surgeons, chemists, gunners, butchers, marshals, sergeants, bailiffs, hangmen, thieves, smiths, bakers, armourers, watchmakers, tailors, cutlers of swords and knives, barbers, dyers, cooks, carpenters, gamesters, bear-wards, tanners, and curriers, according as ♂ may be strong or weak.

Diseases.—The gall, tertian fevers, pestilent burning fevers, meagrims in the head, carbuncles, the plague, and all plague sores, burnings, ringworms, blisters, phrensies, mad sudden distempers in the head, yellow jaundice, bloody flux, fistulas; all wounds and diseases in men's genitals, the stone both in the reins and bladder, scars or smallpox in the face.†

---

* These extremely evil qualities obtain only when the ☽ and ☿ are also very much afflicted.

† ♂ coming to ill aspect of the ascendant by direction early in nativities generally causes either smallpox, measles, or scarlet fever; but if the nativity denote it, he may give hurts, wounds, fevers, &c.

Mars causes all hurts by iron, the shingles, and **such other** diseases as arise by too much choler, anger, or passion.

Places.—Smiths' shops, furnaces, slaughter-houses, places where bricks or charcoal are burned, or have been burned; chimneys, and forges.*

His orb is only seven degrees.

Years.—In man he governs the flourishing time of youth, and from 41 to 56; his greatest year is 264; greater 66, lower 40, and least 15.

Countries.—Saromatia, Lombardy, Batavia, Ferraria, Goth-land.

CHAPTER VIII.

OF THE SUN, HIS GENERAL AND PARTICULAR SIGNIFI-CATIONS.

THE Sun is placed in the middle of all the planets, continually visible to all mortal men. He passes through all the twelve signs of the zodiac in one year : his mean motion is 59 minutes 8 seconds, yet his diurnal motion is sometimes 57 minutes 16 seconds, sometimes more, but never exceeding 61 minutes and 6 seconds. He always moves in the ecliptic, and is ever void of latitude. He has only the sign ♌ for his house, and ♒ for his detriment. He is exalted in the 19th degree of ♈, and receives his fall in 19° ♎.

The Sun governs the fiery triplicity, viz. ♈, ♌, ♐, by day. He is always direct, and never can be considered retrograde.

In nature.—He is naturally hot and dry, but more tem-

---

* To this may be added, cutlers' shops, and places where iron is manu-factured in any manner, armouries, &c.

perate than ♂; is a masculine, diurnal planet, and equivalent if well dignified to a fortune.

Manners when well dignified.—Very faithful, keeping their promises with the greatest punctuality; a kind of itching desire to rule and sway wherever he comes. Prudent, and of incomparable judgment; of great majesty and stateliness, industrious to acquire honour and a large patrimony, yet as willing to spend it again. The solar man usually speaks with gravity, but not many words, and these with great confidence and command of his own feelings; full of thought, secret, trusty, speaks deliberately, and, notwithstanding his great heart, he is affable, tractable, and very humane to all people; one loving sumptuousness and magnificence, and whatever is honourable; no sordid thoughts can enter his heart.

When ill dignified.—Then the solar man is arrogant and proud, disdaining all men, boasting of his pedigree; he is purblind in sight and judgment, restless, troublesome, domineering, a mere vapour, expensive, foolish, endowed with no gravity in words, or soberness in actions; a spendthrift, wasting his patrimony, and hanging on other men's charity; yet he thinks all men are bound to him, because a gentleman born.

Corporature.—Usually the ☉ presents a man of a good, large, and strong corporature, a yellow, saffron complexion, a round large forehead, large goggle eyes, sharp and piercing; a body strong and well composed, not so beautiful as lovely; full of heat, with hair yellowish, and therefore quickly bald; much hair on their beard, and usually an high ruddy complexion; their bodies fleshy; in disposition they are very bountiful, honest, sincere, well-minded, of good heart; healthful constitution; very humane, yet sufficiently spirited, and not loquacious.

Oriental.—We can only say the ☉ is oriental in the figure, or in an oriental quarter of the figure, or occidental, &c.* The planets are oriental when they rise, or appear before him in the morning, and occidental when they set after him.

Quality of Men, and their Professions.—He signifies, kings, princes, emperors, &c. dukes, marquisses, earls, barons, lieutenants, deputy lieutenants of counties, magistrates, gentlemen in general, courtiers, desirers of honour and preferment. Justices of peace, mayors, high sheriffs, high constables, stewards of noblemen's houses, the principal magistrate of any city, town, castle, or country village ; yea, even a petty constable, where no better is ; goldsmiths, braziers, pewterers, coppersmiths, and minters of money.

Sicknesses.—Pimples in the face, palpitation or trembling, diseases of the brain and heart, infirmities of the eyes, cramps, sudden swoonings, diseases of the mouth and impure breath, catarrhs, putrid fevers. Principally in man he governs the heart and the brain; in women, the vital spirit, and denotes hysterics.

Places.—Houses or courts of princes, palaces, theatres, all magnificent structures, being clean and decent ; halls, and dining rooms.

Orb.—Is 15 degrees.

Years. — In age he rules youth, or when one is at the strongest; his greatest years are 1460,† greater 120, lesser 69 and least 19.

Countries.—Italy, Sicily, Bohemia, Phenicia, and Chaldea.

* In nativities the ☉ and ☽ are oriental between the 1st and 10th houses, and in the opposite quarter of the figure ; they are occidental between the 10th and 7th houses, and in the opposite quarter : but in horary questions they are oriental between the 4th and 10th, and occidental after leaving the 10th, until they reach the 4th: oriental when rising, and occidental when setting.

† It is a very remarkable fact, that this period is the *sothic* or *canicular* year of the Egyptians ; whence it is pretty evident that these astrological doctrines came originally from that people, and are, in fact, of the very highest antiquity.

CHAPTER IX.

OF THE PLANET VENUS, AND HER SEVERAL SIGNIFICATIONS AND NATURE.

Name.—After the Sun succeedeth Venus.

Colour in the Element.—She is of a bright, shining colour, and is well known by the name of the evening star, or Hesperus ; and that is when she appears after the Sun is set ; she is commonly called the morning star, but by the learned Lucifer, when she is seen long before the rising of the Sun. Her mean motion is 59 minutes and 8 seconds ; her diurnal motion is sometimes 62 minutes a-day, and 82 minutes she never exceeds. Her greatest latitude is 9° 2′. She is retrograde 42 days, and stationary 2. Her year is 224 days and 7 hours.

Element.—She is a feminine planet, temperately cold and moist ; nocturnal, the lesser fortune, author of mirth and cheerfulness.

Manners and Quality when well dignified.—She signifies a quiet man, not given to law, quarrel, or wrangling ; not vicious ; pleasant, neat and spruce, loving mirth in his words and actions, cleanly in apparel, rather drinking much than gluttonous ; prone to venery, often entangled in love matters, zealous in their affections, musical, delighting in baths and all honest merry meetings, or amusements and theatricals ; easy of belief, and not given to labour, or take any pains ; a company keeper, cheerful, nothing mistrustful, a right virtuous man or woman, often jealous, yet without cause.

When ill dignified.—Then he is riotous, expensive, wholly given to dissipation and lewd companies of women, nothing regarding his reputation, coveting unlawful beds, incestuous,

an adulterer, fantastical, a mere skip-jack, of no faith, no
repute, no credit, spending his means in ale-houses, taverns,
and among scandalous loose people ; a mere lazy companion,
nothing careful of the things of this life, or any thing religious.

Corporature.—A man of fair but not tall stature, his complexion being white, tending to a little darkness * which
makes him more lovely, very fair, lovely eyes, and sometimes
black ; a round face and not large, fair hair, smooth and
plenty of it, and it is usually of a light brown colour ; a
lovely mouth and cherry lips, the face pretty fleshy, a rolling
wandering eye, a body very delightful, lovely, and exceedingly
well shaped ; one desirous of trimming and making himself neat and complete both in clothes and body, a love
dimple in his cheeks,† a stedfast eye, and full of amorous
enticements.

Oriental.—When oriental, the body inclines to tallness or
a kind of upright straightness in person ; not corpulent or
very tall, but neatly composed ; a right Venus person is a
pretty, complete, handsome man or woman.

Occidental.—When she is occidental, the man is more short
in stature, yet very decent and comely in shape and form,
well liked of all.

Quality of Persons, and Employments.—Musicians, gamesters,
silkmen, mercers, linen-drapers, painters, jewellers, players,
lapidaries, embroiderers, woman-tailors, wives, mothers, vir-
gins, choristers, fiddlers, pipers : when joined with the ☽ :
ballad-singers, perfumers, seamstresses, picture-drawers, en-
gravers, upholsterers, limners, glovers, and such as sell those

* This signifies a pale or wan complexion, yet with a dark hue.

† Those who have Venus strong, either in their nativities, or as their
significators in questions, invariably have dimples either in the cheek or
chin.

commodities which adorn women, either in body (as clothes) or in face (as complexion waters).

Sicknesses.—Diseases by her signified are principally in the matrix and members of generation ; in the reins, belly, back, navel, and those parts ; the gonorrhœa or running of the reins, lues venerea or any disease arising from inordinate lust, priapism, impotency in generation, hernias, &c., the diabetes, or an involuntary discharge of urine.

Orb.—Her orb is 7 degrees.

Years.—Her greatest years are 151 ; her greater 82, her mean 45, her least 8. In man she governs youth from 14 to 28.

Countries.—Arabia, Austria, Campania, Vienna, Polonia the Greater, Turin, Parthia, Media, Cyprus.*

CHAPTER X.

OF MERCURY, AND HIS SIGNIFICATION, NATURE, AND PROPERTY.

MERCURY is the least of all the planets, never distant from the Sun above 28 degrees ; by which reason he is seldom visible to our sight.

Colour and Motion.—He is of a dusky silver colour ; his mean motion is 59 minutes and 8 seconds, but he is some-times so swift, that he moves above 1 degree and 40 minutes in one day. He is stationary one day, retrograde twenty-four days. His year is 87 days and 23 hours.

* These observations are retained from respect to our author ; but we must repeat, that it is ♉ and ♎ the houses of ♀, which govern these

Latitude. — His greatest south latitude is 3 degrees 35 minutes, greatest north latitude 3 degrees 33 minutes.

Nature.—We may not call him either masculine or feminine, for he is either the one or the other as joined to any planet ; for if in ♂ with a masculine planet, he becomes masculine :* if with a feminine, then feminine ; but of his own nature he is cold and dry, and therefore melancholy : with the good he is good, with the evil planets, ill ; he is author of subtlety, tricks, devices, perjury, &c.

Manners when well dignified.—Being well dignified, he represents a man of a subtle and political brain and intellect, an excellent disputant or logician, arguing with learning and discretion, and using much eloquence in his speech ; a searcher into all kinds of mysteries and learning, sharp and witty, learning almost any thing without a teacher ; ambitious of being exquisite in every science, desirous naturally to travel and see foreign parts ; a man of an unwearied fancy, curious in the search of any occult knowledge, able by his own genius to produce wonders, given to divination and the more secret knowledge. If he turn merchant, no man exceeds him in way of trade, or invention of new ways whereby to obtain wealth.

Manners when ill dignified.—A troublesome wit, a kind of phrenetic man, his tongue and pen against every man ; wholly bent to fool his estate and time in loquacity and trying nice conclusions to no purpose, a great liar, boaster, prattler, busybody ; false ; a tale-carrier, addicted to wicked arts, as necromancy, and such like ungodly knowledges ; easy of belief, an ass or very idiot, constant in no place or opinion, cheating and thieving everywhere ; a newsmonger, pretending all manner of knowledge, but void of true or solid learning ;

* This applies to aspects also ; but, of course, only in horary questions.

a **trifler,** a mere frantic fellow; if he prove a divine, then a mere verbal fellow, frothy, of no judgment, easily perverted, constant in nothing but idle words and bragging.

Corporature.—Generally he denotes one of an high stature, and straight, thin, spare body; a high forehead, and somewhat narrow long face, long nose, fair eyes, neither perfectly black nor grey, thin lips and nose, little hair on the chin, but much on his head, and of a sad brown inclining to blackness; long arms, fingers, and hands; his complexion like an olive or chesnut colour. You must observe ☿ more than all the planets; for having any aspect to a planet, he partakes more of the influence of that planet than any other does; if with ♄, then heavy; with ♃, more temperate; with ♂, more rash; with ☉, more genteel; with ♀, more jesting; with ☽, more changeable.

Oriental.—When he is oriental, his complexion is honey-colour, or like one sunburnt; in the stature of his body not very high, but well jointed; small eyes, not much hair; in very truth, according to the height of body, very well composed, but still a defect in the complexion, swarthy brown, and in the tongue all for his own interest.

Occidental.—When occidental, a tawny visage, lank body, small slender limbs, hollow eyes, either sparkling, red or fiery; the whole frame of body inclining to dryness.

Quality of Men and Professions.—He generally signifies all literary men, philosophers, mathematicians, astrologians,* merchants, secretaries, writers, sculptors, poets, orators, advocates, schoolmasters, stationers, printers, exchangers of money, attorneys, ambassadors, commissioners, clerks, artificers, generally accomptants, solicitors; sometimes thieves, prattling ministers, busy secretaries, and they unlearned; grammarians, tailors, carriers, messengers, footmen, usurers.

* This more especially if with or in good aspect to *Herschel.*

E

Sickness.— All vertigos, lethargies, or giddiness in the head ; madness, either lightness or any disease of the brain ; phthisic ; all stammering and imperfection in the tongue, vain and fond imaginations, all defects in the memory, hoarseness, dry coughs, too great abundance of spittle, all snaffling and snuffling in the head or nose ; the hand and feet gout, dumbness, foul or diseased tongue ; all evils in the fancy and intellectual parts.

Orb.—His orb is 7 degrees.

Years.—His greatest years are 450, his greater 76, his mean 48, his little or least 20.

Countries.—He has Grecia, Flanders, Egypt. Of towns, Paris.

CHAPTER XI.

OF THE MOON, HER PROPERTIES AND SIGNIFICATIONS.

Name.—The Moon we find called by the ancients Lucina, Cynthia, Diana, Phœbe, Latona, Noctiluca, Proserpina ;* she is nearest to the earth of all the planets.

Motion.—She terminates her course through the whole twelve signs in 27 days, 7 hours, 43 minutes, 5 seconds ; her mean motion is 13 degrees, 10 minutes, and 36 seconds ; but she moves sometimes less and sometimes more, never exceeding 15 degrees and 12 minutes in 24 hours' time.

Latitude.—Her greatest north latitude is 5 degrees and 17 minutes. Her greatest south latitude 5 degrees and 12 minutes. She is never retrograde ; but when she is slow in motion, and goes less in 24 hours than 13 degrees and 11 minutes ; she is then equivalent to a retrograde planet.

-----

* These names prove the various mythological fables to have had their origin in the ancient astrology of the Egyptians.

Nature.—She is a feminine, nocturnal planet; cold, moist, and phlegmatic.

Manners when well placed or dignified.—She signifies one of composed manners, a soft tender creature, a lover of all honest and ingenious sciences, a searcher of and delighter in novelties, naturally inclined to flit and shift his habitation; unsteadfast, wholly caring for the present times; timorous prodigal, and easily frightened; loving peace, however, and to live free from the cares of this life. If a mechanic, the man learns many occupations, and frequently will be tampering with many ways to trade in.

When ill.—A mere vagabond, idle person, hating labour; a drunkard, a sot, one of no spirit or forecast, delighting to live beggarly and carelessly; one content in no condition of life, either good or ill.

Corporature.—She generally presents a man of fair stature, whitely coloured: the face round, grey eyes, and a little lowering; much hair both on the head, face, and other parts; usually one eye a little larger than the other; short hands and fleshy; the whole body inclining to be fleshy, plump, corpulent, and phlegmatic. If she be impeded of the ☉ in a nativity or question, she usually signifies some blemish in or near the eye; a blemish near the eye, if she be impeded in succeedent houses; in the sight, if she be unfortunate in angles, and with fixed stars called nebulæ.

Qualities of Men and Women.—She signifies queens, countesses, ladies, all manner of women, as also the common people, travellers, pilgrims, sailors, fishermen, fishmongers, brewers, tapsters, publicans, letter carriers, coachmen, huntsmen, messengers, mariners, millers, maltsters, drunkards, oysterwives, fishwomen, charwomen, tripewomen, and generally such women as carry commodities in the streets; as

E 2

also midwives, nurses, &c.; hackneymen, watermen, water-bearers.*

Sickness.—Apoplexies, palsy, the cholic, the stomach-ache, diseases in the left side, the bladder and members of generation; the menstrues and liver in women, dropsies, fluxes of the belly, all cold rheumatic diseases, cold stomach, the gout in the wrists and feet; sciatica, worms, hurts in the eyes, surfeits, rotten coughs, convulsive fits, the falling sickness, king's evil, abscess, smallpox, and measles.

Orb.—Is 12 degrees.

Years.—Her greatest years are 320, greater 108, mean 66, least 25.

Countries.—Holland, Zealand, Denmark, Nuremberg, Flanders.

CHAPTER XII.

The Head of the Dragon.—THE head of the Dragon is masculine, of the nature of ♃ and ♀, and of himself a fortune.†

The Tail of the Dragon.—The Tail of the Dragon by nature is quite contrary to the Head, for he is evil. I ever found the ☋ equivalent to either of the fortunes, and, when joined with the evil planets, to lessen their malevolent signification; when joined with the good, to increase the good promised by them. The Tail of the Dragon I always, in my practice, found, when he was joined by the evil planets, their malice or the evil intended thereby was doubled and trebled, or ex-

---

* Generally, all persons who are connected with liquids in their occupation.

† These points are of no consequence in nativities, except as regards the Moon, who brings benefits when she reaches the ☋ in the zodiac by directional motion. and evil when she reaches the ☋.

tremely augmented, &c.; and when he chanced to be in conjunction with any of the fortunes who were significators in the question, though the matter by the principal significator was fairly promised and likely to be perfected in a small time, yet did there ever fall out many rubs and disturbances, much wrangling and controversy, that the business was many times given over for desperate before a perfect conclusion could be had; and unless the principal significators were angular, and well fortified with essential dignities, many times unexpectedly the whole matter came to nothing.

CHAPTER XIII.

ANOTHER BRIEF DESCRIPTION OF THE SHAPES AND FORMS OF THE PLANETS.

Herschel.—THIS is the most distant planet from the Sun; his motion is very slow, as he takes 83 years 151 days to go through the twelve signs. The nature of ♅ is extremely evil. If he ascend or be with the chief significator in any figure, he denotes an eccentric person, far from fortunate, always abrupt, and often violent in his manners. If well aspected, he gives sudden and unexpected benefits; and if afflicted, he will cause remarkable and unlooked-for losses and misfortunes. He is not so powerful as Saturn or Mars, yet can do much evil. Persons under his influence are partial to antiquity, astrology, &c., and all uncommon studies, especially if Mercury and the Moon be in aspect to him. They are likely to strike out novelties, and to be remarkable for an inventive faculty. They are generally unfortunate in marriage, especially if he afflict ♀, the ☽, or the seventh house, either in nativities or questions.

Saturn—Signifies one of a swarthy colour, palish like lead, or of a black earthly brown ; one of rough skin, thick and very hairy on the body, small eyes ; many times his complexion is between black and yellow, or as if he had an affection of the black or yellow jaundice ; he is lean, crooked, or beetle-browed ; a thin weak beard ; great lips, like negroes ; he looks to the ground,* is slow in motion, either is bow-legged or hits one leg or knee against another ; most part a disagreeable breath, seldom free from a cough ; he is crafty for his own interest, seducing people to his opinion ; full of revenge and malice, little caring for religion ; is a foul, nasty, slovenly knave, or a harlot, a great eater and glutton, a brawling fellow ; has broad, great shoulders ; is covetous, and yet seldom rich, &c.†

Jupiter.—We must describe ♃ and a jovialist to be one of a comely stature, full-faced, full-eyed, a sanguine complexion, or mixture of white and red ; a large space between his eyebrows ; usually his beard is of a flaxen or sandy-flaxen colour ; sometimes also, when ♃ is combust, very sad or black ; his hair thick, his eyes not black ; good broad, well-set teeth, but usually some mark of difference in the two fore teeth, either by their standing awry, or some blackness or imperfection in them ; his hair gently curls (if he be in a fiery sign) ; a man well spoken, religious, or at least a good moral honest man ; a person comely, and somewhat fat (if ♃ be in moist signs), fleshy ; if in airy signs, large and strong ; if in earthly signs, a man usually well descended ; but if he be significator, if an ordinary clown, as sometimes he may be, then is he of more humanity than usual in such kind of men.

---

* This downward look, keeping the eyes on the earth, is one of the most remarkable circumstances in the character of the persons described by Saturn, or who have him in the ascendant at birth.

† These evil qualities when Saturn is weak and afflicted.

Mars.—A martial man is many times full-faced, with a lively, high colour, like sun-burnt, or like raw tanned leather ; a fierce countenance, his eyes being sparkling or sharp and darting, and of yellow colour ; his hair, both of head and beard, being reddish (but herein you must vary according to the sign). In fiery signs, and airy, where ♂ falls to be with fixed stars of his own nature, there shews a deep sandy red colour ; but in watery signs, being with fixed stars of his own nature, he is of a flaxen or whitish bright hair ; if in earthy signs, the hair is like a sad brown, or of a chesnut colour. He has a mark or scar on his face ; is broad-shouldered, a sturdy, strong body, being bold and proud, given to mockery and scorn, to quarrel, drink, game, and wench ; which you may easily know by the sign he is in : if in the house of ♀, he wenches ; in that of ☿, he steals ; but if he be in his own house, he quarrels ; in that of ♄, is dogged ; in the ☉'s, is lordly ; in the ☽'s, is a drunkard.

The Sun.—The Sun generally denotes one of an obscure white colour, mixed with red ; a round face, and short chin, a fair stature, and one of a comely body ; his colour sometimes between yellow and black, but for the most part more sanguine than otherwise ; a bold man, and resolute ; his hair curling ; he has a white and tender skin ; one desirous of praise, fame, and estimation among men ; he has a clear voice, and great head ; his teeth somewhat distorted or obliquely set ; of slow speech, but of a composed judgment ; using outwardly a great decorum in his actions, but privately he is lascivious and prone to many vices.

Venus.—Whoever is signified by Venus, whether man or woman, has a good and fair round visage, a full eye, usually we say goggle-eyed : red ruddy lips, the nether more thick or longer than the upper ; the eyelids black, yet lovely and graceful ; the hair of lovely colour, (but most part according to the sign as before repeated); in some it is coal black, in others a light brown; a soft smooth hair; and the body extremely well shaped, even rather inclining to shortness than tallness.*

Mercury.—We describe Mercury to be a man neither black nor white, but between both, of a sad brown or dark yellow colour; long visaged, high forehead, black or grey eyes, a thin, long, sharp nose; thin spare beard, (many times none at all) of an auburn sad colour, next to black; slender of body, small legs; a prattling, busy fellow; and in walking he goes nimbly, and always would be thought to be full of action.

The Moon.—She, by reason of her swiftness, varies her shape very often, but, in general, she personates one having a round visage and full face, in whose complexion you may perceive a mixture of white and red, but paleness overcomes: if she be in fiery signs, the man or woman speaks hastily; in watery signs, he or she has some freckles in his or her face, or is blub-cheeked, not a handsome body, but a muddling creature; and unless very well dignified, she ever signifies an ordinary vulgar person.†

---

* We have always observed that Venus causes *dimples* and a smiling face.

† We have given these descriptions in addition to the former, as it is most material for the student to be able to describe the person inquired of well; as, by that means, the character being known, his conduct may be more accurately foreseen.

CHAPTER XIV.

THE COLOURS OF THE PLANETS AND SIGNS.

♄ GIVES black colour; ♃ a colour mixed with red and green; ♂ red, or iron colour; ☉ yellow or yellow purple; ♀ white or purple colour; ☿ sky colour, or blueish: ☽ a colour spotted with white, and other mixed colours.

♈ White mixed with red; ♉ white mixed with lemon; ♊ white mixed with red; ♋ green or russet; ♌ red or green; ♍ black speckled with blue; ♎ black or dark crimson, or tawny colour; ♏ brown; ♐ yellow, or a green sanguine; ♑ black or russet, or a swarthy brown; ♒ a sky colour with blue; ♓ white, glistening colour.*

CHAPTER XV.

THE NATURE, PLACE, COUNTRIES, GENERAL DESCRIPTION, AND DISEASES SIGNIFIED BY THE TWELVE SIGNS.

ARIES

Is a masculine, diurnal sign, moveable, cardinal, equinoctial; in nature fiery, hot and dry, choleric, bestial, luxurious, in temperate, and violent; the diurnal house of ♂; of the fiery triplicity, and of the east.

Diseases.—All gumboils, swellings, pimples in the face, smallpox, hair lips, polypus, ringworms, falling sickness, apo plexies, megrims, tooth-ache, head-ache, and baldness.

Places ♈ *signifies.*—Where sheep and cattle do feed, sandy or hilly grounds; a place of refuge for thieves, (as unfrequented places); in houses, the covering, ceiling, or plaster·

* Like a fish just taken out of the water.

ing; a stable for small beasts; lands newly taken in or recently ploughed, or where bricks or lime has been burnt.

Description of the Body or Shape ♈ *represents.* — A dry body, not exceeding in height; lean or spare, but lusty bones, and his limbs strong; the visage long, black eye-brows, a long scraggy neck, thick shoulders; the complexion dusky, brown or swarthy.

Countries ruled by ♈. — England, Germany, Denmark, Lesser Poland, Palestine, Syria, Naples.—*Towns :* Florence, Verona, Padua, Marseilles, Burgundy, Saragossa, Bergamo.

TAURUS.

Qualities of the Sign ♉.— It is an earthy, cold, dry, melancholy, feminine, nocturnal, fixed, bestial sign; of the earthy triplicity, and south; the night house of Venus.

Diseases.—The king's evil, sore throats, wens, fluxes of rheums falling into the throat, quinzies, abscesses in those parts.

Places.—Stables where horses are, low houses, houses where the implements of cattle are laid up; pasture or feeding grounds, where no houses are near; plain grounds, or where bushes have lately been eradicated, and wherein wheat and corn are substituted; some little trees not far off; in houses, cellars, low rooms.

Shape and Description.—It represents one of a short, but full, strong and well-set stature; a broad forehead; great eyes, large swarthy face, and broad strong shoulders; great mouth, and thick lips; gross hands; black, rugged hair.

Countries ruled by ♉.—Ireland, Persia, Great Poland, Asia Minor, the Archipelago, and the southern parts of Russia.—*Towns :* Dublin, Mantua, Leipsic, Parma, Franconia, Lorraine: also the islands of Cyprus and Samos, and the port and vicinity of Navarino.

GEMINI.

Quality and Property of ♊.—It is an aerial, hot, moist, sanguine, diurnal, common or double-bodied human sign; the diurnal house of ☿; of the airy triplicity, western, masculine.

Diseases.—It signifies all diseases, accidents, or infirmities in the arms, shoulders, or hands; corrupted blood, windiness in the veins, distempered fancies, and nervous diseases.

Places.—Wainscot of rooms, plaistering, and walls of houses; the halls, or where play is used; hills and mountains, barns, storehouses for corn, coffers, chests and high places.

Countries ruled by ♊.—North America, Lower Egypt, Lombardy, Sardinia, Brabant, Belgium, West of England.— *Towns:* London (especially ♊ 17° 54'), Versailles, Mentz, Bruges, Louvaine, Cordova, New York, and Nuremberg.

Description.—An upright, tall, straight body, either in man or woman; the complexion sanguine, not clear, but obscure and dark; long arms, yet many times the hands and feet short, and very fleshy; a dark hair,* almost black; a strong, active body, a good piercing hazel eye, and wanton, and of perfect and quick sight; of excellent understanding, and judicious in worldly affairs.

CANCER.

Quality and Property of ♋.—It is the only house of the Moon, and is the first sign of the watery triplicity; is a watery, cold, moist, phlegmatic, feminine, nocturnal, moveable sign; mute, and slow of voice; fruitful, northern.

---

* In all cases, I think the hair will be found to be of the colour given by the planet near to or aspecting closely the degree ascending, or on the cusp of the house which signifies the party. I find that ♊ more frequently gives brown hair in questions.—ZAD.

Diseases. — It signifies imperfections all over, or in the breast, stomach, and paps; weak digestion, cold stomach, phthisic, salt phlegms, rotten coughs, dropsical humours, imposthumations in the stomach, cancers,* which are mostly in the breast.

Places.—The sea, great rivers, navigable rivers; but in inland countries it denotes places near rivers, brooks, springs, wells, cellars in houses, wash-houses, marsh-grounds, ditches with rushes, sedges, sea banks, trenches, cisterns.

Shape and Description.—Generally a low and small stature, the upper parts larger than the lower; a round visage; sickly, pale, and white complexion; the hair a sad brown; little eyes; prone to have many children, if a woman.

Countries ruled by ♋.—Holland, Scotland, Zealand, Georgia, and all Africa.—*Towns :* Constantinople, Tunis, Algiers, Amsterdam, Cadiz, Venice, Genoa, York, St. Andrews, Manchester, New York, Bern, Lubeck, Milan, and Vicentia.

LEO.

Quality and Property of ♌.—It is the only house of the Sun; by nature, fiery, hot, dry, choleric; diurnal, commanding, bestial,† barren; of the east, and fiery triplicity; masculine.

Diseases.—All sicknesses in the ribs and sides, as pleuri-

---

* There is little doubt that this disease took its name from the astrological fact, that the sign ♋ rules the breast, in which it generally occurs. Persons born with this sign ascending have always some defect, scar, mark, or disease in the breast.—ZAD.

† This term signifies, that if a person be born under or signified by this sign, or if they have ☽ therein, and at all afflicted by the malefics, they will have less of humane feelings than when under any other sign, except the last half of ♐. They do not sympathize with other persons' sufferings, or feel compassion.

sies, convulsions, pains in the back, trembling or passion of
the heart, violent burning fevers ; all weakness or diseases in
the heart, sore eyes, the plague, the pestilence, the yellow
jaundice.

Places. — A place where wild beasts frequent ; woods,
forests, desert, steep, rocky, and inaccessible places ; king's
palaces, castles, forts, parks ; in houses where fire is kept,
near a chimney.

Shape and Form.—Great round head ; large prominent
eyes, as if staring out, or goggle eyes, quick sighted ; a full
and large body, and more than of middle stature ; broad
shoulders, narrow sides, yellow or dark flaxen hair, and it
curling or turning up ; a fierce countenance, but ruddy high
sanguine complexion ; strong, valiant, and active ; step firm,
and mind courteous.

Countries ruled by ♌ . — France, Italy, Bohemia, Sicily,
Rome.— *Towns :* Rome, Bath, Bristol, Taunton, Cremona,
Prague, Apulia, Ravenna, and Philadelphia ; also the Alps
and the ancient Chaldea, as far as Bussorah.

VIRGO.

Property and Quality of ♍.—It is an earthy, cold, melancholy, barren, feminine, nocturnal, southern sign ; the
house and exaltation of ☿ ; of the earthy triplicity.

Places.—It signifies a study, where books are kept ; a
closet, a dairy-house, corn-fields, granaries, malt-houses, hay,
barley, wheat or peas ricks, &c. ; or a place where cheese and
butter is preserved and stored up.

Diseases.—The worms, wind, cholic ; all obstructions and
croaking of the bowels, infirmities in the testicles, any disease
in the belly.

Countries ruled by ♍.—Turkey in Europe and Asia, Swit-
zerland, Mesopotamia, or Diarbed ; all the country between

the Tigris and the Euphrates, the land of the Turcomans, &c., and the West Indies.—*Towns :* Paris, Lyons, Toulouse, St. Etienne, Basil, Heidelburg, Reading ; also Jerusalem, Candia, Lower Silesia, Croatia or Liburnia, Babylon or Bagdat, Thessaly, Corinth, and the Morea. Also the trade and government of Liverpool, which are ruled especially by the 9th degree.

Shape and Form.—A slender body, rather tall, but well composed ; a ruddy, brown complexion ; black hair,* well favoured or lovely, but not a beautiful creature ; a small, shrill voice, all members inclining to brevity ;† a witty, discreet soul, judicious, and exceedingly well spoken ; studious, and given to history, whether man or woman. It produces a rare understanding, if ☿ be in this sign, and ☽ in ♋ ; but somewhat unstable.

LIBRA.

Nature and Property of ♎.—This sign is hot and moist, sanguine, masculine, moveable, equinoctial, cardinal, humane, diurnal : of the airy triplicity, and western ; the chief house of ♀.

Diseases.—All diseases, (or the stone and gravel) in the reins of the back and kidneys ; heats and diseases in the loins or haunches ; imposthumes or ulcers in the reins, kidneys, or bladder ; weakness in the back, corruption of blood.

Places.—In the fields it represents ground near windmills, or some straggling barn or outhouse, or sawpits, or where coopers work, or wood is cut, sides of hills, tops of mountains, trees, grounds where hawking and hunting is used ; sandy and gravel fields ; pure clear air, and sharp ; the upper

* The early part of the sign gives brown hair.
† If ♅ ascend therein· the limbs will be long and the body taller.

rooms in houses, chambers, garrets, one chamber within another; tops of chests of drawers, wardrobes, &c.

Shape and Form. — It personates a well-framed body, straight, tall, and more subtle or slender than gross; a round, lovely, and beautiful visage; a pure sanguine colour; in youth, no abundance or excess in either red or white; but in age, pimples, or a very high colour; the hair yellowish, smooth, and long, eyes generally blue, and temper even.

Countries ruled by ♎.—China, Japan, parts of India near them; Austria, Usbeck in Persia, towards India; Upper Egypt, Livonia, the vicinity of the Caspian Sea.—*Towns* ᛫ Lisbon, Vienna, Antwerp, Francfort, Spires, Fribourg, Charlestown in America, and its vicinity.

SCORPIO.

Nature and Property of ♏.—It is a cold, watery, nocturnal, phlegmatic, northern, feminine sign; of the watery triplicity; the house and joy of Mars; usually it represents subtle, deceitful men.

Diseases.—Gravel, the stone in the secret parts or bladder; ruptures, fistulas, or the piles; priapisms, all afflictions in the private parts, either of men or women; defects in the matrix, and its diseases; injuries, &c. to the spermatic cord, the groin, &c.

Places.—Places where all kinds of creeping beasts use, as beetles, &c.; or such as be without wings and are poisonous; gardens, vineyards, orchards, ruinous houses near waters; muddy, moorish grounds; stagnant lakes, quagmires, ponds, sinks, the kitchen or larder, washhouse, &c.

Form and Description.—A corpulent, strong, able body, somewhat a broad or square face; a dusky, muddy complexion, and sad dark hair, much and crisping; a hairy body, somewhat bow-legged, short-necked; a squat, well-trussed fellow.

Countries ruled by ♏.—Barbary, Morocco, Norway, Valer tia Catalonia, Bavaria, and the ancient Cappadocia. — *Towns :* Francfort on the Oder, Messina, Ghent, Liverpool, which is especially ruled by the 19th degree.

SAGITTARY.

Quality and Nature of ♐.—It is of the fiery triplicity, east ; in nature hot, dry, masculine, choleric ; diurnal, common, bicorporal or double body, the house and joy of ♃.

Diseases.—It rules the thighs and buttocks, and all fistulous tumours or hurts falling in those members ; and generally denotes heated blood, fevers, pestilence, falls from horses, or hurts from them or four-footed beasts ; also prejudice by fire, heat, and intemperateness in sports.

Places.—A stable for war-horses, or a house where great four-footed beasts are usually kept ; it represents in the fields, hills, and the highest land ; also grounds that rise a little above the rest.   In houses, upper rooms and places near the fire.

Shape and Form of Body.—It represents a well-favoured countenance, somewhat long visage, but full and ruddy, or almost like sunburnt, the hair light chestnut colour, the stature somewhat above the middle size, a conformity in the members, and a strong, able body ; inclined to baldness, and one fond of horses.

Countries ruled by ♐. — Arabia Felix, Spain, Hungary, parts of France near Cape Finisterre, Dalmatia, Istria, Tuscany, Moravia, Sclavonia.—*Towns :* Cologne, Buda, Avignon, Narbonne, Toledo.

CAPRICORN.

Quality and Nature of ♑.—It is the house of Saturn, and is nocturnal, cold, dry, melancholy, earthy, feminine, cardinal, moveable. four-footed, southern : the exaltation of ♂.

Diseases.—It has government of the knees, and all diseases incident to those places, either by strains or fractures; it denotes leprosy, itch, and cutaneous complaints.

Places.—It shows an ox-house or cow-house, or where calves are kept, or tools for husbandry, or old wood is laid up, or where sails for ships and such materials are stored; also sheep-pens, and grounds where sheep feed; fallow grounds, barren fields, bushy and thorny; dunghills in fields, or where soil is laid in low houses; dark places, near the ground or threshold.

Corporature.—Usually dry bodies, not high of stature, long, lean, and slender visage; thin beard, and black hair, a narrow chin, long small neck, and narrow chest. I have found many times, ♑ ascending, the party to have white hair, but in the seventh ever black.*

Countries ruled by ♑.—India, Greece, parts of Persia about Circan, Macran, and Chorassan; Lithuania, Saxony, Albania, Bulgaria, Stiria, Mexico, and parts about the Isthmus of Darien, Santa Martha, Popayan, Pasta, &c.—*Towns :* Mecklenburgh, Hesse, Oxford; and also the Orkney Islands.

AQUARIUS.

Nature and Property of ♒.—This is an airy, hot, and moist sign; diurnal, sanguine, fixed, humane, masculine, the principal house of ♄; western.

Sickness.—It governs the legs, ancles, and all manner of infirmities incident to those members; spasmodic and nervous diseases, cramps, wind, &c.

* This remark of the author confirms our previous opinion, that the colour of the hair in questions depends on the ruler of the term ascending : in nativities, o* the planets aspecting the ascendant, as well as the sign ascending.

F

Places.—Hilly and uneven places; spots newly dug or ploughed, or where quarries of stone are, or any minerals have been dug up ; in houses, the roofs, eaves or upper parts ; vineyards, or near some little spring or conduit head.

Shape and form.—It represents a squat, thick corporature, or one of a strong, plump, well-composed body, not tall : a long visage, sanguine complexion if ♄, who is lord of this house, be in ♑ or ♒, the party is black in hair, and in complexion sanguine, with prominent teeth ; otherwise I have observed the party is of clear, white, or fair complexion, and of sandy-coloured hair, or very flaxen, and a very pure skin.*

Countries ruled by ♒.—Arabia the stony, Russia, Tartary, Prussia, parts of Poland, Lithuania and Muscovy, Lower Sweden, Westphalia.—*Towns :* Hamburgh, Bremen, Piedmont ; also Affghaunistan, and other parts of Asia bordering on Persia; and this sign has rule over the affairs of state in England, especially the 13th degree.†

PISCES.

Property and Quality of ♓.—This is a northern, cold sign, fruitful, phlegmatic, feminine, watery ; the house of ♃ and exaltation of ♀; a bicorporeal, common or double-bodied sign ; an idle, effeminate, sickly sign, or representing a party of no action.

Sickness.—All diseases in the feet, as the gout ; and all lameness and pains incident to those members, mucous discharges, itch, blotches, breakings out ; boils and ulcers pro-

---

* The Princess Charlotte of Wales was born with this sign ascending ; it gives more beauty than any other sign except ♎.

† Eclipses in ♒ cause great innovations in the state in England : comets plunge the nation into war. The greatest changes have occurred in the laws while ♅ has been in ♒.

ceeding from corrupt blood; colds and moist diseases, and bowel complaints caused by wet feet.

Places.— It represents grounds full of water, or where many springs and many fowl are: also fish-ponds, or rivers full of fish ; places where hermitages have been, moats about houses, water-mills. In houses, places near the water, as some well or pump, or where water stands.*

Corporature.—A short stature, not very well made ; a good large face, pale complexion, the body fleshy or swelling, not very straight, but incurvating, or stooping somewhat with the head.†

Countries ruled by ♓. — Portugal, Calabria, Normandy, Galicia in Spain, Cilicia.—*Towns:* Alexandria, Ratisbon, Worms, Seville, Compostella, Tiverton.

CHAPTER XVI.

TEACHING WHAT USE MAY BE MADE OF THE FORMER DISCOURSE OF THE TWELVE SIGNS.

If one demand of the artist, what condition, quality, or stature the person inquired of is, then observe the sign of that house whereby he is signified, and the planet in it, the sign wherein the lord of that house is, and wherein the Moon is ; mix one with another, and by the greater testimonies judge ; for if the sign be humane, viz. ♊, ♍, ♒, or the first half of ♐ that ascends, and the lord of that sign, or the ☽ in any sign of the same nature, you may judge the body to be handsome, and the conditions of the party to be sociable, or very courteous.

---

* This sign denotes standing water, as ♋ does running water.

† I have generally found persons born under this sign have a very delicate skin, and often a white chalky appearance and flabby.—ZAD.

&c. If the query be concerning a disease, and ♈ be either
on the cusp of the ascendant or descending in the sixth house,
you may judge he has something in his disease of the nature
of ♈, but what it is, you must know by the concurrence of
the other significators.

If a person has lost or missed any cattle, or any material
thing, let him observe what sign the significator of the thing
is in ; if in ♈, and it be a beast strayed, or the like, let him
see what manner of places that sign directs into, and let him
repair thither to search, considering the quarter of heaven
the sign signifies ; if it be a piece of goods that without hands
cannot be removed, then let him look into such parts of or
about his house, as ♈ signifies.

If one asks concerning travel, whether such a country,
city, or kingdom will be healthful or prosperous unto him,
see in the figure what sign the lord of the ascendant is in :
if the significator be fortunate in ♈, or if ♃ or ♀ be therein,
he may safely travel or sojourn in such cities or countries as
the sign ♈ represents ; which you may easily perceive in the
above-named catalogue. Those countries subject to the sign
wherein the infortunes are posited, unless they themselves be
significators, are ever unfortunate. Remember, that a gentleman inquires, usually, if he shall have his health and live
jocundly in such or such a country or city ; the merchant
wholly aims at trade, and the increase of his stock ; therefore, in the merchant's figure, you must consider the country
or city subject to the sign of the second house, or where the
part of fortune, or lord of the second house is, and which is
most fortified, and thither let him trade.*

* This implies, that you must judge by the sign on the house which
rules the particular subject of inquiry ; as if it be, where he may gain a
good wife, look to the seventh house.

CHAPTER XVII.

OF THE ESSENTIAL DIGNITIES OF THE PLANETS.

THE exact way of judicature in astrology is, first, by being perfect in the nature of the planets and signs; secondly, by knowing the strength, fortitude, or debility of the significators, and well poising of them, and their aspects and several mixtures, in your judgment; thirdly, by rightly applying the influence of the figure of heaven erected, and the planets' aspects to one another at the time of the question, according to natural and not enforced maxims of art; for by how much you endeavour to strain a judgment beyond nature, by so much the more you augment your error. A planet is then said to be really strong when he has many essential dignities,* which are known by his being either in his house, exaltation, triplicity, term, or face, at the time of erecting the figure. As, for example, in any scheme of heaven, if you find a planet in any of those signs we call his house, he is then essentially strong; as ♄ in ♑, or ♃ in ♐, &c.

Essential Dignity by House.—In judgment, when a planet or significator is in his own *house*, it represents a man in such a condition, as that he is lord of his own house, estate, and fortune; or a man wanting very little of the goods of this world; or it tells you the man is in a very happy state or condition: this will be true, unless the significator be retrograde, or combust, or afflicted by any other malevolent planet or aspect.

Exaltation.—If he be in that sign wherein he is *exalted*, you may consider him essentially strong; whether he be

---

* These apply not to nativities where the angular position and good aspects received by a planet constitute its strength.—ZAD.

near the very degree of his exaltation, or not; as ♂ in ♑, or ♃ in ♋.

If the significator be in his exaltation, and no ways impedited, but angular, it represents a person of haughty condition, arrogant, assuming more to himself than his due; for it is observed, the planets in some part of the zodiac do more evidently declare their effects than in others.

Triplicity.—If he be in any of those signs which are allotted him for his *triplicity*, he is also strong, but in a less degree.

A planet in his *triplicity* shews a man modestly endued with the goods and fortune of this world; one well descended, and the condition of his life, at present time of the question, to be good; but not so much so as if in either of the two former dignities.

Term.—If any planet be in those degrees we assign for his *terms*, we allow him to be slightly dignified.

A planet fortified, only as being in his own *terms*, rather shews a man more of the corporature and temper of the planet, than any extraordinary abundance in fortune, or eminence in the commonwealth.

Face.—If any planet be in his decanate, or face, he has the least possible essential dignity; but being in his own decanate or face, he cannot then be called peregrine.

A planet being in his decanate or *face*, describes a man ready to be turned out of doors, having much to do to maintain himself in credit and reputation; and in genealogies it represents a family at the last gasp, even as good as quite decayed, hardly able to support itself.

The planets may be strong in another way; viz. accidentally; as when direct, swift in motion, angular, in △ or ✶ aspect with ♃ or ♀, &c., or in ♂ with certain notable fixed stars, as shall hereafter be related. Here follows a table of essential dignities: by only casting your eye thereon, you may perceive what essential dignity or imbecility any planet has.

There has been much difference between the Greeks, Araoians, and Indians, concerning the essential dignities of the planets : I mean, how to dispose the several degrees of the signs suitably to any planet. After many ages had passed, and until the time of Ptolemy, the astrologians were not re- solved hereof ; but since Ptolemy's time, the Grecians unani- mously followed the method he left, which the other Christians of Europe to this day since retain as most rational : but the Moors of Barbary at present, and those astrologians of their nation who lived in Spain, do somewhat vary from us to this very day : however, I present thee with a table according to Ptolemy.

TABLE OF THE ESSENTIAL DIGNITIES OF THE PLANETS, &c.

Signs.	Houses.	Exaltations.	Triplicity. Day.	Triplicity. Night.	Terms.					Faces.			Detriment.	Fall.
♈	♂ D.	☉ 19	☉	♃	♃ 6	♀ 14	☿ 21	♂ 26	♄ 30	♂ 10	☉ 20	♀ 30	♀	♄
♉	♀ N.	☽ 3	♀	☽	♀ 8	☿ 15	♃ 22	♄ 20	♂ 30	☿ 10	☽ 20	♄ 30	♂	
♊	☿ D.	☊ 3	♄	☿	☿ 7	♃ 14	♀ 21	♄ 25	♂ 30	♃ 10	♂ 20	☉ 30	♃	
♋	☽ D. N.	♃ 15	♂	♂	♂ 6	♃ 13	☿ 20	♀ 27	♄ 30	♀ 10	☿ 20	☽ 30	♄	♂
♌	☉ D. N.		☉	♃	♄ 6	☿ 13	♀ 19	♃ 25	♂ 30	♄ 10	♃ 20	♂ 30	♄	
♍	☿ N.	☿ 15	♀	☽	☿ 7	♀ 13	♃ 18	♄ 24	♂ 30	☉ 10	♀ 20	☿ 30	♃	♀
♎	♀ D.	♄ 21	♄	☿	♄ 6	♀ 11	♃ 19	☿ 24	♂ 30	☽ 10	♄ 20	♃ 30	♂	☉
♏	♂ N.		♂	♂	♂ 6	♃ 14	♀ 21	☿ 27	♄ 30	♂ 10	☉ 20	♀ 30	♀	☽
♐	♃ D.	☋ 3	☉	♃	♃ 8	♀ 14	☿ 19	♄ 25	♂ 30	☿ 10	☽ 20	♄ 30	☿	
♑	♄ N.	♂ 28	♀	☽	♀ 6	☿ 12	♃ 19	♂ 25	♄ 30	♃ 10	♂ 20	☉ 30	☽	♃
♒	♄ D.		♄	☿	♄ 6	☿ 12	♀ 20	♃ 25	♂ 30	♀ 10	☿ 20	☽ 30	☉	
♓	♃ N.	♀ 27	♂	♂	♀ 8	♃ 14	☿ 20	♂ 26	♄ 30	♄ 10	♃ 20	♂ 30	☿	☿

EXPLANATION OF THE TABLE.

Every planet has two signs for his HOUSES, except Sol and Luna; they but one each. ♄ has ♑ and ♒; and ♃ has ♐ and ♓; ♂ has ♈ and ♏; ♀ has ♉ and ♎; ☿ has ♊ and ♍. One of these houses is called diurnal, noted in the second column by the letter D; the other is nocturnal, noted by the letter N. The planets have their EXALTATIONS, as the third column points out: thus ☉ in 19 ♈; ☽ in 3 ♉; ☊ in 3 degrees ♊, &c. are exalted. These twelve signs are divided into FOUR TRIPLICITIES. The fourth column tells you which planet or planets, both night and day, governs each triplicity; as over against ♋, ♏, ♓, you find ♂, who governs by day and night in that triplicity; and over against ♈, ♌, ♐, you find ☉ and ♃, viz. that ☉ has domination by day, and ♃ by night, in that triplicity: the first six degrees of ♈ are the TERMS of ♃, from six to fourteen, the TERMS of ♀, &c. &c. Over against ♈, in the tenth, eleventh, and twelfth columns, you find ♂ 10, ☉ 20, ♀ 30; viz. the first ten degrees of ♈ are the FACE of ♂; from ten to twenty, the FACE of ☉; from twenty to thirty, the FACE of ♀, &c.

In the thirteenth column, over against ♈, you find ♀ DETRIMENT, viz. ♀ being in ♈, is in a sign opposite to one of her own houses, and so is said to be in her DETRIMENT. In the 14th column, over against ♈, you find ♄, over his head FALL, that is, ♄ when he is in ♈ is opposite to his exaltation, and so is unfortunate, &c. Though these things are expressed in the nature of the planets already, yet this table makes it appear more evident to the eye, and is useful for reference.

CHAPTER XIX.

CONSIDERATIONS BEFORE JUDGMENT.

ALL the ancients that have written of questions do give warn-
ing to the astrologer, that before he delivers judgment he
well consider whether the figure is radical* and capable of
judgment: the question then shall not be taken for radical:
1st, when either the first or second degrees of a sign ascend,
(especially in signs of short ascensions, viz. ♑, ♒, ♓, ♈,
♉, ♊). You may not then adventure judgment, unless the
querent be very young, and his corporature, complexion, and
moles or scars of his body, agree with the quality of the signs
ascending. 2d. If 27 or more degrees of any sign ascend, it
is not safe to give judgment, except the querent be in years
corresponding to the number of degrees ascending, or unless
the figure be set upon a time certain, viz. any event happening, such as a man went away or fled at such a time pre-
cisely; to learn the result: here you may judge, because it is
no propounded question. 3d. It is not safe to judge when
the ☽ is in the later degrees of a sign, especially in ♊, ♏,
or ♑; or, as some say, when she is in *via combusta*, which
is, when she is in the last 15 degrees of ♎, or the first 15
degrees of ♏.

All manner of matters go hardly on (except the principal
significators be very strong) when the ☽ is void of course;
yet sometimes she performs it void of course, if in ♉, ♋, ♐,
or ♓. You must also be wary, when in any *question* propounded you find the cusp of the seventh house afflicted, or

---

* This term signifies, like the *radix* or root, the figure of birth; for
when a person asks his first question of an astrologer, it will generally be
found that the same sign, and often the same degree, will ascend that
ascended at his birth.

the lord of the house retrograde or impedited, and the matter at that time not concerning the seventh house, but belonging to any other house : it is an argument that the judgment of the astrologer will give little content, or nothing please the querent, for the seventh house generally has signification of the artist.   The Arabians, as Alkindus and others, do deliver the following rules, as very fit to be considered before a question be judged :— viz. if ♄ be in the ascendant, especially retrograde, the matter of that question seldom or never comes to good : ♄ in the seventh either corrupts the judgment of the astrologer, or is a sign the matter propounded will come from one misfortune to another.   If the lord of the ascendant be combust, neither question propounded will take, nor the querent be regulated.   The lord of the seventh unfortunate, or in his fall, or terms of the infortunes, the artist shall scarce give a solid judgment.

When the testimonies of fortunes and infortunes are equal, defer judgment : it is not possible to know which way the balance will turn ; however, defer your opinion till another question better inform you.

CHAPTER XX.

WHAT SIGNIFICATOR, QUERENT, AND QUESITED, ARE ; AND AN INTRODUCTION TO THE JUDGMENT OF A QUESTION.

THE querent is he or she that propounds the question and desires resolution ; the quesited is he or she, or the thing sought and inquired after.

The significator is no more than that planet which rules the house that signifies the person or thing demanded ; as if ♈

is ascending, ♂ being lord of ♈, shall be significator of the querent, viz. the sign ascending shall in part signify his corporature, body, or stature : the lord of the ascendant, according to the sign he is in, the ☽ and planet in the ascendant, equally mixed together, shall shew his quality or conditions ; so that let any sign ascend, what planet is lord of that sign shall be called lord of the house, or significator of the person inquiring, &c.

So that, in the first place, when any question is propounded, the sign ascending and his lord are always given unto him or her that asks the question.

Secondly : You must then consider the matter propounded, and see to which of the twelve houses it does properly belong: when you have found the house, consider the sign and lord of that sign, how, and in what sign and what part of heaven he is placed, how dignified, what aspect he has to the lord of the ascendant, who impedites your significator, who is a friend unto him, viz. what planet it is, and what house he is lord of, or in what house posited ; from such a man or woman signified by that planet shall you be aided or hindered, or by one of such relation unto you as that planet signifies ; if lord of such a house, such an enemy ; if lord of a house that signifies enemies, then an enemy verily ; if of a friendly house, a friend.

The whole natural key of astrology rests in the words preceding, rightly understood. By the examples following, I shall make all things more plain ; for I do not desire or will reserve any thing whereby the learner may be kept in suspense of understanding what is useful for him, and most fit to be known. In every question we do give the ☽ as a consignificator with the querent or lord of the ascendant. Having well considered the several applications and separation of the lords of those houses signifying your questions, as also

the ☽, her situation and quality of the aspects she has, and
each significator has to each, you may begin to judge and consider whether the thing demanded will come to pass, yea or
nay; by what or whose means, the time when, and whether
it will be good for the querent to proceed further in his de
mands, yea or nay.

CHAPTER XXI.

TO KNOW WHETHER A THING DEMANDED WILL BE BROUGHT TO PERFECTION, YEA OR NAY.

THE ancients have delivered unto us, that there are four ways
or means which discover whether a person's question demanded
shall be accomplished, yea or nay.

Conjunction.—First, by conjunction : when therefore you
find the lord of the ascendant, and the lord of that house
which signifies the thing demanded, hastening to a ♂, and in
the first house, or in any *angle*, and the significators meet with
no prohibition or refranation, before they come to perfect ♂,
you may then judge that the thing sought after shall be
brought to pass without any manner of let or impediment;
the sooner, if the significators be swift in motion, and essentially or accidentally strong; but if this ♂ of the significators be in a *succeedent* house, it will be perfected, but not so
soon ; if in *cadent* houses, with infinite loss of time, some
difficulty, and much struggling.

Aspects of ⚹ *or* △.—Things are also effected, when the
principal signifiers apply by ⚹ or △ aspect out of good
houses and places where they are essentially well dignified,
and meet with no malevolent aspect to intervene ere they come
to be in perfect ⚹ or △.

Aspects of □ *and* ☍.—Things are also produced to perfection when the significators apply by □ aspect, provided
each planet have dignity in the degrees wherein they are, and
apply out of proper and good houses; otherwise not. Sometimes it happens that a matter is effected when the significators
apply by ☍, but it is when there is mutual *reception* by *house,*
and out of friendly houses, and the ☽ separating from the
significator of the thing demanded, and applying presently to
the lord of the ascendant. I have seldom seen any thing
brought to perfection by this way of opposition, but the querent had been better the thing had been undone; for, if the
question was concerning marriage, the parties seldom agreed,
but were ever wrangling and disputing, each party repining
at his evil choice, laying the blame upon their covetous parents,
as having no mind to it themselves; and if the question was
about portion or monies, the querent did, it is true, recover
his money or portion promised, but it cost him more to procure it in suit of law than the debt was worth; and so have I
seen it happen in many other things, &c.

Translation.—Things are brought to perfection by *translation* of light and nature, in this manner :—When the significators both of querent and quesited are separating from ♂,
or ⚹, or △ aspects of each other, and some other planet
separates himself from one of the significators, of whom he
is received, either by house, triplicity, or term,* and then this
planet applies to the other significator by ♂ or aspect, before
he meets with the ♂ or aspect of any other planets; he thus
translates the force, influence, and virtue of the first significator to the other, and then this intervening planet, (or such
a man or woman as is signified by that planet,) shall bring the
matter in hand to perfection.

Consider what house the planet interposing or translating

* This means being in these dignities of that significator.

the nature and light of the two planets is lord of, and describe him or her ; and say to the querent, that such a party shall do good in the business of, &c. ; viz. if lord of the second, a good purse effects the matter ; if lord of the third, a kinsman or neighbour ; and so of all the rest of the houses ; of which more hereafter.

Collection.—Matters are also brought to perfection, when the two principal significators do not behold one another, but both cast their several aspects to a more weighty planet than themselves, and they both receive him in some of their essential dignities ; then shall that planet, who thus *collects* both their lights, bring the thing demanded to perfection ; which signifies that a person somewhat interested in both parties, and described and signified by that planet, shall perform the thing which otherwise could not be perfected ; as many times you see two fall at variance, and of themselves cannot think of any way of accommodation, when suddenly a neighbour or friend accidentally reconciles all differences, to the content of both parties ; and this is called a collection.

In all questions, you are generally to observe this method following :—The ascendant represents the person of the querent, and the second his estate, the third his kindred, the fourth his father, the fifth his children, the sixth his servant or sickness, the seventh his wife, the eighth the manner of his death, the ninth his religion or journeys, the tenth his estimation or honour, mother, trade, &c. ; the eleventh his friends, the twelfth his secret enemies : also understand, that when one asks concerning a woman, or any party signified by the seventh house and the lord thereof, that then the seventh house shall be her ascendant, and signify her person ; the eighth house shall signify her estate, and be her second ; the ninth house shall signify her brethren and kindred ; the tenth shall represent her father ; the eleventh her children, or whe-

ther apt to have children ; the twelfth her sickness and servants ; the first house her sweetheart ; the second house her
death ; the third her journey ; the fourth her mother, or
trade, &c. ; the fifth her friends ; the sixth her sorrow, care,
and private enemies. Let the question be of or concerning a
churchman, minister, or the brother of the wife or sweetheart,
the ninth house shall represent each of these ; but the tenth
house shall be significator of *his* substance ; the eleventh
house of his brethren ; and so in order : and so in all manner
of questions, the house signifying the party quesited shall be
his ascendant or first house, the next his second house, and
so continuing round about the whole heavens of twelve houses.
If a question be made of a king or nobleman, the tenth is
his first house, the eleventh his second, &c. ; but in nativities,
the ascendant always influences the party born, whether king
or beggar. These things preceding being well understood,
you may proceed to judgment ; not that it is necessary you
have all that is written in your memory exactly, but, that you
be able to know when you are in error, when not ; when to
judge a question, when not.

Of the true Time of erecting a Figure.

The proper time is that when you feel most anxious about
any matter, and first form the resolution to erect a figure on
the subject : if you find the figure radical, and lay aside all
self-love and prejudice, you may safely judge a figure erected
for that instant of time.

If a person apply to an astrologer, the figure must be taken
for the exact time he first speaks on the subject ; or, if it be
by letter, when it is first read and understood by the artist.
If it be not a question, but an event suddenly happening,
then the moment of its commencement will shew, by a figure,
its result &c. ; as the first setting off on a journey, beginning

a letter, or any business, &c.; or when you first discover the loss of any article, or hear of any event happening: in all these cases, the first impression on your mind is the true moment for the figure.

Of the Planet or Planets which hinder or impedite the Thing demanded in any Question.

In all questions consider carefully what planet it is which obstructs or hinders the perfection of the thing desired. We receive judgment herein from that planet with whom the lord of the ascendant be joined, (whether by bodily ♂ or by aspect), or the significator of the thing inquired after, whether it be the ☽ herself, or that she be partaker with the lord of the ascendant or not, or signify the thing demanded.

Carefully observe the planet to which the querent's significator is joined, or the ☽; and observe how that planet is disposed, and unto whom *he* is joined; for if the lord of the ascendant, ☽, or significator of the thing propounded, be joined to an evil planet, evilly disposed, without reception, or if he be not evilly disposed, but be joined to an infortune, and that infortune receive him not, it denotes the destruction of the thing demanded.

A planet is ill-disposed when he is *peregrine, retrograde, combust;* also if *cadent* and behold not the lord of the house or the cusp of the house of the thing demanded. The aspect to the cusp is better than to the lord of the house.

If the significator, as above, be joined to an unfortunate planet, viz. one retrograde, combust, or cadent; then observe whether mutual reception intervene; which shews the perfection of the matter, though with much labour and solicitation. If there be no reception, the affair will come to nothing though there may have been much probability of its performance.

G

If the lord of the ascendant, the ☽, or lord of the thing demanded, or the planet who receives any of them, be free from affliction, though without mutual reception, it perfects the matter with facility.

If any one of them be free from the infortunes, and joined with any benevolent planet, who is himself aspected by a malevolent, without mutual reception, the matter will be brought to a good conclusion.

Consider carefully whether planets in aspect be without reception, for when they are in reception, things are ever brought to pass; though, if the aspect be evil, with degree of trouble, delay, &c.

Consider also, whether any other planet *prohibit* before the significators join in perfect ♂ with an evil planet; if so, it hinders the thing from happening: but if no such prohibition or cutting off the light of the *infortune* occur, by which its malevolence may be taken off, the thing will be effected.

If an infortune *collect* the light of other planets, or if light be translated to an infortune, the matter will not be effected unless there be reception; viz. that the infortune be received by, or disposed of, or ruled by, (which is all one thing), the significators.

THE RESOLUTION OF ALL MANNER OF QUESTIONS AND DEMANDS.

CHAPTER XXII.

QUESTIONS CONCERNING THE FIRST HOUSE. IF THE QUERENT BE LIKELY TO LIVE LONG—YEA OR NOT?

Signs of Health and long Life.

CONSIDER whether the sign ascending, the lord thereof, and ☽, be free from affliction; viz. combustion or ☌, □ or ☍ of the lords of the 8th, 12th, 6th, or 4th houses; whether they be direct, strong in dignities, swift in motion, angular, especially in the 1st, or 10th houses; or if in the 11th or 9th, and in good aspect with ♃, ♀, or ☉, or in the terms of ♃ or ♀: these are arguments of health and long life; and the contrary, viz. the asc. ☽, or lord of the 1st, in bad houses, and afflicted, shew mischief at hand.

If the lord of the ascendant be under the Sun's beams, or going to combustion, which is worse than when he is leaving ☉; or ☽ cadent and unfortunate, by being afflicted by those planets having rule in the 8th, or 6th; or ♄, ♂ or ☊ in the ascendant or 7th house peregrine, or in their detriments or retrograde, judge that the querent will not be long lived, but is near some danger or misfortune, according to the quality of the significators, and of the houses those planets are lord of, which afflict the ☽, &c.

G 2

The Time when any of those Accidents shall happen.

If the lord of the ascendant be going to ♂, &c. of ☉, or
.ords of the 8th, or 4th, see how many degrees he is distant,
and in what sign either of them are; and for each degree
allow one week in a moveable sign, one month in a common
sign, and one year in a fixed sign ; this is only for example ;
for the measure of time must be limited according to the other
significators concurring in judgment herein.

Secondly.—Consider also how many degrees ☽ is from any
infortune, or the lords of the 6th or 8th, according to the
signs and houses in which they are found, and their nature
and quality.

Thirdly.—If there be an infortune in the ascendant, see
how many degrees the cusp of the 1st house wants of the
place of the evil planet ; or, if he be in the 7th house, how
far it is from the cusp of that house, and compute the time
of death, sickness, or misfortune, by the degrees, as they may
be in fixed, common, or moveable signs.

If the lord of the ascendant be most afflicted by the lord
of the 6th, and in the 6th, or come to combustion in the 6th,
the querent will have very many and tedious sicknesses, which
will scarce leave him till his death.   This will be more certain
if the lords of the ascendant, 8th house, and ☽, be all placed
in the 6th.

If the ☽, lord of the ascendant, or sign ascending, be
most afflicted by the lord of the 8th, or by a planet situated
in the 8th, judge that the sickness which now afflicts him,
or shortly will, will end fatally, and that death is approaching.   But if the ☽ and other significators are chiefly afflicted
by the lords of other houses, judge the misfortune from the
nature of the house or houses of which the afflicting planets
are lords ; and the first origin thereof from some person or

thing belonging to that house, wherein you find the afflicting planet posited. Judge thereby a misfortune, but not death.

If there be any fixed star, of much power, near the ☽, lord of the ascendant or the degree ascending, or with the planet which afflicts any of these, you may judge evil thereby, according to the nature of that star; for which, see the chapter on Fixed Stars.

Caution.

Avoid rash judgments; especially of death. This should never be judged by one single testimony, however strong. And though the lord of the ascendant be going to combustion in the house of death, observe whether the ☽, ♃, or ♀ (or ☿ if well aspected and strong), throw any good aspect to the lord of the ascendant, before he come to perfect ♂ with ☉; for then either medicine or natural strength will contradict that malignant influence, or take off part of that misfortune. When two or more of the rules aforesaid occur, you may be more bold; yet concerning the absolute time of death, I have found it best to be wary. Though you may safely judge that the querent will not be long-lived, or else subject to many calamities; and this I know by many verified examples. This knowledge will be useful to those who will use their reason to avoid those casualties their nature or inclinations would run them into.*

---

* The student will perceive, by this observation of the author, how false is the assertion, that astrology teaches or upholds fatality. On the contrary, it expressly teaches that the worst influence may be overcome by the use of reason, which, of course, implies by the assistance also of God's blessing, which both reason and revelation inform us we should pray for when we perceive any impending evil.—ZADKIEL.

To what Part is it best the Querent should direct his Affairs or where may he live most happily ?

The 12 houses are divided into the four quarters of heaven, east, west, north and south.   From the cusp of the 1st, where the ☉ and planets rise, to the cusp of the 10th, is the south-east quarter.   The 1st, is due east ;   the 12th, is about two points south of east ;   the middle of the 11th, is south east ;   the cusp of the 11th, is about two points east of south ;   and the 10th, is due south.   In like manner, from the 10th to the 7th house is the south-west quarter ;   and from the 7th to the 4th is the north-west quarter ;   and, lastly, from the 4th to the ascendant is the north-east quarter.   In that quarter wherein you find ♃, ♀, ☽, or ⊕, or most of them, direct the querent to proceed in that direction, especially if ⊕ and ☽ be free from combustion and be strong.   If ♃ or ♀ be lords of the 8th, 12th, or 6th houses, you must avoid them ;   and avoid that quarter wherein the evil planets are, unless they be essentially strong, and lords of the 1st, 2d, 10th, or 11th houses, when they may prove friendly.*

If the querent desire to live where he may most enjoy *health,* look to the quarter of the lord of the ascendant, or ☽ ;   and whichever is strongest, or casts the best aspect to the degree ascending, to that quarter repair for health.   If an increase of *wealth* be considered, see where the lord of the 2d, the ⊕, and its dispositor, or any two of them, be, and thither repair for that end.   Of this I shall speak in other judgments.

What Part of LIFE *is like to be best ?*

See in what angle or quarter of heaven the fortunate and

---

* I should not myself choose the directions of the infortunes in any case.—ZADKIEL.

promising planets are; for in this way of judging we usually give to every house five years, more or less, as the significators promise life or death. Begin with the 12th, then the 11th, then the 10th, &c., and so round to the ascendant. If ♃ or ♀ be in the 11th or 10th, judge the querent to have lived happily from the 5th to the 15th year of age: if they be in the 8th or 7th, he will or hath lived contented from fifteen to thirty; if ♃, &c. be in the 6th, 5th, or 4th, house, say that after his middle age, from 30 to 45, he may do well; but if the benefics be in the last quarter, his greatest happiness will be in his last days, or after 45. If you find the significators very strong, you may add a year to each house. Lastly, the aspects the ☽ and lord of the ascendant are separated from shew what and what manner of accidents have preceded the question; their next application what may be next expected. If you consider the house or houses the planets they separated from are lords of, it acquaints you with the matter, nature, person, and quality of the things already happened—evil if the aspects were evil, and good if they were good. Also if you note the quality of the next aspect by application, and the well or ill-being and position of the planets applied to, it shews the character of the next succeeding accidents and events, their nature, proportion, &c., and the time when they will happen.

Fig. 2.

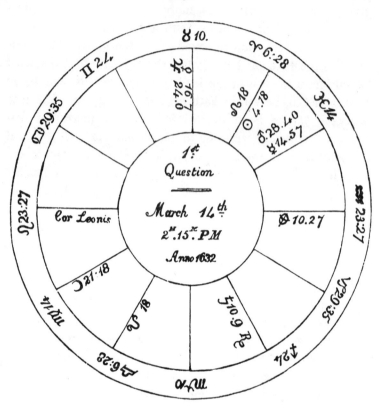

An ASTROLOGICAL JUDGMENT *concerning these Demands by the Querent.*

1. If he were likely to live long, yea or not?
2. To what part of the world he were best direct his course?
3. What part of life was likely to be most fortunate?
4. He desired I would relate some of the general accidents which had happened to him already?
5. What accidents in future he might expect?
6. The time when?

The stature of the querent is shewn by ♌, the sign ascending; a fixed star of the 1st magnitude, of the nature of ♂ and ♃, called *Cor* ♌, the lion's heart, is near the cusp of the 1st house, in ♌ 24° 34' ;* both the cusp of the 1st house and the degree wherein ☉ lord of the ascendant is, are the terms of ♃; the ☽ is in △ aspect to both ♃ and ♀, and they in the 10th house; so that the form and stature of the querent were decent. He was of middle stature, strongly compacted, neither fat nor fleshy, but comely and graceful, a fair visage, reddish hair, clear skin, some cuts on his right cheek (he was a soldier), and certainly the presence of the fixed star in the ascendant, which represents the face, occasioned those hurts or scars.†

As the sign ascending, and its lord, were in the *fiery* triplicity, and by nature hot and dry, so was this gentleman's temper and condition, being exceedingly valiant, choleric, high-minded, and of great spirit: for ☉ is in his exaltation; yet ☽ being in △ to the two fortunes, he was sober, modest, and excellently educated, thereby having great command of his passion; but as ☽ was in ☍ to ☿, he had his times of anger and folly, whereby he much prejudiced his affairs.‡

1st QUERY.—*If live long, &c. ?*

The ascendant not vitiated by the lords of the 6th or 8th; the lord of the ascendant in his exaltation no way impeded, pretty quick in motion, in the 9th house, and in terms of ♃;

* This star has now advanced to about 27° 30' of the sign Leo.

† I differ from the author on this point, and believe that the lord of the ascendant being in ♈, which rules the head, shewed them; it being a *masculine* sign, caused them to be on the right side; and, being *above the earth*, they were in front of the head, or in the face. The ☉ being afflicted by the ☌ of ♂, caused them to be scars or wounds: if he had been alone, they would have been merely *moles.*—ZADKIEL.

‡ The ☉ in ☌ with ♂ would render him very fiery, and at the same time very brave and fortunate, as a soldier.

☽ separating from △ of ♀ applying to △ of ♃, he strong
in the midheaven, and the malice of ♂ restrained by the ⚹
of ♃ ; ☉ above the earth, the fortunes angular and more
potent than the infortunes; I concluded that, according to
natural causes, he might live many years; that nature was
strong, and he subject to few diseases. This has hitherto
proved true; he being yet alive this present March, 1646.

2d QUERY.—*To what part of the world he were best direct
his course?*

☉ lord of the ascendant near the cusp of the 9th, (and the
sign thereof moveable), the house of long journeys; I intimated that he was resolving suddenly upon a *journey* south-
east: south, because the quarter of heaven wherein the lord
of the ascendant is, is south; east, because the *sign* where ☉
is, is east, (*this he confessed*); and as ☉ was but 2° 10' distant
from the cusp of the 9th, he went away within two months.

I judged those countries subject to ♈ might be propitious.
Had his resolution been to stay in England, it might have
been good for him, for England is subject to ♈ : I would have
advised him to steer towards Kent, Essex, Sussex or Suffolk;
for they lie south-east from London.   But if sometimes you
find a city, town or kingdom, subject to the *sign* which promises good, stands not in the direction the sign or quarter of
heaven points out as above, observe this rule—that if enforced to live in that country, city, &c., then direct your
actions or employment *to those parts* of that country, &c.,
which lie east, west, &c., as in the figure is directed.

As the ☽ applied strongly to the △ of ♃, and he and ♀
were in ♉, which rules *Ireland*, I advised him that *Ireland*
would agree with his constitution, and that he might get *honour*
there, as the planet to whom ☽ applies is in the house of
honour.   And the querent did go into Ireland, and there performed good service, and obtained a notable victory against
the rebels.

3d QUERY.—*What part of his* LIFE *would be best?*

Considering the two fortunes were placed in the 10th, and ☊ and ☉ in the 9th, I judged his younger years would be the most pleasant; and ♂ being in the 8th, which comes to about the 24th, 25th, or 26th years of his age, I judged about that time many crosses, and that his afflictions first began. And seeing no fortunate planet either in the 7th, 6th, 5th, 4th, or 3d houses, I said the remainder of his life, for many years, would be little comfortable, and full of labour and trouble. Yet I judged those calamities should not suddenly come upon him, because ☽ applied to △ of ♃, and wanted almost 3° of coming to a perfect aspect. Therefore I conceived by means of some person in authority represented by ♃, he should be supported or assisted in his affairs for almost three years after the question. Had ♃ been essentially dignified, I should have judged him a more durable fortune.

4th QUERY. — *What general* ACCIDENTS *had happened already?*

Although it is not usual to be so inquisitive, yet, seeing the figure so radical, I considered from what planets ☉, lord of the ascendant, had last separated. The ☉ had lately been in ☌ ♂, then □ ♄, then ✶ ♃. Now as ♂ is lord of the 4th house, signifying lands, &c., and was now in the 8th, which signifies the *substance of women*, I judged he had been molested of late concerning some lands, or the jointure or portion of his wife, or a woman; wherein I was confirmed the more, as ☽ applies to ☍ ♂ in the 8th house; she being in the querent's house of property, which shewed that the quarrel or strife should be concerning money or things signified by that house. (*All this was very true.*)

As ☉ had lately been in □ ♄, significator of the querent's wife, I told him that his wife and he had been at great variance; and because her significator ♄ did dispose of his ⊕, I judged that she had no mind that he should have any of her estate or manage it, but kept it to her own use. For ♄ is retrograde in a fiery sign, and the sign of the 7th fixed, all which shews her to be a woman not willing to be curbed or to submit. (*This was confessed.*)

Lastly, as ☉ was lately in ⚹ to ♃, and ♃ in the 10th, I told him that some great lawyer or courtier* had endeavoured to reconcile the differences between them ; and as ☉ and ♄ did now apply to △ aspect, there seemed, at present, a willingness in both parties to be reconciled. Nor did I see any obstruction in the matter, except ☿, who is in □ aspect to ♄, did impedite it. I judged ☿, in general, to signify some lawyer, attorney, or writings ; but, as he was lord of the querent's 2d, it might be because the querent would not consent to allow her such a sum of money as might be asked ; or that, his purse being weak, he had not wherewithal to solicit his cause ; or ☿ being lord of the 11th, some pretended friend would advise the contrary, or some of her lawyers ; or, as the 11th is the 5th from the 7th, a *child* of the querent's wife might be the occasion of continuing the breach. (*I believe every particular herein proved true ; however, this was the way to find the thing which disturbed their unity.*)

Observe, that as ♀, lady of the 10th, doth dispose of ♃, lord of the 8th, viz. the wife's fortune, so she had entrusted her estate to a great nobleman.

5th QUERY.—*What* ACCIDENTS, *in future, he might expect ?*

In this query, I first considered ☉, lord of the ascendant, no ways unfortunate or in ill aspect with any planet ; but, on the contrary, excellently fortified : I judged he had the wide world to ramble in, (for a planet strong, and in no aspect with others, shews a man at liberty to do what he will) ; and, for many years he might (*quoad capax*) live in a prosperous con-

---

* It was the *Lord Coventry.*

dition, and traverse much ground, or see many countries. For ♈, the sign which ☉ is in, is moveable and on the cusp of the 9th, the house of long journeys ; which denoted many changes and variety of action in sundry parts.

2dly : I observed ☽ in his house of substance, applying to ♃ in the 10th, and ♃ lord of the 5th and 8th ; the former the house of children ; the latter that of the wife's substance. Hence I gathered, that the querent was desirous to treat with some nobleman (♃ being in the 10th) about the education of his children ; and that there might be a salary payable out of the wife's jointure. (*Such a thing he did settle before he left England.*)

3dly : I found ☽ in ♍ *peregrine.*

4thly : ☿ lord of his 2d, signifying his estate in ♓, his *detriment ;* yet, in his own terms, afflicted by ♂, and having lately had the ☍ of ☽ . Hence I judged that he had been in great want of money a little before the question was asked. And if we note the distance between the ☍ of ☽ and ☿, we find 6° 21', shewing that he had been in want of money about six months and somewhat more, previously to asking the question. (*This was confessed.*)

5thly : Seeing ☽ was applying to △ of ♃, and then, before she got out of the sign ♍, did occur the ☍ of ♂, I acquainted the querent that, after some years of pleasure, he would be in great danger of losing his life, goods, lands, and fortune. His *life,* because ♂ is in the 8th : his *estate,* because ☽ is in the 2d ; and his *lands* or *inheritance,* because ♂ is lord of the 4th and situated in the 8th house ; for the 4th house denotes *lands,* &c.

6th QUERY.—*The time when ?*

In this query, I considered the application of ☽ to △ ♃ ; which wanting about 3 degrees, I judged that he might live pleasantly for about three years to come

2dly : Seeing that ☉ lord of the ascendant, during his motion through ♈, did not meet any malevolent aspect, and had got 26 degrees to run through the sign, I gave this nature of judgment: I told him that for about 26 months, or until over two years to come, I judged he should live in a free condition, in those parts in which he intended his journey, &c.

Lastly : I considered how many degrees ☽ wanted of the ☍ of ☽ .

Longitude of ♂	28°	40
Longitude of ☽	21	18
Difference	7	22

This difference, if in proportion unto time, and neither give years, because the *significators* are in common signs and not in fixed ; nor months, because the signs signify somewhat more ; but proportion a *mean* between both : the time limited in this way will amount to about three years and three quarters ere the ☍ of ♂ to ☽ should take effect. But as this query was general, I might have allowed for every degree one year.* After, or about which time, he was in several actions, both dangerous to his person and fortune ; and since that time till the present, he has had his intervals of good and ill, but is now under the frown of fortune, &c.

As the ☉ at the time of the question was strong, he did overcome all manner of difficulties for many years, and has, in our unlucky differences, had honourable employment on his Majesty's part. But as ☽† is in ☍ to ♂, so it was not without the general outcry and exclamations of the people ; nor was it his fortune, though in great command, ever to do his Majesty any notable piece of service. And he is now for

* I should certainly always do so.—ZAD.

† In all questions ☽ signifies the people, where they are at all concerned.

ever, by just sentence of the Parliament, deprived of the happiness of ending his days in England; which might, in some measure, have been foreseen by the ☍ of ☽ to ♂, he being lord of the 4th, the end of all things.*

N.B. All young beginners should at first write down their judgments on each figure at full length, and afterwards contract their opinions into a narrow compass; by this means they will soon acquire experience. It is well to enter every figure in a book for farther reference, and to remark and register such things as have occurred according to their predictions or otherwise; by which they will be able to correct their future judgments.

CHAPTER XXIII.

If one shall find the Party at Home he would speak with ?

THE ascendant and its lord are for the querent, the 7th and its lord for him you would speak with; but if it be with any relation, take the house signifying that relation and its lord; as, for the father the 4th, for a child the 5th, and for an intimate friend the 11th; if the lord of the 7th, or quesited's significator, be in any of the four angles, the party is at home; but if he be in a succeedent house, he is not far from home; but if in a cadent house, then he is far from home.

If you find the lord of the ascendant apply to the quesited's perfect aspect the same day you intend to visit him, you may be assured either to meet him going to his house, or hear of him by the way; or, if any planet separate from the lord of the quesited's house, and transfer his light to the lord of the ascendant, you will learn where he is by a person signified by

---

* I should say also, by ♄ being in the 4th house and retrograde, for such a position ever denotes a final catastrophe

that planet. Describe the planet, and it personates the individual ; and the nature of the planet, sign, and quarter of heaven it is in, will, by the plurality of testimonies, shew whether it be male or female.

Of a thing suddenly happening, whether it signifies Good or Evil?

Erect your figure of heaven at the exact time of any event happening, or when you first heard of it : then consider who is lord of the ascendant, and which planet disposes of ☉ and ☽ ; and see if either of these be in the ascendant, and, if more than one, take the most powerful ; and let his position be well considered. If he be in good aspect with ☉, ♃, or ♀, there will no evil arise from the accident, rumour, or whatever the event may be ; but if you find that planet weak in the scheme, combust, or in evil aspect to ♅, ♄, ♂, or ☿, there will be some evil occur. If you consider the afflicting planet and his nature and position, you may learn the nature of the misfortune. If it be the lord of the 3d, it will come through some kinsman or neighbour, or by some short journey ; if the lord of the 2d cast the ray, or the evil planet be in the 2d, it denotes loss of money ;* if the lord of the 4th. trouble about houses, &c., or by means of a father or wife's mother ; if the 5th, by intemperance, or by children, &c., and so of the rest.†

* the same if ⊕ receive evil rays approaching.

† The nature of the planet casting the ray, also may be expected to shew the nature of the evil ; ♂ shews robbers, &c., ♄ elderly persons, ☿ young persons and lawyers, ♅ unlooked-for and uncommon events, ♀ females, ☉ men in power, ♃ clergymen and magistrates, ☽ sailors. low people, mobs, &c. But note, that unless the benefic planets be lords of evil houses, their ill aspects do not import much evil. And if they be lords of good houses, or placed in good houses and strong, their good aspects denote benefits in the same manner ; and in all cases ⊕ shews gain or loss, as it may be aspected ; and ☊, with the chief significator, imports benefits, and ☋ the reverse.

QUERY.—*What Mark, Mole, or Scar has the Querent on any Part of his Body? This is useful to prove that a question is radical, and to satisfy sceptics of the truth of the science.*

When you have, upon any demand, erected the querent's figure, observe what member of man's body the ascending sign represents; for upon that part of his body will the querent have a mole, mark, or scar; as, if the ascendant be ♈, the same will be on the head; if ♉, it will be on the neck; if ♊, on the arms or shoulders, &c.* And also in the part ruled by the sign in which the lord of the ascendant is, will there be another mark.

The signs on the cusp of the 6th house, and that in which the lord of the 6th is, will give other marks on the parts they rule. Also the sign in which ☽ is found will give a mark in that part it governs.

If ♄ give the mark, it is dark, obscure, or black; ♂ usually gives a red mole; but if he be in a fiery sign, it is generally a cut or scar.

If the sign or planet signifying the mark or mole be much afflicted, the mark, &c. will be more obvious and eminent.

If the sign or planet be masculine, the mark is on the *right* side of the body; but if they be feminine, on the *left* side. And if the significator of the mole, &c. be *above* the horizon, the mark or mole will be on the *fore part*, or visible to the eye, or on the outside of the member, &c.; but if the planet be *below* the earth, it will be found on the inside, or

---

* PARTS *of* MAN'S BODY *ruled by the* TWELVE SIGNS.

♈ *Head and face.*	♎ *Reins and loins.*
♉ *Neck and throat.*	♏ *Secret members.*
♊ *Arms and shoulders.*	♐ *Hips and thighs.*
♋ *Breast and stomach.*	♑ *Knees and hams.*
♌ *Heart and back.*	♒ *Legs and ancles.*
♍ *Bowels and belly.*	♓ *Feet and toes.*

H

hinder part, or not visible.　If few degrees are on the cusp of the house, or the planet signifying the mole, &c. be in few degrees of the sign, the mark, mole, &c., will be in the upper part of the member.　If they be in the middle of the sign, it will be in the middle of the member or part ruled by the sign.　But if the latter degrees ascend, or are on the 6th, or their lords, or ☽ be in the latter degrees of a sign, then will the mark, mole, or scar be near the lower part of the member.　If your question be radical, and the time rightly taken, the above rules will always exactly hold good.　And so will they (*mutatis mutandis*) upon the body of the quesited ; for if a person inquire concerning his wife, then the sign on the 7th and its lord will shew the woman's marks ; and the sign on the 12th, (the 6th from the 7th), and its lord will shew two other marks.

Many times if the ☽ be in ♂ or ☍ ☉, the querent has some blemish in or near his eyes : and this is ever true, if the ♂ or ☍ be in angles, and ☽ or ☉ be afflicted by Mars.*

Whether one absent be dead or alive?

If the quesited have no relation to the querent, then the

---

* If ♃ give the mark, it will be bluish or purple ; ♀ gives it yellow ; ☿ a pale lead colour ; ☉ olive or chesnut ; and ☽ a whitish hue, or partly of the colour of the planets she aspects.　The infortunes ♄ and ♂, especially when together, or in exact aspect, mark according to their position.　If they be in the ascendant, a mole, &c. will be in the face ; if in the 2d, on the neck · in the 3d, on the arms, &c.

And all these rules apply to the figure of birth, as well as horary figures ; but *defects*, such as protrusion of the breast bone, or a humped back, &c. (to persons born with ♋ or ♌ rising), may sometimes be found in lieu of moles or scars.　For example, her present majesty, having ♄ in ♓, which rules the feet, and situated near the cusp of the 12th *house,* at her birth, she has a *weakness* in her feet.　Had *one* testimony only existed, and ♄ been in ♓ elsewhere, she would have merely had a mole on her foot.

ascendant, its lord, and ☽ shall signify the absent person.*
But if the party inquired after be a relation, then take the
house and its lord which signifies that relation ; as the 3d for
a brother or sister, fhe 4th for a father, the 6th for a paternal
uncle or aunt, the 10th for a mother, &c.

In judging this question, see whether the quesited's lord of
the 1st and 8th be joined corporally together in the 8th, or be
in ☍ from the 6th or 8th. These are tokens of his being
sick or near to death. See if there be any translation of light
between the lord of his ascendant and the 8th, or if the lord
of the 8th being in his ascendant, the lord of his ascendant
be also in the 8th ; or the lord of the 8th in the 4th, and the
lord of the 4th in the 8th ; these are all tokens that the party
is dead ; especially if his significator be much afflicted by ill
aspects, and the evil planets be angular, and the good ones
cadent.

If the lord of his ascendant be separating from ill aspect
of the lord of the 6th, the absent party has been lately sick ;
if from the lord of the 8th, he has been near death, but is not
dead, without other striking testimonies, as above, concur. If
from the lord of the 12th, he has been troubled with anxietv
about arrests or fear of imprisonment ; and if his significator
be in the 12th, he is in much trouble by means of a private
enemy ; and if in a fixed sign, and other testimonies of trouble agree, he is in prison. If he separate from the lord of
the 2d by ill aspect, he is now suffering by want of money
If from the lord of the 7th, he has had some quarrel or contention. If the 9th, trouble on journeys or by law, &c.
and so of the other houses. I have ever found that if the
lord of his ascendant be in the 9th, 10th, or 11th, though re-

* We should always take the ascendant, &c. for the querent, and the
7th and its lord for the quesited. But if the figure be erected by an artist
at his own suggestion, let the ascendant, &c. shew the absent person.

ported dead, he was alive.   If you find him alive, and would know when you will hear from or see him, observe in the Ephemeris when the lord of the querent's 11th and the quesited's ascendant come to ✳ or △ aspect: about that time news of him will arrive.   If the ☽ apply to ✳ or △ of his significator, then allow a day, week, or month, for each degree she be distant, according as the significators may be placed in angles, succeedent or cadent houses, and the signs be moveable, common, or fixed.*

---

* The most difficult thing in all questions is to judge of *time* with accuracy.   I should advise the young student to be cautious of giving any judgment on this head, unless where it is the chief point desired to be known.   In this case, and if the figure be very radical, and if *the planet which is applying* to the other be taken, the following rule will hold good :—

Each Degree gives

In Moveable Signs and Angles........ ..... DAYS

In Common Signs and Angles.. .... WEEKS.

In Fixed Signs and Angles........ .....MONTHS.

Succeedent houses give *weeks, months,* and *years,* as the sign is *moveable, common,* or *fixed ;* and *cadent houses* give *months* in *moveable signs. years* in *common,* and an indefinite time in *fixed signs.*--ZAD

Fig. 3.

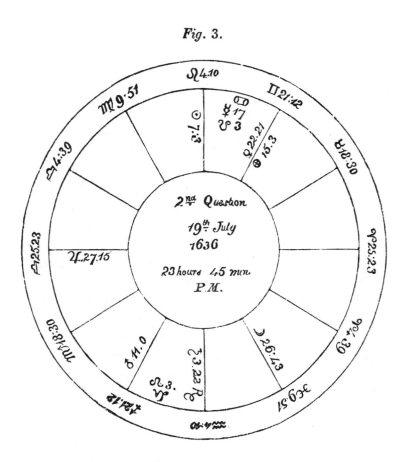

THE ABOVE FIGURE WAS FOR RESOLUTION OF THE FOLLOWING
QUERIES.

1st. *If a Party might be found at Home?*

2d. *A Thing suddenly happening, whether Good or Ill is
about to follow?*

3d. *What Moles or Marks the Querent has?*

4th. *If one absent be dead or alive?*

1st Query.—*A Woman demanded whether her Son was with his Master at her own House ?*

In this figure, ♀ lady of the ascendant denotes the querent. The 5th house is that of children, and describes the matter inquired of. I found ♃, lord of the 5th, youth's significator, in the east angle ; one argument that the party was at home at his mother's house. The ☽ was applying to ⚹ of ♄ lord of the 4th, the significator of the querent's dwelling : I judged that she would find him there at her coming home : which she did. Now, had I found ♃, lord of the 5th, in the 10th, which house signifies the master ; or had ☽ separated from ♃, the youth's significator, and then applied to ☉, the ☽ being in an angle, I would have judged him at his master's house. I considered further, that the 25th of July following at 2 P.M., the significators of the mother and son (♃ and ♀) came to △ aspect ; and therefore I judged that she should see him at that time : which she did. For usually about that day when the *significators* come to ⚹ or △ aspect (which may be seen in the *Ephemeris*), it is very probable that news of, or a letter from, the quesited will arrive, if the distance will permit. But if the querent and quesited be not far asunder, without question they meet on that very day.

Had the party inquired for been a stranger, he would have been denoted by ♂ lord of the 7th ; and being in the 2d, a *succeedent* house, I should have said he is not at home, but yet not far from home. And as the sign ♐ is eastern, and the 2d house is north east, I should judge him in that direction ; and as ♐ governs fields, hills, or high grounds, I should direct a messenger, if sent for him, to go in that direction, and look for him in such places ; but if it were in a town, as ♐ governs stables, fire-places, &c., I should cause him to be sought near a stable, smith's or butcher's shop, &c., as ♂ delights in such places.

2d QUERY.—*A Thing suddenly happening, whether* **Good** *or Ill is about to follow?*

The ☉ is here lord of the sign he is in ; ♃ is lord of ♓, where ☽ is ; ♀ is lady of the ascendant, and is casting a △ to the ascendant, and is in △ to ♃, and he in the ascendant ; from all which we might safely have judged, had this been the time of a sudden accident, or thing done, that it could not have redounded to the querent's injury. But had ♀ been nearer to ☍ of ♂, he being in the 2d, I should have judged that the querent would have received some loss of money shortly, and so of the rest.*

3d QUERY.—*What Moles or Marks the Querent has?*

I find 25° of ♎ ascending and ♃ in the ascendant, which signifies the face. This querent had a wart or mole on the right side of her face, near her mouth ; for ♃ and ♎ are *masculine.* And as the latter degrees of ♎ ascend, so the querent confessed a mole on the lower part of her reins towards the haunches. ♈ being the sign of the 6th, shewed she had one on the forehead, near the hair, for the cusp of the house is but 4 degrees. ♂ lord of the 6th, being in ♐ a masculine sign and under the earth, shewed a mole on the right thigh, towards the middle of it, on the back part, or

---

* We consider that our author has been rather brief on this point, for numerous occasions occur where the mind is desirous of knowing the result when events happen. If ♀ had been within orbs of ♂ opposition, that is, *half the distance of their united orbs,* or 7° ; we should have judged loss of money by a party shewn by ♀, and her situation considered with the houses she governs. As, for example, ♀ ruling the 12th, some private female enemy, among the relations of the wife or husband, because ♀ is in the 3d from the 7th house. And as ♂ is ☍ to ⊕, we should predict a loss by a servant (since ♂ rules the 6th) ; and as ⊕ is in the 8th, it might be by one who comes to char or go messages ; if ⊕ had been in a watery sign, a washerwoman. But the general testimonies being good, we should say the evil will be but trifling. Experience will teach the student these points.

that part which is not visible. The ☽ in 27th degree of ♓,
a feminine sign, under the earth, I told her she had one mole
under and towards the extremity of her left foot.

The quesited being her son, had ♓ for his ascendant, which
denoted a mole on the left side of his cheek ; and as ♓ signifies the foot, so he had one on the left foot a little below the
ancle, as few degrees ascend. The 6th from the 5th is the
10th in the figure, which having 4° ♌, shewed that near his
right side, below his breast, he had some scar, mole, or mark.

In this way follow the directions of the rule.

4th QUERY.—*Whether one absent be dead or alive ?*

In the aforesaid figure, the ascendant ♃ therein and ♀
its ruler, as also ☽, are the significators of the party absent.
The ascending sign and ♃ therein describe his person ;* and
☽ and ♀ shew his condition.

The ☽ and ♀ are free from any evil aspect of the lord of
the 8th, and a benefic is in the ascendant, and ♀ in the 9th;
I should therefore pronounce the absent in health. But ♀
having been recently in ☍ to ♂, lord of the 2d and 6th, he
had been lately in trouble about money, and also inclined to a
feverish state. But by ♃ in the ascendant, and in △ to ♀,
I should say that medicine, or such a person as is described
by ♃, had relieved him. And as ☿ lord of the 11th applies
to a □ of ♃, (both of them in signs of long ascension, which
is equivalent to a △,)† I should judge the querent to have
news of the absent about ten weeks from the time of the

---

* If no planet be in the ascendant of the party, look to the lord of the
ascendant for a description of his person, according to the sign it is in,
and judge by that and the sign ascending; but if the lord of the ascendant
be much *afflicted*, the ☽, according to the sign she is in, must be taken.

† This doctrine of the signs of long ascension, causing a ⚹ to be equal
to a □, and a □ to a △, and the reverse in signs of short ascension, can
only be received in horary and mundane astrology ; and not in nativities.

question, because ☿ wants ten degrees of the □ of ♃ . **If the absent be known to be at a short distance from the quesited, I should have judged that in ten days they should hear of him, because the signs are moveable.***

CHAPTER XXIV.

OF A SHIP, AND HER SAFETY OR DESTRUCTION.

THE ascendant and the ☽ signify the ship and cargo ; the lord of the ascendant, those that sail in her.   If you find a malevolent, having dignities in the 8th, placed in the ascendant, or the lord of the ascendant in the 8th in ill configuration with the lords of the 8th, 12th, 4th, or 6th, or if the ☽ be combust, and under the earth, you may judge that the ship is lost, and the men drowned.   But if you find reception between the significators at the same time, the ship was wrecked, but some of the crew escaped : if all the preceding significators be free from affliction, then both ship and cargo are safe ; and if there be reception, the more so.   If the ascendant and ☽ be unfortunate, and the lord of the ascendant fortunate, the ship is lost, but the men saved.

But when the querent demand, of any ship setting forth, and the state of the ship ere she return, and what may be hoped of the voyage ; then, behold the *angles* of the figure, and see if the fortunes are therein, and the infortunes remote from angles, cadent, combust, or under the ☉ beams, then you may judge the ship will go safe with all her lading.   But if you find the infortunes in angles, or succeeding houses,

---

* We should, in this latter case, prefer looking to the Ephemeris for day when ☿ formed a △ of ♃ for hearing news, and when ♀ and came to ♂ for his return.

there will chance some hinderance unto the ship. If the infortune be ♄, the vessel will strike ground. If ♂, and he
be in an earthy sign, he will signify the same, or very great
danger and damage. But if the fortunes cast their benevolent
rays to the place of ♄ or ♂, and the lords of the angles and
of the dispositor of the ☽ be free, then the ship shall labour
hard, and suffer damage, yet the greater part of the crew and
cargo shall be preserved. If ♂ afflict the lords of the angles,
and dispositor of ☽, the crew will be in danger by enemies
or pirates ; and if there be any additional evil configurations
among these significators, there will be quarrels on board,
thieving, and purloining, &c., with bloodshed: ♄ causes
thefts only, if so situated, but no bloodshed.

If the signs afflicted by ♄, ♂, ♉ (and ♅, if he be ill aspected), be those that signify the vessel's bottom, or parts
under water, she springs a leak ; if the signs be unfortunate
in the midheaven, fiery signs, and ♂ therein, there is danger
of lightning or fire ; if airy signs and ☿ afflict, damage by
high winds. If ♂ be in the 4th, and afflicted, it denotes fire
beneath : and if ♅ be with him, spontaneous combustion.
If the sign be ♊, ♎, or ♒, she may be set on fire by an
enemy.

If ♄ be in the midheaven, and shew damage, it will be by
rotten sails or gear, and bad weather, foul winds, &c. An infortune in the ascendant shews damage to the fore part of the
vessel ; and if the lord of the ascendant be retrograde, it denotes that she will put into some harbour ; and if he be in a
moveable sign, she returns to the very port she sailed from.
If the lord of the 8th afflict the lord of the 1st, and he in the
8th, the ship will be injured according to the nature of the
planet afflicting. If he impedite the ☽'s dispositor, the lord
of the ascendant and ☽, it shews the death of the master,
and probably of his mate. If it be ⊕ which is afflicted, it

foreshews evil to the cargo or a bad market; but if ♃, ♀, or ☊ be in the second, or assist its lord, or the lord of ⊕, it shews good profit, which will be according to their strength.

If the lords of the ascendant, of the ☽ and their dispositors be slow in motion, the voyage will be long; if they be swift, the ship will return quickly. If there be ill aspects between the lord of the 1st and the dispositor of ☽ without reception, there will be discord among the seamen, and with them and the owner. If the lord of the ascendant be strongest, the seamen will prevail; but if the lord of the house where ☽ is, then the owner. If the dispositor of ⊕ be not with it, or the lord of the 2d be weak, there will be scarcity of provisions, and, if they be in watery signs, of fresh water.

PARTS of a SHIP ruled by the SIGNS.

♈ The breast, or bows of the ship.

♉ The cutwater, and parts beneath.

♊ The rudder, or stem.

♋ The bottom, or floor.

♌ The upper works.

♍ The hold.

♎ The parts about the water's edge.

♏ The seamen's berths, or cabin.

♐ The seamen themselves.

♑ The ends of the vessel.

♒ The master, or captain.

♓ The oars, in galleys; the wheels, in steam-vessels; and the sails in others.

Fig. 4.

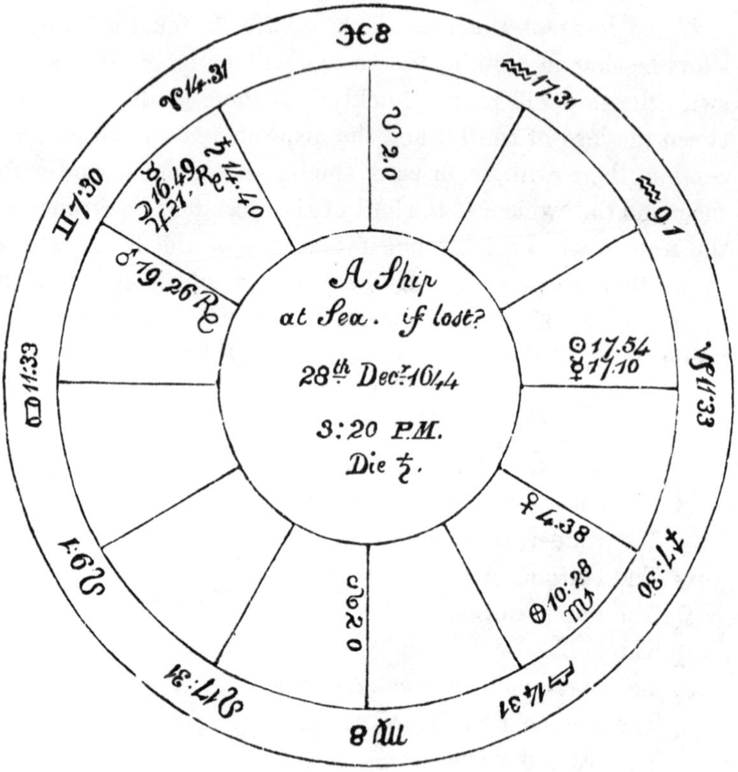

AN EXAMPLE OF A SHIP AT SEA.

In December 1644, a merchant, in London, having sent a ship to the coast of Spain to trade, had several times news that his ship was wrecked. He would have given £60 per cent. to insure her, but no insurance company would meddle, no, not upon any terms. A friend of the merchant asked, *What I thought of the ship, if sunk or living?* I gave my opinion, *that the ship was not lost, but did live, and though f late in some danger, yet was now recovered.* My judgment was founded on the considerations in *act* following :—

In the first place, the ascending degrees of Cancer shewed the bulk or body of the ship. I find ♄ casts his ☐ from a cardinal sign, out of the 11th house, very near to the ascendant. After his ☐ I find ☽ in her exaltation, casting a ⚹ to the ascendant, interposing her ⚹ between the ☍ aspects of ☿ and ☉ in the 7th, which otherwise had been dangerous, for all ☍ aspects to the ascendant in this judgment are dangerous. From the ascendant afflicted by ☐ of ♄, and presence of fixed stars of his nature, I judged the ship was of ♄'s nature, sluggish, heavy, and not very sound. And ♋ being a weakly sign, made me judge the ship was of such nature ; (*and it was so confessed*). From hence, and ☊ in the 9th, I judged that the ship had been in some distress in her voyage, occasioned by such casualties as ♄ signifies, viz. some leak or damage in or near her breast, as ♈, the sign ♄ is in, represents that part.

But as ☽, lady of the ascendant, is in the 11th in her exaltation, in no way impeded, and by a benevolent △ aspect applying to ☉ and ☿, and is so near the body of ♃, and as all the significators are above the earth, and no infortunes in angles ; I judged the ship, sailors, and officers, were safe, and in good condition. The next QUERY was—

Where the Ship was, upon what Coast, and when any News would come of her ?

Herein I considered the ☽ was fixed, and in the 11th house ; ♉ is a southern sign, but in an east quarter of heaven, verging to the south ; her application is to △ of ☿, and he in ♑ a south sign and west angle ; all this made me judge that the ship was *south-west* from London, and upon our own coasts, or near those which lie between Ireland and Wales. I judged her at that time to be in some harbour, because ♉, where ☽ is, is fixed, and in the 11th, or house of comfort and relief, and that she was put in to repair. (*It proved that she was in a harbour in the west.*)

Because ☽ applied to △ of ☿ and ☉, and they in an angle, and all three very swift in motion, and did want but a few minutes of a perfect △, I judged there would be news, or a certain discovery of the ship in a very short time. The significators being so near a perfect aspect, I said, either that night, or within two days, the news would arrive. (*And so it proved.*) And, observe, that it gave me good encourage- ment when I saw ⊕ disposed of by ♂, and that ☿, to whom ☽ applied, was in reception with ♂; also, that ☽ did so well apply to ☉, lord of the 2d, or house of *substance :* a sign that the merchant should gain by that adventure.

Besides, usually when ☽ applies to a good aspect of a *re- trograde* planet, it brings the matter to an issue one way or other speedily, and when least expected ; and it is a general maxim, that if ☽ apply to the fortunes, or by good aspect to any planet or planets in angles, it is reason that we hope well, &c.

Fig. 5.

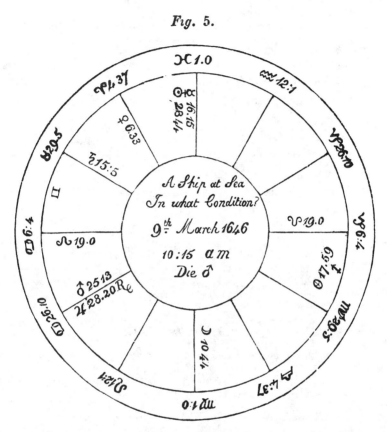

EXAMPLE *of another* SHIP *at* SEA.

Here the ascendant and ☽ are significators of the ship.
and those who sail in her. The ☽ lately separated from a
□ of ♄, lord of the 8th and 9th, and afterwards applied to
△ of ♄, then to ☍ of ☿, lord of the 12th and 4th houses.
This shewed that the ship had lately been in danger of ship-
wreck: and as the ☽ had been void of course, so had no
news been heard of her; for, after being in □ of ♄ in fixed
signs, and at the time in a cadent house, and then not next

applying to the good aspect of any benefic planet, but being
void of course, and then again continuing her application out
of the 4th to ♄, who is still lord of the 8th, though it was
by good aspect; and then to ☍ of ☿, her dispositor, who is
in his detriment and entering combustion; and ♃, dispositor
of ☿, subterranean, and ♂ with ♂ and in term of an infortune; and, moreover, as ♂ is in his fall near the cusp of
the 2d, I judged, by all this, loss to the merchant. Besides
⊕, is in the 6th disposed by ♃, he retrograde and afflicted
in the 2d in no aspect to ⊕, the ☽ also in □ to it, as also
☿. There being so many ill testimonies, I judged he would
lose much, if not all, in this ship; and so consequently that
she was cast away. (*And so it proved.*) The principal significator in the 4th and afflicted, was a sure sign of the ship
sinking.

CHAPTER XXV.

JUDGMENTS CONCERNING THE SECOND HOUSE.

WHETHER *the Querent shall be rich? or have a competent
Fortune? By what Means attain it? The time when? and
if it shall continue?*

Whoever interrogates, the lord of the ascendant and the ☽
are invariably his significators.

Consider the sign on the 2d, its lord, and the planets therein,
or aspecting the cusp or its lord; also the ⊕.

If you find the planets all angular or even succeedent, if
direct and swift in motion, it is a good sign. If in good
houses, direct, and moderately well dignified, it is also a good
sign. Those two rules are general.

If the lord of the 1st, the ☽, and lord of the 2d, be joined
together, or if they have good aspect to the lord of the 2d, or

if ♃ or ♀ cast a good aspect to ⊕, or if the lord of the 2d or ☽ be in the ascendant, or lord of the 1st in the 2d, or benefics do ascend or be found unafflicted in the 2d, or ☍ be there, all these are testimonies that the querent need fear no poverty. As the significators may be strong, and the testi monies numerous, the querent shall be in proportion rich. Always remember to judge according to his condition in life ; for, *quoad capax*, it shall happen to the interrogator.

By what Means attain it ?

If the lord of the 2d be in the ascendant, he may gain a fortune unexpectedly, (especially if well aspected by ♅, and this planet be strong), or gain it without much labour. If the lord of the 2d or the Moon promise substance by any mutual aspect, observe from what house the aspect is, or what house ☽ rules ; if neither of these promise substance, see what house ⊕ and its dispositor be in.

If the planet assisting be in the ascendant, the querent will gain by his own industry, and, if he be a mechanic, by his own labour, care, or invention. But if the assisting planet be not lord of the 2d, he will gain by well managing his own affairs, estate, &c. ; or by such things as are of the nature of that planet, the sign he is in being also considered.

If the lord of the 2d be in the 2d, he shall profit by his own industry. If the lord of the 3d benefit the lord of the 2d, ⊕, or other significators of wealth, he will be assisted by his neighbours, brethren, or kindred ; or by removing to that quarter from whence the lord of the 3d throws the aspect.

The lord of the 4th gives wealth by means of his father, or some aged person ; or by taking lands, or purchasing houses, &c. ; or by well managing money lent him by his kindred or neighbours ; or property left him by his ancestors.

I

The lord of the 5th promises gain by cards or other gambling; or stock-jobbing; or by holding office as an ambassador or messenger. If a man of low quality ask, by keeping an inn, &c., or being porter to some institution, or connected with theatres, &c., and such things as the 5th house denotes. It may be by well managing his father's estate, or receiving something thereout.

The lord of the 6th gives gain by servants, dealing in small cattle, &c., or by turning surgeon, &c., if capable.

The lord of the 7th gives gain by means of a wife, by the sword or warfare, by contracting bargains in his way of business, or by gaining some lawsuit, &c.

The lord of the 8th or planet therein denotes legacies, or a wife's portion, which may be unexpected at the time, (especially if ♅ assist), or he may suddenly go and settle in some country wherein he shall thrive and grow rich.

The lord of the 9th, &c., gives property by the wife's relations, or some neighbour of her's when he did marry; or some clergyman or lawyer shall befriend him; or if ♋ or ♓ be in the 9th, he may thrive by a distant sea voyage. But if an earthy sign be there, he may gain by removing to the part signified by that sign, and by dealing in the commodities belonging to that country, &c.

The lord of the 10th, &c. promises gain by the service of the king or some great man, holding office, &c. If the querent be young and of small fortune, let him learn some trade or business that may be shewn by the sign and planet in the 10th.

The 11th and its lord denote unexpected benefit by friends, or the employment of some king, nobleman or other great person.

If the fortunate aspect be cast from the 12th or by its lord, the querent will advance his fortune by great cattle or horse-races; or if the sign be human, that is, ♊ or ♒, by means of prisons, &c., such as being governor or turnkey of a jail, a sheriff's officer, &c. If the sign be ♈, ♉, or ♑, by cattle; if ♍, by corn. Herein mix your judgment with reason.

The most assured testimonies of riches are if the lords of the 1st, 2d, and ♃ be joined in the 2d, 1st, 10th, 7th, 4th, or 11th houses; or if not in ♂, if they apply by ⚹ or △ and be in mutual reception. If they apply by □ or ☍, yet have reception, the querent will gain wealth, though with much labour and pains.

Signs of Poverty, and its Cause.

If you find that the querent will *not* be rich, and he desire to know *why*, that he may the better order his affairs and be wary of such difficulties as may threaten, then carefully observe as follows. The planet afflicting most the lords of the 2d and 1st, the ☽, ⊕, or their dispositors, or the cusp of the 2d or planet therein, shews the cause. If the lord of the 1st, then the querent himself is the cause, and the house in which he is found may shew how. The lord of the 2d shews want of money or sufficient capital to set up with. The lord of the 3d shews that his kindred or neighbours will oppose him much, or undersell him, &c. And in this way you may go through the twelve houses, judging the reverse of what you were instructed when the aspects, &c. were good.

Caution.—If the lord of the 2d or the dispositor of ⊕ be infortunes, yet be strong and well aspected, they may denote gain as well as ♃ or ♀, though with less satisfaction and more painstaking. Also ♃ or ♀ being afflicted, may obstruct as well as any other; for every planet must do the work for which he is by Providence assigned. Again, wherever ☋ may be found, he denotes evil by that house, as if in the 6th, by evil servants, sickness, &c. ɪ 2

If the querent shall obtain the Substance he hath lent, or
which he demands?

The lord of the ascendant and ☽ are the querent's significators, the lord of the 2d denotes his substance.*

The 7th and its lord denote the person of whom he means
to ask the money, and the 8th and its lord, &c., his property. Observe whether the lord of the ascendant or ☽ be
joined with the significator of the quesited's property, or be
in good aspect with such significator. If this be so, and that
significator be a fortune or very strong, he shall assuredly
receive the money. If he be an infortune, and there be reception between him and the querent's significator, the
querent will also receive his money, &c. ; but if the quesited's
significator be an evil planet, and there be no reception, he
will hardly ever gain his desire, or with so much delay and
difficulty, he would rather wish the thing undone.

In like manner if the lord of the 8th be in the 2d with
reception, it is a sign he shall gain his money, &c. But if
the lord of the 7th or 8th be in the 1st or 2d without reception with the querent's significators or lord of the 2d, he
shall not have his desire, but may rather expect prejudice in
the thing demanded.

If the lord of the 1st and ☽ be joined to a fortune that has
dignity in the sign ascending or *intercepted* in the *ascendant*,
the matter will be effected ; or if joined to an infortune
having such dignity, *with reception*, the business will be dis-
patched. Or, if the significators be joined to a fortune in
the 10th or 11th, though without reception, the matter shall
be perfected.

* When any planets are found in a house signifying anything, they may
be taken as well as the lord of the house

If one shall acquire Gain, or Profit, Salary, &c., from the Government, or any Nobleman, or Person of high Rank, &c. ?

This question will serve for any other of the like nature, where the querent is much inferior in rank to the person he looks to for accomplishing his desires.

The ascendant, its lord and the ☽, represent the querent as usual, and the 10th and its lord the quesited. The 2d is the house of property for the querent, and the 11th for the person inquired about.

If you find the lord of the 1st or the ☽ joined to the lord of the 11th, or to any fortune in the 11th, not afflicted, you may affirm that the querent shall obtain his money, salary, or debt, &c. Or if it happen that the ☽ and lord of the ascendant be joined to an evil planet with reception, he may expect to succeed, but not without much solicitation, and many weary efforts. If there be any evil aspect between the significators, one being an infortune and without reception, the querent will never gain what he desires.

In this question be very careful to observe the planets' true essential dignities, and their mutual receptions, and by which of their mutual dignities they receive each other.*

Of the Time when the aforesaid Events treated of in this Chapter may happen.

Herein diligently note to what planet the lord of the ascendant or ☽ applies, by ♂ or aspect. Consider how many degrees are wanting of the perfect aspect or ♂, and say that it shall be as many days as there are degrees, if they be *both in cadent houses;* if both in *succeedent* houses, so many weeks ; if both in *angles,* so many months. But if the matter cannot possibly be effected in days or weeks, but requires

* Reception by house is the most powerful ; then exaltation, triplicity term. and face : the latter is very weak

much time, instead of months say years, and of weeks say months, and of days say weeks, &c.   And if one planet be in an angle, and the other in a succeedent house, they shall signify months ; one succeedent, and the other cadent, they denote weeks ; and when one be angular and the other cadent, months.*

Some of the ancients have said, that if, at the time of a question, the planet which signifies the perfection of the thing demanded be in the same sign with the lord of the ascendant, the matter shall be brought to conclusion when they come to bodily conjunction ; if the lord of the ascendant be the heavier planet, and whether there be reception or not.   But if the lord of the ascendant be the lighter planet, not without reception, unless they be in an angle when the conjunction hall be effected, or that the other planet be in one of his own houses, especially that which is termed his joy.†

I have observed that reception by house, though the aspect were a □, or even ☍, brings things to perfection; but that other receptions avail not in this case.

As regards the time when ; I find that if a fortune, or the ☽, or lord of the thing quesited, be in the ascendant, and have any essential dignities therein, the number of degrees between the planet and the cusp of the ascendant denote the time ; days, if a moveable sign, and the business capable of being quickly perfected ; months, or years, according to the sign and quality of the business.

---

* There appears a species of confusion in this arrangement, which is the reverse of the usual system, of allowing angles to produce events quicker than cadents.   We should advise the student to be careful in his experiments before he adopt it.

† *Joys of the Planets :*

♒, ♄; ♐, ♃; ♏, ♂; ♎ ♀; ♍, ☿.   These are not usually noticed by modern astrologers.

Fig. 6.

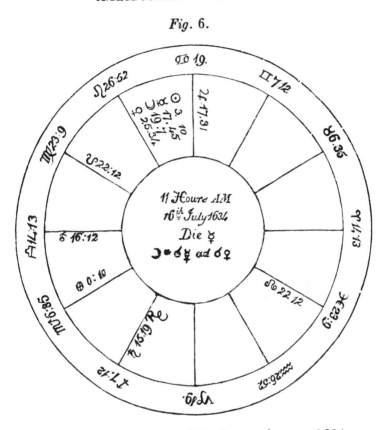

EXAMPLE.—A tradesman of *London*, in the year 1634, propounded the following queries. I have seen the experience
of my judgment.

QUERIES.—1st. *If he should be Rich, or subsist himself
without Marriage?*

2d. *By what Means he should attain Wealth?*

3d. *The Time when?*

4th. *If it would continue?*

1st QUERY.—*If the Querent should be Rich, or subsist
himself without Marriage.*

I first cons·dered the general disposition of the planets,

and found the major number, especially the fortunes, swift in motion, well posited, and not afflicted. Also, that ♀, lady of the ascendant, was near *Cor Leonis*, a star of great virtue and influence ; ☽ increasing in light, ♃ almost culminating. Hence I formed this general judgment, that he should live in good rank and quality among his neighbours, &c. (*quoad capax*) according to his calling. Secondly, whether he should be rich or not ? I considered that the lord of the 2d is in the ascendant, and being also lord of ⊕, is near *Spica Virgina*, in 18° ♎.* Then ♃ (a general significator of wealth) was in his exaltation and angular, casting his □ to the cusp of the ascendant, which □ in signs of long ascension we usually repute a △.† Also, that ☽ separated from a ⚹ of ♂, lord of the 2d, &c., significator of the thing demanded, and ♂ of ☿, and applied to ♂ ♀, the querent's significator ; transferring the light and virtue of both ♂ and ☿, to the proper significator of the querent. The dispositor of ☽ is ☉, and he strong and powerful, the ⊕ in a fixed sign, and in the terms of ♂ ; from all which I judged that the querent would acquire an estate, and have a competent fortune ; but as it is signified by an infortune, that he would attain it by labour and care. (*And so to this day he hath.*) And as ♂, lord of the 7th (the house of marriage), hath the most material signification of the thing demanded, viz. wealth, I advised him to marry, and said, that without marriage he should not so well subsist.

2d QUERY.—*By what Means he should attain Riches?*

In this scheme, ♂ being the planet signifying wealth, as lord of the ⊕ and the second house, and placed in the as-

---

* This star has now advanced to 22° ♎.

† Signs of long ascension, are ♋, ♌, ♍, ♎, ♏, ♐. Signs of short ascension, are ♑, ♒, ♓, ♈, ♉, ♊. In the former a ⚹ is taken for a □, and a □ for a △ ; and in the latter, a ⚼ is taken for a ⚹, and a △ for a □. We advise the student to reject these distinctions, which only tend to create confusion.

cendant, signifies property got by the querent's own industry. And as ♂ is lord of the 7th, I said, he would marry a woman who would produce him a good fortune ; and it more than he could well look for, and of a settled nature ; which I judged by ♀, lady of his wife's house of property, being so well fortified. And as ☽ was lady of the 10th, (house of trade), and was transferring the light of ☿ and ♂ to ♀ his significator, I advised him to be diligent in his profession, and that he would thereby gain a good estate. (*He has since had a good fortune with his wife, money, and land, and been very successful in trade*). Jupiter, so strong in the 10th, was an infallible sign (according to natural causes) of plenty of trade, or a gainful profession.

3d QUERY.—*The Time when?*

All the significators oriental, and five planets swift in motion, promise property in a short time after the question ; and ♂, the chief significator of the thing inquired after, being swift in motion, argues the same. The distance from the ascendant to ♂ being about two degrees, signified about two years, at which time he had a portion with his wife. The ☽ wanted 6° 27' of her ♂ with ♀ : hence I concluded that about 1640 he should have very great trading, and live in excellent repute ; and as ♀ is seated on the cusp of the 11th, (or house of friends), that he should have many good friends, &c., by whom he should increase his estate.

4th QUERY.—*If the Querent should continue rich?*

This I resolved by the cusp of the 2d, which being a fixed sign and ⊕ therein, and ♃ in his exaltation and angular, and ♀, the dispositor of ♂, being in ♌, a fixed sign, as also the ☽ in ♌, all implied that he should continue in a plentiful estate, and that the riches God should bless him with would be permanent, and that he should never be reduced to want or poverty.

There was only one thing arising out of the figure, of which I cautioned him. The ⊙, lord of the 11th, beholds ⊕ by □, as also the cusp of the 2d; and as ⊙ here signifies friends, I exhorted him to avoid confiding in solar men, though of much friendship with him. In all such cases describe the planet afflicting, and you give caution sufficient.*

CHAPTER XXVI.

OF THE THIRD HOUSE, VIZ. OF BRETHREN, SISTERS, KINDRED, NEWS, SHORT JOURNEYS, ETC.

THE chief, but not the only, questions regarding this house are those concerning brethren, cousins, or neighbours, and short journeys.

QUERY.—*Shall the Querent agree well with his Brother or Neighbour ?*

The querent has the usual significators; the quesited is shewn by the lord of the 3d, the cusp of the 3d, and the planets therein. If the lord of the 3d be a benevolent planet, or be in the ascendant, or there be a fortune in the 3d, or the respective lords be in good aspect or mutual reception, or the lord of the ascendant throw a good aspect to the cusp of the 3d, no doubt unity will endure between the parties. If the evil planets, or ☌, be found in the 3d, unless very well dignified and aspected, it denotes discord, and the querent may expect little good from the quesited. If there be evil aspects between their significators, the same judgment holds; and if the significators are afflicted by being peregrine, retrograde, or combust, it shews hatred or untoward conduct.

* The description of ⊙ in ♌, would herein answer the exact kind of persons who might injure the querent's property.

♄ or ☌ in the third, shews the neighbours are ill-mannered and the kindred selfish ; if ♂ be there, the neighbours are dishonest, and the relations treacherous. If they be out of their dignities, these evils are increased ; and if ill planets be in the ascendant, or ☌ be there, the querent is himself ill conducted.

Of an absent Brother ?

The 1st, and its lord and ☽, are for the querent ; the 3d for the quesited ; and the 4th, his house of substance, &c.

Consider in what condition the lord of the 3d is, in what house, and how aspected. If he be in the 3d, free from evil aspects of the infortunes, you may judge that the absent brother is in health. If he be in his own house, but afflicted by the evil planets, without reception, judge that he is in health, but in great perplexity and sorrow ; but if they so aspect him with reception, say, that he is in distress, but that he will shortly evade it, and rid himself of his troubles. If the fortunes aspect him by ⚹ or △ without reception, or by □ or ☍ with reception, you may judge him to be in health, and well contented ; and if they aspect him by ⚹ or △, and there be reception, you may tell the querent that his brother is healthy and happy, and wants nothing in this world.

If the lord of the 3d be in the 4th, without aspects of the malefics, he is endeavouring to get property in the country where he then lives. If he be in the 5th, and joined by ♂, or good aspect to the lord of the 5th, if the latter be not much afflicted, he is healthy, jocund, and merry, and likes the society he is in. If it be a fortune, and there be a reception between the lords of the two houses, the 3d and 5th (his 3d), you are assured of his happy condition. Yet if it be a malefic, or he be in evil aspect with a malefic in the 5th, without reception, or if he be void of course while in the 5th, you may judge that he is restless, and discontented in his present abode. Generally, if he be afflicted in any but the 6th, 8th, or 12th houses, he is not very comfortable, yet not in ill health.

If he be in the 8th, and well aspected by a fortune, he is not in danger, yet he is indisposed. If he be joined to evil planets by bad aspects out of the 6th, he is in an infirm and dangerous state. The same, if the lord of his 6th be in the 3d, unless he have dignities therein. If, in this case, the lord of the 3d be ♂ with the lord of the 8th, or entering combustion at the same time, with other testimonies of his being ill, there is reason to fear that he will die.

If you find his significator in the 7th, he is still in the country he went to, and indifferently well.

If the lord of the 3d be in the 8th, he apprehends that he shall die ; and there is great fear of his death if his significator be combust, in ♂ with the lord of the 8th, or afflicted by evil planets.

If his significator be in the 9th, he is gone to some country further off than when he first went, or is forming some clerical, legal, or scientific connexion, or is employed travelling.

If he be in the 10th, and well aspected by the fortunes, especially if with reception, he has got some good employment, or office, in the country to which he is gone. If combust and afflicted, there is fear that he is dead.

If he be in the eleventh, and joined to the lord of the 11th, it denotes he is well situated, with his friends, and happy ; though if evil planets afflict him, he is not so well pleased with his present condition.

If he be in the 12th, and well aspected, he is engaged with horses or cattle, &c., keeping an inn, or is turned grazier, &c. If ill aspected in this or the 2d house, he is in trouble, and if in a fixed sign, probably in prison ; yet, if his significator be retrograde, he will manage to escape. If in the ascendant, he is very pleasantly situated; and, unless ill aspected, he is much respected.

If any other person than a brother be inquired of, his condition may be known by applying the foregoing rules to that person's significator. As, for example, if the quesited be the querent's father, let the lord of the 5th (the 2d from the 4th) be considered for his substance. And if the quesited be a friend, let the 11th house represent him, and then the 12th will be his 2d, or house of property; the 8th will be his 10th, or house of honour, &c.; and so all round the 12 houses. But understand that, though every house has its 6th, 8th, and 12th, yet of every person inquired after, the 6th house of the figure shall signify his sickness, the 8th his death, the 12th his imprisonment.

Of Reports, News, Rumours, &c. whether true or false? and whether importing Good or Evil?

That which I found true by experience (in our late sad times of war) was this: if I found ☽ in the ascendant, 10th, 11th, or 3d house, separating by benevolent aspect from any planet, and then applying by good aspect to the lord of the 1st; I say, I found the report or rumour true, but always tending to the good of the parliament, let the report be good or ill. But if ☽ applied to the lord of the 7th by any good aspect, I was sure we had the worst, and our enemies the victory. If the ☽ was void of course, the news proved of no moment, usually vain and false, and soon contradicted. If the ☽ and ☿ were in □ or ☍, without reception, and neither casting a good aspect to the degree ascending, the news was *false*, and reported purposely to alarm us.

The time of erecting the figure was ever the hour when I

first heard the rumour; but, if another propounded it, then that very minute when it was first proposed.

If, on hearing of any matter, you desire to know whether it will be prejudicial to you or not, observe whether ♃ or ♀ be in the ascendant, or ☽ or ☿ in any of their essential dignities, in ✶ or △ to the lord of the 11th; you may then judge that the party inquiring shall receive no damage thereby. But if the lord of the 6th, 8th, or 12th, be in the ascendant, or in evil aspect to the lord of the ascendant, or a malefic retrograde in the ascendant, or afflicting its lord, or the degree ascending, then the querent will be prejudiced by the matter. But if it concern the public, some damage has happened to their ministers or friends. In this case, if ♄ denote the evil, he shews plundering, loss of corn, or cattle, &c.; ♂ causes straggling parties to be cut off, and military violence, bloodshed, &c.; ☿ the miscarriage of letters, or evil to the literary community, messengers, &c.; ☉ causes distress to the king, or some chief or leader; ♀ causes ill to some gentlemen or their friends. The ☽ denotes violence by mobs, and if she be afflicted, injuries are done to the people.

If Rumours be true or false, according to the ANCIENTS.

If the lord of the ascendant, the moon, or her dispositor, be in an angle or a fixed sign, and in good aspect to the fortunes, or the ☉, you may judge the rumour is true. If they be in moveable signs, cadent, and ill aspected by the infortunes, judge the reverse; and consider the majority of the testimonies. When the angles of the figure, the ☽, and ☿, are in fixed signs, and these latter separate from infortunes and apply to fortunes, the rumour is true. Evil rumours hold true, or will be in some way verified, if the angles of the 4th and 10th are fixed, and the ☽ therein. If you have evil uews, yet if either fortune be in the ascendant, or the ☽ fortunate, it is a strong argument that the r·mours are false, and that they will turn rather to good than evil. Mercury, or the planet to whom he or ☽ applies, being retrograde or afflicted, or if either of these two be lord of the ascendant, it signifies that the rumour shall vanish to nothing, or shall be converted to good. If the lord of the ascendant be under the beams of ☉*, the matter is kept secret, and few shall ever know the truth.

Of Counsel or Advice given by a Neighbour, or Relation, Friend, &c.

Erect the figure when first the party begins to break their mind, and you shall know whether they really wish you well or not, and whether it be good to follow their advice.

If there be in the 10th house either ☉, ♃, ♀, or ☋, or if ☽ apply by good aspect to the lord of the ascendant, judge they come with an honest heart, and the advice is intended for your good. If ♅ ♄, ♂, or ☋ be there, or if ☽ apply by evil aspect, they intend deceitfully. *Haly* affirms, that if the sign ascending be moveable, and the ☽ and lord of the ascendant are both in moveable signs, the party comes to deceive.†

Of short Journeys, whether good to go or not?

By a short journey, I mean such distances as a person may go and come back in a day or two. Consider the lord of the ascendant, and whether he be swift in motion, and in the 3d,

---

* This signifies within a distance of 12 degrees of ☉. Modern authors say 17 degrees.

† If the advice be intended for your benefit, yet it may not be well to follow it. This may be seen by the lord of the 4th, and planets therein ; for if malefics be there, or the lord of the 4th afflict the lord of the ascendant, it will end ill : if good planets be there. it ends well.—*Z* ir

or in any of the dignities of the lord of that house; or in good aspect with its lord, or a planet therein; or if the ☽ apply to such aspect, or be in the 3d, or cast her ⚹ or △ to the degree ascending, or be swift in motion; all these are arguments that the party shall go his short journey, and have success.   The part of heaven in which the place lies to which he would go is known by the situation of ☽, the sign on the cusp of the 3d, or its lord, whichever may be strongest in essential dignities.   If the chief significator be in a northern sign, he goes north, and so of the rest.

EXAMPLES.

In November 1645, a citizen of *London* having gone into the west of England, and no news being heard of him for many weeks, his brother, with great importunity, moved me to give my judgment concerning these particulars.

The figure, erected at the moment of the question, is on the following page ; and the particulars of the judgment on each of three queries, which were put on the occasion, will be found to follow.

Fig 7.

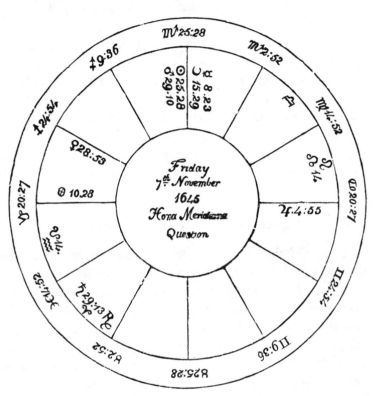

QUESTIONS REGARDING AN ABSENT BROTHER.

1st.—*If Living or Dead? if Dead, whether Killed by Soldiers? for at this time our miserable kingdom was full of soldiers.*

2d.—*If Living, when he should hear of him? and where he was?*

3d.—*When he should come Home?*

———

1st QUERY.—*If Living or Dead?*

The ascendant doth here represent the shape and form of

K

him who asked the question, with consideration had to ♄, lord of the sign. The querent was lean, spare of body, and a real *saturnine* man, &c.

♉ is the ascendant of the 3d house, and ♀ being lady thereof, represented the absent brother.

♀, the significator of the quesited, being noways afflicted, either by ☿, lord of the 8th in the figure, or ♂, lord of the quesited's 8th : and the separation of the ☽ being good, *viz.* a △ of ♃, and ♂ of ☿, who is in good aspect to ♃, and going to ♂ of ☉ on the cusp of the midheaven, I judged the absent brother was alive, and had had no manner of accident, but was in good health.

2d QUERY.—*When he should hear of him?*

♀ lady of the 3d applies to a friendly △ of ♄, lord of the ascendant, and ♄ being retrograde, applies also to the aspect of ♀ ; a very good argument that the querent should hear news of his brother very suddenly. And if you look into the *Ephemeris* for 7th November, 1645, you will find that, about four o'clock on that very day, the △ aspect between ♀ and ♄ was formed. I therefore advised the querent to go to the *carriers* of those countries where he knew his brother had been, and ask when they saw the quesited ; for l told him that it was probable that he should hear of him that very day. (*He has since confidently affirmed, that about the very moment of time, viz, about four, a carrier came casually where he was, and informed him that his brother was living, and in health.*)

Where he was?

His journey was into the *west*. At time of the question I find ♀, his significator, leaving ♐, a north-east sign, and entering ♑, a south sign ; whereon I judged he was in the south-east part of the county unto which he went.   And as ♀ was not far out of the ascendant, and was in the oriental quarter of heaven, that he was not above one or two days' journey from London; and as ♀ was leaving ♐, and entering a sign in which she has dignities by *triplicity* and *term*, I judged the man was leaving the country where he had no possession or habitation, and was coming to his own house in London, where he had good property.   As ♀ wanted one degree of getting out of the sign, I judged he would be at home in less than *one week;* for ♐ is a common sign, and one degree therein in this question might well denote one week.   He came home on the following *Tuesday*, when ☽ came to ☌ ♀, she being then got into ♑, in her own *term* and *diurnal triplicity*.   The two significators being in △, these two brothers always did, and do, live very amicably together.

Fig. 8.

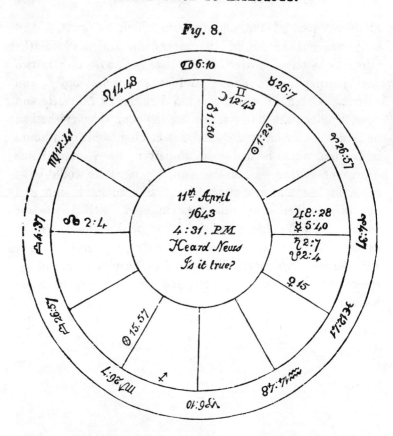

QUERY.—*If a Rumour or Report were true or not?*

In 1643, his Majesty's army being then *rampant*, several reports were given out that his Majesty had taken Cambridge, &c. : a well-affected person inquired of me if the news were true or false? whereupon I erected this figure, and gave judgment :—" *All that we heard was untruth, and that the town neither was or should be taken by him or his forces.*"

A Report that Cambridge was taken by the King's Forces; if true?

First, I considered that the angles were all moveable, and

that the evil ♂ vitiated the cusp of the 10th, and ♄ that of
the 7th ; one argument that the report was false.

Secondly, the ☽ was cadent, and in ♊, a sign wherein she
is very weak : a second such argument.

Thirdly, the ☋ on the cusp of the ascendant was a sign of
good to the Parliament, for the first house signified that honourable society. ♀, lady of the ascendant, was in her exaltation, but ♂, lord of the 7th, our enemies, in his fall, viz. ♋,
and afflicted by □ of ♄ . The ☽ separating from ♃ in the
7th, and transferring his light to ♀, gave reason to expect
that there would come good to our side by this report or
rumour, and no benefit to the enemy. The □ of ♄ and ♂
assured me that our enemies were so full of division and trea-
son, and so thwarting one the other's designs, that no good
should come unto them by this report. And so, in short, I
judged that Cambridge was not taken, and that what we heard
was false.*

———

Had this question been, *Whether the querent would have
brethren or not ?* then you should judge as follows :—

The sign on the 3rd ♏ is fruitful; ♋, the sign in which
the lord of the 3d is found, is fruitful, and the ☽ applies
to ♀; signs that the querent might expect both, but chiefly
sisters, as the signs are mostly feminine.

———

* If the student erect a figure for 10h. 53m. A.M. Dec. 23d, 1834, he
will find ♐ 15 on the 10th, and ☽ in ♎ 0 : 15 in the 7th, applying
to □ of ☉, lord of the 7th. We erected this figure on hearing a rumour
of several persons being cruelly slaughtered by soldiers at Rathcormac, in
Ireland, for the purpose of collecting tithes. The ☽ being angular and
afflicted, shewed that the *evil* report was true ; and ♅ being exactly on
the cusp of the ascendant, ♒ 23 : 30, was a similar testimony. ☋ was
in ♐ 16 : 35 on the cusp of the 10th, shewing discredit to the government, arising out of the transaction. The coroner's jury found a verdict
of *wilful murder*

CHAPTER XXVII.

OF THE FOURTH HOUSE, AND JUDGMENTS DEPENDING THEREON.

This is the House of Parents, Lands, Tenements, Cities, Towns, Villages, Farms, Castles, Treasure found, &c., or of any Thing hidden in the ground ; also of the Grave.

RULE.—*To Find a Thing hidden or mislaid.*

BE careful to consider to whom the thing hidden, &c. may belong : if the goods did belong to the querent, take the lord of the 2d ; but if to his brother or sister, regard the lord of the 4th ; if to his father, the lord of the 5th ; if to his mother, the lord of the 11th, and so of other persons ; if to a stranger to the querent, or one who is no relation, take the lord of the 8th. If you find the lord of the house of pro- perty is in any angle, judge the thing missing is within the house of him who is the owner. And if the lord of the property is in the ascendant, or disposed of by the lord of the ascendant, by house, or in the same sign with him, say it is in that part of the house wherein he most frequents, or lays up his goods, or such things as he most delights in. But if the lord of the quesited's property be in the 10th, it is then in his shop, if he keep one, or, if he be a gentleman, in his dining-room ; if he be a farmer, it is in the common room of the residence, or first room after you enter the house. If the lord of the property be in the 7th, it is then in that part where the quesited's wife or his maid-servants have most to do. If in the 4th, it is where the most aged of the house lodges, or formerly did most frequent ; or in the middle of the house, or in the most ancient part, or where his father or some elderly man lodged. The nature and quality of the place are known by the signs the significators are in; for it the sign of the second be *airy*, or the greater part of the significators, including the sign where ⊕ is, be the same, the thing is hid in the eaves, or the upper part of the room where it is, or on high from the ground; and if the thing be in an orchard or garden, it is higher than the ground, or upon some tree, line, &c., or is on the highest hill or part of the ground. If the said significators be strong, and in *watery* signs, it is in the dairy, or washhouse, brewhouse, or near water. If they be in *fiery* signs, it is near the chimney, or the walls of the h ise, or where iron is found. If in *earthy* signs, the thing is on the ground or earth, or near some pavement or floor; and if the thing lost be out of the house, it will be found near the bridge, stile, or gate, where people come into the grounds.

If the significator be going out of one sign into another, the thing is behind something, or fallen between two rooms, or near the threshold; and it is higher or lower, according to the sign being airy, &c.

If a thing be lost, and not stolen, consider the following points :—

1. The sign ascending, its nature, and the quarter of heaven it denotes.

2. The sign the lord of the ascendant is in.

3. The sign of the 4th house.

4. The sign the lord of the 4th is in.

5. The sign the ☽ is in.

6. The sign of the 2d house.

7. The sign the lord of the 2d is in.

8. The sign ⊕ is in.

Then examine the greater number of testimonies to discover what quarter of heaven the thing is in, as regards the parts of the house. Having found the bearing, or point of the compass, observe the nature of the sign, viz. *airy* signs, above ground ; *fiery*, near a wall, or partition ; *earthy*, on the floor ; *watery*, near a moist place in the room, &c.

Bearing by Compass of the Signs.

♈ East	♌ E. by North	♐ E. by South
♎ West	♊ W. by South	♒ W. by North
♋ North	♏ N. by East	♓ N. by West
♑ South	♉ S. by East	♍ S. by West.

Of Buying and Selling Lands, Houses, Farms, &c.

The ascendant, its lord, and the ☽ , are for the buyer, and the 7th, its lord, and planets therein, for the seller. The 4th. its lord, and planets therein, signify the land, or house, &c. And the 10th house, its lord, and planets therein, signify the price ; that is, whether it will be sold cheap or dear.

If you find the lords of the 1st and 7th in good aspect, and the lord of the 7th apply by good aspect (or if by evil aspect with reception) to the lord of the ascendant, you may judge the seller has good will to the buyer ; and if they are at all dignified, the purchase will be effected; but if the aspect be evil, there will be much bargaining and dispute before all be settled.

If the lord of the ascendant, or ☽ , apply to the lord of the 4th, or this planet apply to them, or if they be in each other's places, viz. the lord of the 1st, or ☽ , in the 4th, or the lord of the 4th in the ascendant, and there be any reception, the purchase will be effected.

But if there be no dwelling in houses as above, yet the ☽ transfer the light of the lord of the 4th to the lord of the ascendant, the bargain will be concluded, though by brokers or agents, rather than by the principals.

If none of the above rules hold, there will be no bargain made.

Of the Quality of the Land or Houses, &c.

If you find the infortunes in the 4th, especially if they be peregrine, or the lord of the 4th retrograde or afflicted, it will never continue long with the buyer's posterity, or benefit him.

But if ♃, ♀, or ☊, be in the 4th, or the lord of the 4th be strong and well aspected, the purchaser may expect good success with the property; and if a fixed sign be in the 4th, it will continue in the family of the purchaser.

If an infortune possess the ascendant, the tenants or occupiers are evil and deceitful, and will give trouble. If a fortune be there, or ☊, judge the reverse. In the former case, if the evil planet be retrograde, the tenants will decamp without paying their rent, or will throw up their leases.

If in the 10th house there be a fortune, and it direct, the timber will be profitable, or the house will let well. If it be retrograde, there are many trees, but they not profitable. If there be an infortune direct, there are few trees, or the house will not let well; and if he be retrograde, the timber will be stolen, or the rent will be either stolen after payment, or no payment be well and truly made. If there be no planet in the 10th, consider the lord of the house, and, as he may be strong or weak, judge the result of the profits, whether by timber, &c., or by letting the house, &c. But the angle of the 7th must be considered in like manner, to judge the quality of the grass, corn, or herbage, &c. As regards the description of the ground, look to the 4th house; and if you find a fiery sign on its cusp, the ground is in general hilly, dry, and hard; the more so, if the lord of the 4th be in a fiery sign, viz. ♈, ♌, ♐. If there be an earthy sign on the cusp, the ground is plain, level and good pasture land, or for tillage. If there

be an airy sign thereon, the ground is of a mixed nature, part
hilly and part plain, partly good and partly bad.   If the sign
be watery, then there is plenty of water, a brook, or rivulet,
&c., thereon.   And if an infortune be in the 4th, and retrograde or peregrine, the land will partake greatly of the nature
of that infortune ; as if ♏ be the sign, and ♄ in it, the land
is marshy or boggy, and full of rushes ; if he be afflicted, so
much worse is the land.   And if the land lie near the sea,
you may fear an overflow, or that the banks are damaged, &c.
If ♄ be in the 4th in a fiery sign, the land is barren, and
wants water ; if he be afflicted, it is utterly stony and worthless.   If ♄ be there in an airy sign, the land is defective ;
and if he be afflicted, especially in ♊, the management of it
has been bad and unthrifty.   If he be there in an earthy sign,
the land is tolerably good, but heavy, clay land ; and if he be
afflicted, the farmers are dull, and too poor to manage it well.

In like way judge of the standing of a house or building :
if it be a watery sign, there will be much damp ; and if ♄
be there in ♏, it is overrun with rats.

Of the Cheapness or Dearness of the Land or Houses, &c.

This is known by the lord of the 10th ; for if he be angular and strong, the price will be high, and the seller will stand
upon his terms ; but if he be weak, cadent, afflicted, &c., the
price will not rise high.

If it be good for the Querent to take or lease the House, Farm, or Land, &c.

The 10th house, &c., will herein shew the profit or advantage to be made by the undertaking, having regard also to
the usual significators of property, viz. the lord of the 2d,
and ⊕, &c.

The 4th house will shew the end of the matter as regards the taking the property.

If there be a fortune ascending, or ⊕ be in the ascendant, or the lord of the ascendant be there, or be in ⚹, or △ to the degree on the cusp and not afflicted, the querent will take the house or farm, &c., and find it a good bargain.

If an infortune ascend, the querent will not take the property; or if he have already taken it, he has no mind to it, and will quickly put it off to another party.

If you find the lord of the 7th in the 7th, or casting a good aspect to its cusp, or there be benefics therein, the man will keep his word in the bargain, but he will profit by it more than the querent.

If an infortune be in the 7th and not lord of the 7th, have great care of the covenants or agreements between you; for the landlord will be too hard for you, as he minds nothing but his own ends in the matter.

Consider the 10th house; and if a fortune be there or behold its cusp by good aspect, the parties, notwithstanding some rubs, will proceed in their bargain, and the land, &c. will be let to the querent.

If you find an infortune in or in evil aspect to the 10th, the bargain will be broken off. If it be land, they differ abcut the timber, &c., or upon the erecting of some new buildings; and if the thing be a house, &c., they differ about the repairs.

As to the end of the matter, see to the 4th house. If fortunes be there, or the lord of the 4th behold the cusp favourably, it will end well, and both parties will be pleased; but if an infortune be there, or the lord of the house aspect it by □ or ☍, the whole matter will end ill, and will please neither party.

QUERY.—*Shall the Querent enjoy the Estate of his Father?*

If in this question you find the lords of the 2d and 5th in reception and in each other's houses, there is no doubt that the querent shall have a competent fortune out of his father' estate. But if the lord of the father's property be retrograde or afflicted, then some part of the estate intended for the querent will be wasted or otherwise disposed of. If you would know why or how, see what planet impedites the lord of the 5th, and what house he is lord of. If it be the lord of the 6th, it may be one of the father's brothers, or sisters, or neighbours shall prevail on the father to alter his intentions towards the querent. If it be the lord of the 7th, it may be some female, or his wife, or some person with whom the querent has quarrelled, that will cause his father to alter his mind. If it be the lord of the 12th, it is some one of the mother's kindred, or it may be (especially if ♃), some minister or clergyman. Now, if, upon describing the party, the querent is well informed of who it is, and is desirous to gain the person's good will, and so to diminish their malice, let him do as follows : on the approach of any ⚹, △, or ☌ between the planet signifying that party and the lord of the ascendant, let the day be observed in the Ephemeris when the ☽ separates from one and applies to the other, (by good aspect if possible), and on that day endeavour a reconcilement : and it is not to be doubted that he may obtain his desire, as I have found many times by good experience.*

If the lord of the 5th dispose of the ⊕, and be in the ascendant or 2d, the querent shall gain his desires. ♃ or

---

* This method of electing times for application to individuals for any favour, or to gain any point, may be safely practised after any other horary question, as well as this particular one.—ZᴬD.

♀ in the 5th, casting a ✳ or △ to any planet in the **2d,** argues the same.

If ☽ separate from the lord of the 5th, and go immediately to ✳ or △ of the lord of the 2d or of the ascendant, it shews assured hopes of acquiring the property of the father.

If you find an infortune ill dignified in the 4th, the father has no inclination to part with his money ; nor will it be well to move him much thereto, until that unfortunate planet be transited out of the sign. But if you cannot stay so long, observe when that planet is direct, swift in motion, oriental, in ✳ or △ with ♃ or ♀ or the lord of the ascendant, and then let the father be moved in the business. The observing those influences will not *compel* the father's mind, but will cause more benevolent intentions.

If the lords of the 2d and 5th apply to any good aspect by retrogradation, the querent will receive some property from his father suddenly, before he thinks of it. If there be any good aspect, reception, &c., between the lord of the 4th and any other planet, stronger than there is between the lord of the 4th and the lord of the ascendant, the father regards the party signified by that other planet better than the querent : if it be the lord of the 3d, or any planet in the 3d, then it is one of the querent's brothers, &c.

Of removing from one House or Place to another.

Observe the ascendant, the 4th and 7th houses, and their lords, planets therein, &c.

If the lord of the 4th be in the 7th, and he a good planet, and the lords of the 1st and 7th be good also and strong, it is then better to remain where you are. But if the lord of the 7th be with a good planet, and the lord of the 4th with an evil one, it is then not well to remain. If the ☽ or lord of the ascendant separate from ill aspects of the infortunes, and they lords of the 4th or 7th, or from the lords of the 6th, 8th, or 12th ; or if an evil planet be in the ascendant or 4th ; or if the lord of the 2d be weak, I advise the querent to remove. And if the lord of the 6th be in the ascendant, or afflict its lord or the ☽, I have found that the querent has ill health where he is, or is troubled by evil servants. If the lord of the 12th be the afflicting planet, he has backbiting, treacherous neighbours. And if the ⊕ was in the 6th, 8th, or 12th, or the lord of the 2d was in ill aspect to the lord of the ascendant, I have found that he went back in the world, &c. If the lord of the 10th afflict, I judged that he was unfortunate in trade, or had lost his credit. If the lord of the 4th afflict, he has been injured by repairing the house, &c. The lord of the 7th shews injury by an opposite neighbour, who undersells him, &c.

In giving advice which way to steer his course in hopes of better success, I observe what planet in the scheme is strongest, and has the best aspect to the lords of the ascendant or 2d ; and according to the quarter of heaven the sign that planet is in signifies, I advise the querent to remove. I do not remember that any ever repented the following my advice, though many have afterwards returned me both thanks and rewards.*

If ☽ separate from a fortunate planet, stay; if she separate from an infortune, remove. An infortune in the ascendant, or a fortune in the 7th, remove; but a fortune in the ascendant, or infortune in the 7th, remain.

Of Treasure, Mines, &c. concealed in the Ground.

To discover mines or any other thing supposed to be concealed in any place, the querent must observe whether there

* Let the querent also attend to the places ruled by the sign in which the planet is; as London for ♊, Dublin for ♉, &c.

be any planet strongly dignified in the 4th house; and the nature of the treasure, mine, &c. may be judged of by that planet, if he have any affinity with the 7th house. The nature of the mine, &c. will depend on the nature of the planet. If ♄ be lord of the 7th and in the 4th dignified, he signifies good coal mines; or if the question were of stone, then there is a good quarry. And so judge of the others according to their nature and strength in essential dignities.

EXAMPLE.

If I should purchase the Houses of Master B.?

The inheritance of the house wherein at this present 1647 I live, and some others, being proffered me to buy in 1634, I had a desire to know if I should deal with the seller, and procure money in convenient time to pay for the purchase, my own money being in such hands that I could not call it in under six months' notice. Being desirous, I say, to purchase the said houses, and fully resolved upon it, I took my own question myself, at the time I found my mind most perplexed and solicitous about it. The time of the query to myself fell out according to the position of heaven following.

Fig. 9.

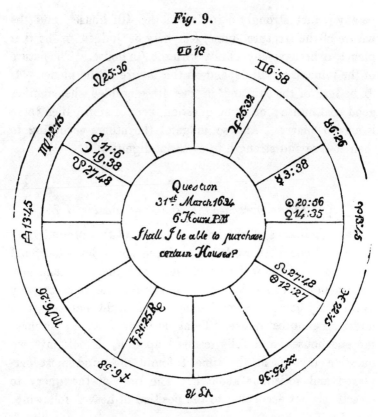

Resolution of the above Question.

The sign ascending is ♎, and the degree ascending the place of ♃ in my *radix :* I looked upon that as a good omen in the first place.   ♀ is for myself, ☉ locally placed in the 7th is for the seller.   ☉ receives ♀ in his exaltation ; and as ♀ is near the cusp of the 7th, and no other planet there but the ☉, this signified that there was no other purchaser about it at present but myself. The ☉ so exalted and angular, denoted that the seller was high in his demands, (*and so he was,*) nor was he necessitated to part with it.   Finding my signi-ficator received of ☉ and so near the cusp of the 7th, was an argument that I should proceed in the business, notwithstanding the many debilities of ♀. For as ☉ was lord of the 7th, so also was the lord of the 11th; signifying that my *hopes* should not be frustrated. And ♀ also was applying to △ of ♄, lord of the 4th, viz. the houses inquired after, and had no frustration, &c., before the perfect aspect; a strong argument that I should buy the houses. Both significators applied to the aspect, ♄ being retrograde, I also considered that ☉ was in △ to ♄, the ☉ being lord of my 11th and ♄ of the 4th; and as ♄ beholds the ascendant and has dignities therein, he, therefore, had signification of myself. Now, whether you consider him as having dignities in the ascendant or as lord of the 4th, the lord of the 11th and he applying by a △, argued assuredly that I should proceed and in the end conclude for the houses. The ☽ in the next place translating the influence of ♂, lord of the 7th, to ♄, having virtue in the ascendant, though by a □ out of signs of long ascension, did much facilitate the matter; but argued my contracting leisurely and slowly, because of the □ aspect. And as ☽ is afflicted and ♀ unfortunate, so I had much trouble and many meetings about it; the seller not abating one penny of £530, being the first money he demanded. As ☉ is near to a ⚹ of ♃, so did a *jovial* man endeavour to procure the purchase (after I began), but ♃ is cadent and in detriment, which shewed he should not prevail. ♀ angular and in aspect with ♄, and ☉ lord of the 11th (or 5th from the 7th), shewed that a daughter of the seller was my very good friend in this business, and suffered no interloper to intervene, though some offered fair to hinder me. As ♂, lord of my 2d, was retrograde, it denoted that I should get none of my own money to supply my occasions. ♃, lord of ⊕ in ⚹ to ☉, no ways impeded, but by being in detriment, in platic ⚹ with the lady of the ascendant, gave me such hopes.

L

that I doubted not of procuring money when he entered ♋, his exaltation, and ♂ became direct; which he did twelve days after, when a friend lent me £500.

The qualities of the houses are shown by ♑, the sign on the 4th, and by ♄, lord thereof, who having no material debilities (except being retrograde and cadent), and being also in △ to ☉, the houses were really old, but strong and able to stand many years. When ♀ and ☉ came to ♂ in ♉ (25th April), I bargained; and on the ☽ to ♂ ♀ (May 17th), I paid in £530, and my conveyance was sealed. As ♀ wanted 6 degrees of being ♂ with ☉, so was it six weeks and some days from the time of the question until I perfected what the figure promised.

As to the moles and scars on my body, it exactly agrees; for as ♀ is in ♈, which represents the face, so have I a mole on my cheek, about the middle of it; and as ♎ ascends, I have one on the reins of my back. The ☽ in ♍, afflicted by ♂, I have a red mole below the navel. ♃, lord of the 6th in ♊, a masculine sign, I have a mole near my right hand, visible on the outside; so have I one on the left foot, as ♓, the sign on the 6th signifies.

I had a hard bargain, as the figure every way considered manifests; and shall never live to see many of the leases yet in being expire. And as ♀ is in ♈, the sign opposite her own house, so did I do myself injury by the bargain; I mean in matter of money; but the love I bore to the house I now live in, wherein I lived happily with a good master full seven years, and therein obtained my first wife, and was bountifully blessed with the goods of this world, made me neglect a small hinderance; nor now, I thank God, do I repent it, finding God's blessing in a plentiful measure upon my labours.

CHAPTER XXVIII.

OF THE FIFTH HOUSE AND ITS QUESTIONS.

If one shall have Children, yea or nay ?

HEREIN generally consider whether the signs ascending and on the 5th house be fruitful ;* whether the lord of the ascendant, or the ☽ be in aspect with the lord of the 5th, and if so, whether the lord of the 5th be strong, and also the planet or planets in the 5th or in aspect with its lord. These are signs the querent shall have children before they die. Also if the lord of the 5th be in the ascendant, or the lord of the ascendant be in the 5th, it is a strong argument of children. If there be translation of light or collection between the significators, you may still judge that there will be children, but not so speedily as if it had been foreseen by the former manner of judgment.

If a Woman ask, whether she may have a Child ?

If a married woman ask, consider whether the lord of the ascendant be in the 5th or 7th, or the lord of the 5th be in the ascendant or 7th, or lord of the 7th in the 5th, or the ☽ with him, or good planets in the ascendant, or with the lord of the 5th or in the angles ; she may then conceive. But if none of these testimonies concur, and you find barren signs and planets in the aforesaid situations, (especially if infortunes be angular and fortunes cadent), she neither has conceived at present nor will hereafter. If good and evil planets be mixed, she may have children, but they will not live. If ♊, ♌, or ♍, be on the ascendant or 5th, and ♅, ♄, ♂, or ☉ in the 5th, it is a strong sign of barrenness. But ☉ rather causes the death of children than prevents their birth.

* Fruitful signs are the watery triplicity ♋, ♏, and ♓.

Whether a Man shall have Children by his Wife, or his intended Wife? Or, whether a Woman may by her Husband, &c.

Observe the ascendant, its lord, and the ☽; and if the lord of the ascendant or ☽ be joined to the lord of the 5th, they shall have issue by the party inquired of. If this be not, observe whether *translation* or *collection* of light occur between the significators, or whether ☽ or lord of the ascendant be in the 5th, or the lord of the 5th in the ascendant. These are all testimonies in the affirmative. If ♃ or ♀ be in the 5th no way afflicted, a child will be very speedily born; and if they, or either of them, be in the ascendant or 11th, there will be children, but not so speedily. But if the fortunes be afflicted while in those places, there is danger of the child being born dead, or dying shortly after birth. If there be signs of children, yet ♀ be afflicted by ♄ or ♂, there is danger of some accident, &c. to the mother before the birth.

If ♄, or ♂, or ☋, (and ♅, if afflicted), be in the 5th, or the two former cast their ☍ to its cusp, the woman is not with child, nor will be. The □ of the infortunes to the cusp of the 5th denotes no conception, unless they be strong and there be other good testimonies. The lord of the 5th, weak, &c., denotes a sickly child.

Whether a Woman be with Child or not? if she ask the Question.

She is so, if the lord of the ascendant, or ☽, behold the lord of the 5th by any aspect, or translation of light have passed between them. If the lord of the ascendant, or ☽ be in the 5th, free from affliction by the infortunes, or lords of the 6th, 8th, or 12th, or ☋. If ♃ be in the 1st, 5th, 7th or 11th, not in aspect to ♄, or ♂, and they slow in motion, or retrograde. If the lord of the ascendant, or 5th be in good aspect to a planet in an angle, with mutual reception. If the ☽ be in reception with any planet in an angle, and be essentially fortified. If the lord of the ascendant behold its cusp by good aspect, out of a good house; or if ☽ be in the 7th, and behold the lord of the 7th in the 11th; or if ☽ be in the 11th, and behold the lord of the 7th in the 7th. If the lord of the ascendant be in mutual reception by house, triplicity, exaltation, or term, with a planet who has the same reception exactly; that is, if each be in the other's house, &c. If the ☽ apply to the lord of the ascendant, or lord of the 5th, by good aspect from the 10th house, or by evil aspect if with mutual reception. If the sign ascending be fixed, and a fortune therein, or if the lord of the 5th be strong in the ascendant, or 10th, you may ever predict true conception.

She is not so, if you find none of the above testimonies, or barren signs on the 5th, or ascendant; or evil planets there, or afflicting their lords and the ☽ .

If the Man ask the Question, unknown to the Woman.

She is with child, if the lord of the 5th behold a planet in an angle, with reception; or if the lords of the ascendant, or 5th, or 7th, or ♃, ♀, ☉, ☽, ☿, or ☋, be in the 5th, and be fortunate.—N.B. ☿ if in aspect to a malefic, and not in any aspect to a benefic, cannot be relied upon.

She is not with child, if ♃ or ♀ be afflicted. If ♀ be joined to ♄ or ♂, (or to ♅, if he be ill aspected), and they be combust, retrograde, or in ♌, ♍, or ♑. If ♄ or ♂ be in the 5th, in □, or ☍, to its lord, they denote no conception; but if other testimonies be more powerful, and denote conception, they shew danger of abortion.

The lord of the ascendant joined to a retrograde planet, or

to one in a cadent house, or received by a retrograde or combust planet, or if no aspect or translation of light be between the lords of the 1st and 5th, are all signs of no conception ; but judge by the majority of testimonies.

Is the Child Male or Female ?

The lords of the ascendant, the 5th, and the ☽, and the signs on the ascendant and 5th being masculine, denote a male ; if they be, on the contrary, feminine, the child will be a female.—N.B. Unless this be a part of the question, do not attempt to give a judgment ; nor then either, unless there be a great majority of testimonies on one or the other side. The sign the dispositor of the ☽ is in may also be considered.

Whether the Child shall live or die ?

The lord of the 5th retrograde, combust, or cadent, or being in his fall or detriment, and afflicted by the lord of the 8th of the figure, or the 8th from the 5th, (which is the 12th), are signs of death. Or if the lord of the 5th, being weak, be afflicted by an evil planet in the 8th or 12th, unless some opposite testimonies occur, it may be expected the child will speedily die. If the lord of the ascendant be in the 5th, and be afflicted as above, or if ♅, ♄, ♂, or ☊, be in the 5th, especially if retrograde, they denote the same.

Whether there shall be twins ?

If suspicion be of twins, and you find, upon that question, the ascending sign be double-bodied, and a fortune therein, or the same of the 5th house, and ☉ and ☽ be in double-bodied signs, and the lords of the ascendant and 5th be the same, you may judge twins. But unless all, or nearly all, these testimonies concur, it is not safe so to judge.—N.B. The dispositor of the ☽, that is the planet in whose house she is, may also be considered. Moreover, if the ☌ be with either ♃, ♀, or the ☽, or that all these be in either ♊, ♍, ♐, or ♓, it is a farther testimony of the woman bearing twins.

How long the Woman has been pregnant ?

Observe the lord of the ascendant, the 5th, or the ☽; see which is nearest from any aspect which is past, and then judge according to the nature of the aspect. If the separation be from a △, say she is in the 5th month of her conception, or the 3d; if it be a ⚹, she is in the 2d or 6th month; if a □, she is in the 4th month; an ☍, gives the 7th month; and if it be a ☌, then she has been pregnant only *one* month.

Of the Time when the Birth shall take place ?

Observe when ♂ or ☉ are in ☌ with the lord of the 5th, or there be a ☌ of the lord of the 5th with the lord of the ascendant in the 5th house; about that time the birth may be expected. Observe, also, when the lord of the ascendant goes out of one sign into another; that is also a probable period for the birth. See, also, how far the lord of the 5th is from the cusp of the 5th, and give to every sign one month. Judge according to the majority of these testimonies.*

Of Ambassadors or Messengers.

The lord of the 5th and the ☽ may be considered to represent the ambassador or messenger. The planet to whom

---

* This is rather a difficult point to decide; and unless the querent have great anxiety on the subject, which in some cases may happen, we advise the student to avoid giving judgment, or at least till he has well satisfied himself, by experience, of the right method. We believe it will generally be found, that at the time of the birth the ☉ is passing some aspect of the cusp of the 5th, or its lord.

either of them apply shall shew the cause and nature of the message.

If you find the application be from a fortune by $\square$, σ, or σ, and there be reception between them, or collection or translation, and that planet be in the 10th, or lord thereof, the embassy is on some high and important matter of a political nature. If the planet who is received, or translates, or collects, be lord of the 11th, he comes to renew leagues of friendship. If the lord of the 5th be afflicted or weak in the 7th, and the lord of the ascendant and he be in evil aspect, and σ aspect either of them evilly, there is no sign of any peace or permanent benefit arising from this embassy or message. According as the lord of the 5th and $\mathbb{D}$ be well affected to the ascendant, its lord, and planets therein, you may predict advantage to the querent or his nation, according as it be respecting a public or private matter.

Of a Message sent for Money.

The message is shewn by the $\mathbb{D}$, the messenger by the lord of the 5th: the other significators as usual.

If the lord of the 5th separate from the lord of the 7th, and apply to the lord of the ascendant, you may judge the messenger has effected the thing he went for, and is returning home. If the lord of the 5th separate from the lord of the 2d, he brings money. The answer the messenger brings is of the nature of that house from whose lord the lord of the 5th separates, and also of the nature of the planet himself. Therefore, if he separate from a good planet, it gives hopes of a good answer; the contrary, when he separates from evil planets. If the lord of the 5th apply by $\square$, or σ, to an infortune, before he is separated from the lord of the 7th, the messenger has had some impediment in effecting his business by the party to whom he was sent, and has also sustained some hinderance on his journey before he arrived at the place. But if this application to an infortune happen *after* the lord of the 5th was separated from the lord of the 7th, the messenger will have delays and misfortunes on his return. If you find an infortune (especially ♂) in the 9th, he will hardly travel safe for thieves ; but if a fortune be there, his going and returning will be safe.

If there be reception, (though they apply by □ or ☍) between the lords of the 5th and 7th, the messenger will be well received ; but the evil aspect shews some delay or excuse framed by the party to whom the messenger is sent.

As to the messenger's return ; when the lord of the 5th comes to a ⚹ or △ of the lord of the ascendant, that day, or near it, the messenger is heard of ; or when ☽ separates from the lord of the 5th, and applies to the lord of the ascendant, the querent shall have intelligence of his messenger. The application of the *significator* to a ponderous planet shews more certainly the day. Use discretion in judging the nature of the journey, its length, &c. And, according to the nature of the signs and houses in which the applying planet may be found, expect the return to be in days, weeks, months, &c.

Fig. 10.

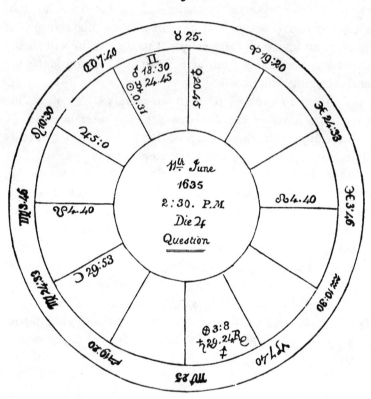

QUERY.—*If the Person asking the Question should ever have Children ?*

Judgment upon the preceding Figure.

The ascendant is here ♍, a barren sign; the sign of the 5th is ♑, an indifferent sign in this question, but rather barren, as being the house of ♄. The lord of the 5th, ♄, is retrograde in ♐; and the lord of the ascendant, ☿, is in ♊, both signs more barren than fruitful. The ☽ is in the terms of ♂, and in □ to ♄, lord of the 5th.   ☿, lord of the ascendant, is in the terms of ♄, and afflicted by ♂, and going to ☍ of ♄, who is lord of the 6th as well as 5th; ☌ also in the ascendant.   All these are strong arguments of barrenness; and I therefore delivered the following judgment, viz., that the querent neither had been, nor ever would be, pregnant, being naturally barren; for finding the chief angles afflicted by malefics, it was certain that the evil which prevented her from conceiving had been long upon her, and would continue.   I found no one promising testimony; so I declared, positively, that she never would have any children, according to the rules of the science.

The ☽ being in □ to ♄, and ☿, lord of the 1st, applying to his ☍, the querent was very sickly, afflicted with wind and cholic; ☌ in the ascendant, shewed great pain in the head; and ☿ in ♊, shewed the same.*

The querent's moles, &c. agreed exactly with the figure, viz. one mole close by the navel: one upon the right ancle; one towards the right knee, on the inner side of the thigh; one near the member shewn by the ☽ in ♍; and one on the outside of the right arm.

* See the Table of the Parts in Man's Body the planets rule for each sign

Fig. 11.

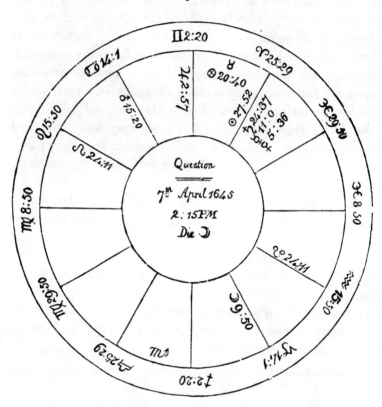

QUESTION.—*A Female being with Child, whether it were a Male or Female; and about what Time she should be delivered?*

————

1st QUERY.—*Is the Child a Male or Female?*

In this case I followed the method of taking only the plurality of testimonies of the proper *significators*, whether masculine or feminine, and so gave judgment.

Arguments of a Girl.

♍ the sign ascending ....*feminine.*

♑ the sign on the 5th house .... do.

☽ in a sign .... do.

☿ lord of the ascendant, with ♀ a planet .. do.

Arguments of a Boy.

☿ lord of the ascendant in a sign...... *masculine.*

♄ lord of the 5th, a planet .... do.

♄ lord of the 5th, in a sign .... do.

☽ in a house .... do.

♄ in a house .... do.

♃ a benefic in an angle, in a sign...... do.

☿ applying to aspect of ♂, a planet .. do.

Here are seven testimonies of a boy, and only four of a girl; I therefore affirmed that the lady carried a son; (*and so it proved*).

2d QUERY.—*How long ere she should be delivered?*

The sign of the 5th is moveable; so is ♈, wherein both the lords of the 1st and 5th are situated. These argued but a short time; but as ♄, lord of the 5th, is a ponderous planet, and was slow in motion, I considered him much in this query; and also ☽, because she was situated in the 5th I took the distance between

♄ in ♈ .... 24° 37

☽ in ♑ 9 50

Difference 14 47

Also between ♄ and ☿ :

♄ in ♈ .... 24° 37

☿ in ♈ 11 0

Difference 13 37

Finding only one degree and ten minutes between the as‑
pect of the ☽ and ♄, and that of ☿ and ♄, I gave for
every degree one week, and so judged that, about *fourteen*
weeks from the time of the question, she should be deli‑
vered.

The birth took place on the 11th July following, when
♂ transited the degree ascending, and ☿ the ☍ of ☽, viz.
♋ 9°. The ☉ also was that day in ♋ 27° 48', the perfect
□ to his own place in the figure, and ☽ in ♂ with ☿ in
♋. The time was thirteen weeks and four days after the
question.

CHAPTER XXIX.

OF THE SIXTH HOUSE.

Viz. Sickness, Servants, Small Cattle, &c.

IN the first place, we ought to take the figure for the exact
moment of the person falling sick, or rather of being obliged
to take to his bed.*

Secondly, if that cannot be had, accept of that time when
first any person spoke to a physician, &c. regarding the pa‑
tient. And if it was with his consent, the ascendant will
signify him; but if unknown to him, the ascendant will
denote the querent; and the house describing his relation to
the person speaking of the sickness will describe the patient.
(This is, supposing the physician to be an astrologer, which
they formerly were; but if the patient's friend speak to an
astrologer, the same rule holds.)

Thirdly, or let the physician note the time of his own first

* If the illness be produced by an accident, then take the time at
which it occurred.

speaking with the patient,* and let a figure be erected for that moment.

Then consider carefully, first, the ascendant and planets therein; secondly, the 6th house, and planets therein, thirdly, the sign and house wherein the Moon is; fourthly, how she is affected or afflicted, by what planet, in what house that planet is, and of what house he is lord.

What Part of the Body is afflicted?

If the ascendant be afflicted by an evil planet, and he retrograde, combust, peregrine, slow in motion, or in □ or ☍ to the lord of the 4th, 6th, 8th, or 12th, the disease is then *in the head*, or in that part or parts of the body which the planet or planets signify in the sign then ascending.

For example; if ♋ ascend, and ♄ therein, the sick party is afflicted in the head, because the ascendant signifies the head; and also has some disorder in the bowels, reins, or secrets, because ♄ in ♋ signifies those parts; or else with some rotten cough, as ♄ denotes coughs, and ♋ rules the breast. If the lord of the ascendant, ☽, or lord of the 6th, be in a sign signifying the same member or parts as ♄, or if the sign on the 6th represent the same, your judgment will be more certain; I may say, infallible.†

I also would observe, in like manner, the 6th house, its

---

* Our author adds, "or when first the *urine* was brought to him." This makes it evident that the water doctors, as they were termed, even until a very recent period, had recourse to astrology to ascertain the nature and result of their patients' diseases. We are quite sure, from long experience, that these may be accurately learned by the science; and we believe that many medical men call it to their aid even now. The day is coming when this will be generally the case.

† In all cases where the ☽ is afflicted by either ♄ or ♂, we should regard the rules for that situation as of the chief importance; we have ever known them fail.

sign, lord, and planet in it. Also observe carefully the sign
and house where ☽ is, her separation and application. And
you may then venture safely to give judgment as to what part
of the body of the sick person is grieved, and of the nature
and quality of the sickness.

The Cause and Nature of the Sickness.

The significators in *fiery* signs, and *fiery* signs on the ascendant and 6th, shew feverish and hot complaints, hectic
fevers, erysipelas, &c.

Earthy signs argue long and tedious diseases, agues, inter-
mittent fevers, and such complaints as proceed from melancholy, consumption, &c.

Airy signs shew corrupt blood, gout, cutaneous diseases,
scrofula, &c.

Watery signs shew diseases that proceed from cold and
moisture, coughs and disordered stomach, &c.

Diseases signified by the Houses.

1st. All diseases in the head, eyes, face, ears, nose, mouth,
    foul breath, &c.
2d. The throat, scrofula, quinsey, glandular swellings in the
    neck, sore throat, &c.
3d. The shoulders, arms, and hands.
4th. The stomach, breast, and lungs.
5th. Back, hind parts of the shoulders, liver, heart, sides,
    and stomach.
6th. Lower part of the abdomen, the intestines, liver, and
    reins.
7th. The hams, the flank, the small intestines, bladder, mat-
    rix and members of generation.
8th. The spine, rectum, and groin.
9th. The hips and thighs.

10th. The knees and upper part of the leg behind **the** knees.

11th. The leg from the knee to the ancle, the shin-bone, shank, &c.

12th. The feet, ancles and toes, with all hurts or disease incident to them.*

Whether the Disease will be long or short.

Have regard to the time of year, and consider that diseases commencing in the winter are usually longer, and those in summer shorter.

Diseases which proceed from ♄ are more permanent, and are generally regulated much by the motion of the ☉. Those of a hot and dry nature, which are influenced by ♂ and ☉, are short, and regulated by the motion of ☽. ♄ causes long chronic complaints, falls, bruises, blows, &c.; ♃ and ☉ shorter; ♂ short, violent, and quick, such as cuts, bleedings, &c. ♀ a mean between both, and such as proceed from intemperance; ☿ various and changeable, such as fits, &c.; ☽ such as return at periods, as the falling sickness or epilepsy, giddiness, swimming in the head, gout, periodical illness in females, &c.†

Signs of a short Disease.

When the cusp of the 6th, the ☽, and the lords of the 1st and 6th, be in *moveable* signs, or the lord of the ascendant swift in motion, or going out of his own house into another, so that it be not the sign of the 6th or 12th, or if a fortune be in the 6th, you may judge that the disease will soon terminate.

* For the diseases signified by the *signs*, see CHAPTER XV; and fo. those of the *planets*, see the nature, &c. of each, at page 35.

† ♅ causes all uncommon and extraordinary complaints; or gives remarkable features to the sickness

M

Signs of a long Disease.

The lord of the 6th evil or afflicted, and placed in the 6th, fixed signs on its cusp, or the significators, especially the ☽, in fixed signs, are testimonies of a long and durable disease: and if ♄ be lord of the 6th and in a fixed sign, or retrograde and slow in motion, he extremely prolongs the disease; but if he be in a moveable sign, or in any of his own terms, or be swift in motion, he is not then so unfortunate.

General Signs.

The disease continues but a short time if ♓ be on the cusp of the 6th. If the ☽ apply by ill aspect to the lord of the ascendant, the disease will increase. If ☽ be in the 6th in ill aspect to ♀, the disease is brought on by intemperance, either evil diet or surfeit; and if ♀ be in ♏, there is evidence of a scandalous disease. But if the patient be a female, it may be the whites or other diseases of the matrix.

The last degrees of any sign being on the cusp of the 6th, denotes that the disease is almost at an end. If the lord of the 6th apply by ill aspect to the lord of the ascendant, it is a token of the disease increasing; the same, if the lord of the 6th be in the 8th or 12th house. If the lord of the ascendant be in the 6th, and the lord of the 6th in the ascendant, the disease has been of long continuance, and will continue until one of the significators leaves the sign where he is. And if, at the time of transiting out of the sign, he meet the evil aspects of the infortunes or lords of the 4th or 8th, and they slow in motion, and it be from signs evilly aspecting one another, it is a strong sign that the sick person will then depart this life. The lord of the 6th afflicted by the □ or ☍ of the lord of the ascendant, the disease is grievous and hard to cure. If the lord of the 6th be in the ascendant, the disease will continue, but the pain at times is small. If he be in a cadent house, the disease is not important, nor w.ll it endure. Good planets in the 6th promise a good end to the disease; evil, the contrary. The lord of the 6th, afflicted in the 6th, 8th, or 12th, or an infortune in the 6th, denotes a disease not easily curable. The lord of the ascendant *and* ☽ free from ill aspects, both being unafflicted and strong, and not in the 6th, 8th, or 12th, is a fair testimony of recovery and health. The lord of the 1st in the 4th or 8th, if not afflicted, denotes not death; but if unfortunate, it shews great difficulty ere the party be cured. If, however, he be unfortunate by retrogradation, being combust, &c., he may possibly be cured, but will afterwards relapse. If he be in evil aspect with ☽, there is danger; but, above all, if ♄ be lord of the ascendant, and be slow or retrograde, there is reason to fear a long and tedious sickness. If ♄ be strong and well qualified, the reverse.

When the lord of the ascendant is angular, strong, and unafflicted, the querent is in no danger. The ☽ slow in motion and in any aspect with him, it prolongs the infirmity, though there be at present hopes of a cure. If she be swift in motion when aspecting the lord of the ascendant, the cure will be effected in a little time. The ☽ decreasing in light, and coming to ♂, □, or ☍ of ♄, unless the disease be already leaving the patient, is very dangerous. The ☽ in ♂ with an oriental planet, who is swift in motion and direct, denotes a orief sickness; if joined to a retrograde and occidental planet, the contrary.

If ♏ ascend, the patient has been the cause of his own sickness by folly, anger, peevishness, or the like; especially if ♂ be therein. Both lights cadent and their dispositors unfortunate, the sickness will be severe; but if the fortunes assist, though the disease will be of long continuance, the party will recover beyond all expectation : the **stronger the** fortunes are, the more confident you may be in your judgment. If ♂ be lord of the ascendant and in the 6th, but in **good** aspect to ♀, there is no danger; if even in □ or ☍, not much.

The lord of the 6th combust, retrograde, in his fall or detriment, and in the 8th, in ♂, □, or ☍ of ♄ or ♂, you may fear that the disease will never leave the patient till death. If the ☽ also be applying to the same aspects of the lord of the 8th, your judgment will be certain. The ☽ or lord of the 1st, in ♂, □, or ☍ to a benevolent planet, but he retrograde, the patient will recover, but not speedily, for it denotes relapsing out of one disease into another. When ☽ leaves ☍ of ☉, and is swiftly applying to the □ or ☍ of ♂, it threatens a fatal end to the disease ; but if she receive a ⚹ or △ of ♃ or ♀, the sick shall recover. If the ☽ be in the ascendant, and in ♂, □, or ☍ to ♄ or ♂, or any other evil planet, it is a token of severe illness and danger, unless she be in mutual reception with the planet afflicting.

Testimonies of Recovery.

The ☽ applying to a fortune, powerful, denotes that the party will be restored to his former health. If reception be between the lords of the ascendant and 8th by house or triplicity, the fortunes assisting the degree ascending, or that on the 6th, or the ☽ by ♂, ⚹, or △, the sick will perfectly recover. The lord of the ascendant, being a benefic planet, or any fortune in an angle and no ill aspects cast thereto, signifies health. A certain sign of recovery is, when ☉, ♃, ♀, or ☽ be in the ascendant, and no ways afflicted by the lord of the 6th or 8th house ; the more so if in the houses of the lights or benefics. The ☽ in her own house, or the houses of ♃ or ♀, and in any aspect to those benefics, and no **way** afflicted by ♅, ♄, or ♂, denotes health and life. Wheneve. ☽ ☌ ♃ occurs, it denotes recovery, but if in ♑, less than in any other sign. If ☽ apply to the lord of the ascendant by good aspect, and be unafflicted (by the lord of the 8th or 6th especially), recovery is promised.

When, at the first falling sick of the party, ☽ is void of course, and at her next crisis meets a ⚹ or △ of ♃ or ♀ in the exact degree which forms the perfect critical aspect, the patient will undoubtedly recover, be he never so ill at time of asking the question. If at the commencement of a disease, ☉, ☽, and the lord of the ascendant, are free from ill aspects of the infortunes or lord of the 8th, there are assured hopes of life.

Arguments of Death.

The lord of the ascendant and ☽ in ☌ with the lord of the 8th, without interposing aspects of fortunes.

The lord of the ascendant cadent, and the lord of the 8th in an angle, especially if the latter be an infortune. The ☽ applying to a planet in the 8th, and afflicted; and the lord of the ascendant applying to the lord of the 8th or to evil planets therein, are very dangerous. The ☽ transferring the light of the lord of the 8th to the lord of the ascendant, usually denotes death. So when the lord of the 8th is in the ascendant, the lord of the ascendant and ☽ both being afflicted; or the lord of the ascendant being in the 8th and afflicted, and ☽ also weak and in no dignity. The lord of the ascendant under the Earth, and in ill aspect to the lord of the 8th in the 8th, or if the two lords be in ☌ in the 4th house. It is a very ill sign when the lord of the ascendant is in ☌ with the lords of the 4th, 6th, 8th, or 12th.

The lord of the ascendant combust in the ascendant, or the lord of the 8th in the 10th, and the lord of the ascendant in the 4th, 6th, or 12th, and afflicted by malefics, are very evil.

The lord of the 8th retrograde and conjoined with the ☽, or in □ or ☍ to her, shews death. The lord of the accendant in ♌ or ♒, and evilly affected by the lords of the 6th or 12th, shews little hopes of recovery; and his being conjoined with *Aldebaran*, *Antares*, *Caput*, *Algol*, or other violent fixed stars, is also evil. And if both lights be afflicted by ♄ in an angle, it is testimony of a tedious, long illness.

The ☽ in the 4th with ♂, or the ☉ with ♄, are testimonies of death; also the ☽ near the cusp of the ascendant in □ of ♂ from the 4th. The ☽ combust in the 8th, or if lady of the 6th and combust in the ascendant or 4th, the same; and especially if the lord of the 8th be afflicted.

The ♂ of ☽ with ☉ is a very ill sign, especially when she has not yet passed ☉; however, when the ♂ is in ♈ or ♌, it is not quite so evil.*

In all cases the multiplicity of testimonies must be observed, the strength of the afflicting planets, and the absence of assistance to neutralize the evil influence, before you predict death.

To know whether the Querent be really ill or not.

If the ascendant be not afflicted, nor its lord out of all his essential dignities, nor afflicted by ♄, ♂, or the lord of the 6th, he is not. Or if no planet afflict the 6th house by its presence, or the ☽ be not afflicted in the 8th or 12th, or if you find ♃, or ♀, or ☋ in the ascendant, or ☉ in the 6th, or the ☽ and lord of the ascendant in good aspect, or ♃ or ♀ casting a ⚹ or △ to the cusp of the ascendant or 6th, the party is not really sick, but at the utmost some slight indisposition has occurred, which will shortly be rectified.

Whether the Disease be in the Body or Mind, or both.

If the ascendant, ☉, and ☽ be all afflicted, the disease is

---

* We should say, if it be in ♋, where ☽ disposes of ☉, it is not so evil.

then through the whole body ; but if the planets which dispose of ☉ and ☽, or if the lord of the ascendant, or two of
them, be afflicted, the disease is more in the mind.   If the
ascendant the ☽, and lord of the ☉ are all, or two of them,
afflicted, and the lord o.̈ the ascendant and the dispositor of
the ☽ free, the affection is in the mind and not in the body.

If ♄ afflict the ☽, he shews trouble in the mind, vexation
and care ; but if ♃ be in the planet afflicting the ☽, the
contrary ; for he never oppresses the mind, but always the
body.

If the lord of the house in which ☽ is, and the lord of the
ascendant are afflicted by ☉, or combust, or under the beams
of ☉, the distemper is bodily.   But if the ruler of ☽ and the
ruler of the lord of the ascendant be *much* afflicted, the grief
is more mental than bodily.   Also if the degree ascending
and that degree where ☽ is be more afflicted than the lords
of those signs, the disease is more in the mind ; but if the
lords be more afflicted, the reverse.

When the dispositors of the lights are very much afflicted
and very weak, and the degree ascending have a □ of ☽ but
no ill aspect of ♄ or ♂, the person is much tormented in
mind.   In these cases ☉ causes the mind to be troubled by
pride, self-conceit, haughtiness, &c.   ♀ argues luxury, or a
lasciviousness which disturbs both body and mind.   ☿ shews
foolish fancies and fearful imaginations.

Of the Crises, or of Critical Days.

If the disease be not chronic, you will find great alteration
in the patient near those times when ☽ arrives at a distance
from her first place, when the patient was taken ill, of 4ᵒ,
9), or 13.5 degrees.   To learn whether these *crises* will be
good or evil, see how she is aspected at those times.   If she

be in good aspect with a benevolent planet, it promises **ease** and an improved condition; but if she there meet with **evil** aspects of malevolent planets or the lords of the 6th or 8th, he will be worse, and the medicines do little good. I have always observed that, when the ☽ came at the *crises* to ♂, □, or ☍ of that planet which did afflict the ascendant, ☽, or lord of the ascendant, or when she came to such aspect of the lord of the 6th or planets placed in the 6th, the patient suffered much, the disease ran high, and medicines given about that time worked little or no good. When she came, however, to ⚹ or △ of the lords of the ascendant, 9th, 10th, or 11th houses, I observed some interval of ease or amend‧ment. So when the lord of the ascendant came to any good aspect of the ☉ (if he had not power or dominion in the disease), I found the patient's *mind* much relieved.

How long it may be before Recovery.

When there is reason to believe that, by God's blessing, the sick person shall recover, and it be desired to know when, observe which planet is lord of the ascendant, and what benevolent planet he is in aspect with; then see what house they are in, (that is the one which *applies* to the other's aspect), whether angles, &c., and what signs they possess, whether moveable, &c. Then according to discretion and quality of the disease, so frame the measure of time. In general, I judge in so many days as the aspect wants degrees of being perfect, if the sign be moveable and the planet angular; but if swift in motion, I am the more certain that the patient will begin to amend in so many days. If the sign be common, in which the application is, I neither judge days, weeks, nor months, but use discretion, having first observed the nature of the disease.

The ancient rule was as follows :—

Moveable signs shew . . . . *days.*

Common ditto . . . . *weeks.*

Fixed ditto . . . . *months.*

Angles are equivalent to . . . . . . *moveable signs.*

Succeedent houses to . . . . *common signs.*

Cadent houses to . . . . *fixed signs.*

It is well to observe, also, the quick or slow motion of the ☽, the sign she is in, and her situation as to angles, &c. I often find that when the lord of the ascendant quits the sign he is in, and enters a sign in which he has dignities, the patient recovers at that time, or feels an alteration for the better. If a common sign be on the 6th, 28° or more, I say, that the disease will *vary* in two weeks.

JUDGMENT OF THE DISEASE FROM THE AFFLICTION OF THE MOON AT THE FIRST ILLNESS OF THE PATIENT, OR THE TIME OF ASKING THE QUESTION.*

Whoever shall be first taken ill, or compelled to take to his bed when the ☽ *is afflicted by* ♄ *, or by* ☿ *, if he have the nature of* ♄ *, will, in a great measnre, suffer as here described.*

The ☽ *in* ♈, *in* ☌, □, *or* ☍ *of* ♄ .—Headache or heaviness in the head, much discharge at the nostrils, dulness, or weariness of the eyes, humours falling into the throat; weak pulse, and a heavy drowsiness of mind ; loathing at the stomach, violent unseasonable perspiration, internal heats, and externally cold. The patient more afflicted at night than by day.

The ☽ *in* ♉, *in* ☌, *&c. of* ♄ .—Fevers proceeding from obstructions near the heart, liver, and lungs, occasioned by sur-

---

* The student may rely that he will find these rules, when they apply, to be infallible.—ZADKIEL.

feits, high living, &c. The pulse high and immoderate, the
body inflated, lungs oppressed, ulcerated, &c. If the ☽ be
not supported by benefics, there is danger of death within 14
days.

The ☽ *in* ♊ *in* ♂ ♄ . *&c.*—The disease has its origin in
the mind by too much care, or a multiplicity of business, or
otherwise by fatigue in travelling or over-exercise. There is
danger of a small fever ; the pain is dispersed over all the
body, but chiefly in the joints. The vitals are afflicted, the
pulse rare, and weak ; there are frequent perspirations, symp-
toms of spleen and consumption. If ♂ also afflict, without
assistance, the patient will hardly live 10 days ; but if ♃ or
♀ assist, the sick person may recover after a long period.

The ☽ *in* ♋ *in* ♂ *of* ♄ , *&c.*—The breast is much afflicted
with tough phlegm, or slimy matter ; there is cough, and
much salivary discharge. Hoarseness, catarrhs, &c., with
humours falling into the breast ; the windpipe obstructed ;
slight fevers, agues, &c. holding a long time ; also pains in
the bowels, infirmity in the reins or secrets. If ☽ be decreasing, and near the body of ♄ , the disease will continue a
long time.

The ☽ *in* ♌ *in* ♂, *&c. of* ♄ .—The sickness arises from
bad blood, the patient suffers with heat in the breast, heart-
burn, violent fevers, troubled pulse, much external and internal heat, faintness at the heart, swoonings, the stone ; and
sometimes the black jaundice. If there be no good aspects
to prevent it, they frequently die when ☽ comes to ☍ of ♄ .

The ☽ *in* ♍ *in* ♂, *&c.* ♄ .—The illness arises from indi-
gestion, obstructions in the bowels, &c. ; shooting pains are
felt under the ribs, &c. ; flatulency, gout, or aches in the
thighs or feet, &c. The patient generally is sick a long time.

The ☽ *in* ♎ *in* ♂, *&c. of* ♄ .—The disease has its origin in
some surfeit of wine or rich food, meat ill digested, &c., or

from excess of venery; the breast is affected, also he head, there is no appetite, a loathing in the stomach, cough, hoarseness, &c., and often great pain in the joints, knees, and thighs, with an itching in those parts, and fear of sciatica.

The ☽ *in* ♏ *in* ♂, *&c. of* ♄.—Denotes a disease in the *rectum* or *sphincter muscle,* piles, hemorrhoids, or fistula. There is very likely a retention of urine, or the reverse; stone in the bladder, dropsical humour, &c. It may be that it is gonorrhea, &c., or the diseases of the matrix.*

The ☽ *in* ♐ *in* ♂, *&c. of* ♄.—The patient suffers by pains in the joints, &c., or fever, extremes of heat and cold. Illness often happens by too great exertion of body or mind, and cold taken afterwards; there is much melancholy also. And if it be an ☍ of ♄, there is generally a spice of gout, tumours or swellings in the hands, thighs, or feet, &c. If ♂ have any ill aspect to ☽, it proves a violent burning fever.

The ☽ *in* ♑ *in* ♂, *&c.* ♄.—The disease proceeds from cold or melancholy. It brings heaviness of the breast and stomach, difficulty of breathing, dry coughs, the lungs oppressed, and a fever is approaching. The pain is greater at night than in the day. The patient continually complains of headache, or pain in the left ear, or of a rumbling noise in his head.†

* These latter especially, if ♀ throw an ill aspect, or the lord of the 5th house.

† We can speak personally as to this effect. We were taken ill in the evening of the 1st March, 1829, when ☽ was in ♑, 19°, and ♄ in ♋ 28°, and we suffered extremely during the night, and had violent pains in the left side of the head, and sensations of noises, as of the working of the piston of a steam-engine. A fever ensued, which confined us to bed for three weeks, having caught cold after taking mercury. The direction in our nativity was M.C. ♂ ☉, who, being in ♂ with ♂ at birth, partook of his ill qualities, and afflicted the ascendant by his mundane square.

The ♓ in ♒ in ♂, &c. ♄.—The illness is occasioned by too much toil of mind or body, want of sleep, or due refreshment. The malady comes on unequally with remission or intension.* The patient suffers by noise in the head, by wind, or faintness at the heart, or a rising and danger of suffocation by hysterical fits, &c. ; and by sore throat.

The ♓ in ♓ in ♂, &c. ♄.—The complaint arises from cold,† and the patient is afflicted with continual fever, frequently sighs, suffers pains under the nipples of the breast, and about the heart ; the throat suffers from much phlegm, or there is water in the chest, rotten cough, &c.

Whoever is taken ill when ♓ is afflicted by ♂ or the ☉, suffers in the following manner :—

The ♓ in ♈ in ♂, &c. of ♂.—The disease is from some distemper of the membranes, &c. of the brain. There is continual fever and restlessness, extreme thirst, foul tongue, or inflammation of the liver, heat and pain in the breast, high pulse, and often delirium. The patient is generally almost mad with pain, either cholic or cholera pains, &c. in the bowels. If after the ♓ leave ♂ she go to ♂ or ☍ of ♄, there is small hope of life ; and if she decrease in light, and be slow in motion, there is scarce any.

The ♓ in ♉ in ♂, &c. of ♂.—There is an abundance of blood, continual fever, the whole frame disordered ; sore throat, with inflammation in the neck, or hind part thereof ; pain in the bones, broken sleep, and a foolish longing after wine and cold water. There is often putrid sore throat and also hoarseness, and strangury, stone, or gravel, with pain in the reins or kidneys, or disease therein.

---

* This till ♓ is past ☍ of her own p'ace, when, if there be good aspects the sick is recoverable.

† Especially wet feet, damp linen, &c.

The ☽ *in* ♊ *in* ♂, *&c.* ♂.—A violent fever, high and inordinate pulse; there are obstructions and corrupt blood, pains all over the body, heat in the reins, and sometimes spitting of blood; also lameness or fractures in the arms, pains in the joints, &c.

The ☽ *in* ♋ *in* ♂, *&c.* ♂. This shews a disordered stomach by having taken too much to drink, &c., riot, and excess. It often turns to dysentery, cough, and spitting of blood.

The ☽ *in* ♌ *in* ♂, *&c.* ♂.—Too much blood abounds, weak pulse, a disturbed brain, raving, and strong fits; loss of or depraved appetite; distempers of the heart, heaviness all over the body, and drowsiness. There is danger of consumption. The blood is over-heated, the body dry and parched; there is probability of pleurisy, fainting, and swooning. I ever fear this ♂ or ☍ more than in any other sign.

The ☽ *in* ♍ *in* ♂, *&c.* ♂. Flux in the bowels, small fevers, a failing pulse, cholic, flatulence, weakness in the legs, or near the ancles. If ☽ be afflicted by ♂ in ♍, diseases are not easily removed.

The ☽ *in* ♎ *in* ♂, *&c.* ♂.—The patient is grieved with plentitude of blood, and, from that cause, has high pulse, no rest, is feverish, and an inflammation all over the body. The patient has taken some surfeit by excess or disorder in his diet, or the blood is over-heated; or there is stone or gravel in the kidneys. Violent burning fevers often follow.

The ☽ *in* ♏ *in* ♂, *&c.* ♂.—There is generally some ulcer, lues, gonorrhea, &c., or, if a child, measles; it may be piles, or hemorrhoids. There is frequently some stoppage in the head by grievous colds; and as the blood is corrupt, so we find blotches, breakings out, &c. If there be reason to believe it, some scandalous disease may be judged, especially if ♀ afflict ☽.

The ☽ *in* ♐ *in* ♂, *&c.* ♂.—The disease is in general vio lent, and caused by gluttony or repletion. There is fever frequently very high, or choleric passion; but the pulse is often faint, and beats slow and feeble. Inordinate exercise has frequently been the cause of the disease; and he suffers pestilent fever, &c. It shews hand and foot gout, breakings out, sore throat, &c., and, at times, sore and inflamed eyes. Also, hurts by horses.

The ☽ *in* ♑ *in* ♂, *&c.* ♂.—Nausea abounds, vomiting and flux. A puffing up of the sinews, (such as cholera cramps), inflammation of the breast, and humours in the hands or fingers. The face is yellow and sunken, the body extremely wasted, and the blood corrupt. The pulse remits, and is slow. The yellow jaundice happens under these aspects.

The ☽ *in* ♒ *in* ♂ *&c.* ♂.—If ☽ be slow in motion, and decreasing in light, the disease proceeds from sharp and violent affections, or vehement passions. There is pain at the heart, swooning fits, high pulse, great pain in the chest, and much difficulty in breathing.

The ☽ *in* ♓ *in* ♂, *&c.* ♂. The body is full of gross humours, the disease is from too much drinking and excess, and is most prevalent in the night time. The party is troubled with a kind of delirium, (frequently it shews that they are yet drunk), they have vehement thirst, sharp burning fevers, and are desirous of wine. They have generally a looseness and much pain in the bowels, or a violent cough and great expectoration, and are almost suffocated with phlegm; the body is swollen, and there is danger of dropsy.*

---

* Where various diseases are named, the student must look to other testimonies to ascertain the exact complaint.

Fig 12.

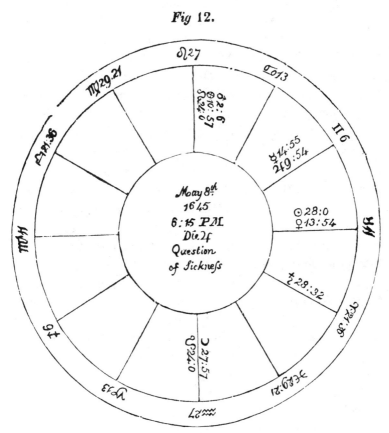

QUESTION.—*A sick Doctor, what is his Disease? Is it curable?*

To learn what part of the body is affected, observe that, as the ascendant is not afflicted, you must look to the 6th house, and see if it be so. Therein we find ♄ in his fall; and as he naturally signifies diseases by his presence, I concluded that, from thence and that house I must require the part aggrieved.

♈ represents the head.

♄ in ♈ shews the breast.*

♂, lord of the ascendant, in ♌, signifies the heart.* The lord of the ascendant has just separated from a □ of ♄, being at that time in ♋, which signifies and rules over the breast and stomach. From all these testimonies I concluded that the parts of the body grieved were the head, breast, heart, and stomach; and that there was lodged in the breast or stomach some obstruction, which caused all his disease and suffering.

From what Cause the Sickness was.

The principal significator being ♄, and he in his own terms, and ☽ disposed of by him and applying to him, shewed such diseases as he causes, and which might exist in the head and breast. ♂, lord of the ascendant, was also in the terms of ♄, and applied to □ of ☉, who was in the terms of ♂. So that dry, melancholy diseases were shewn by ♄, and heat or fever by ♂. And, indeed, when I came to speak to him, he was suffering great pain and rumbling in his head, was very silent, dull, and melancholy; he slept very little, had a very dry cough, and complained of great weakness and pain in his breast and at his heart. His complexion was between black and yellow, as if inclined to jaundice; and he had also a lingering consumption and great weariness all over him, with pains in his joints, shewn by ☽ in an airy sign. The ascendant is ♏, which signifies the secrets, stone in the bladder, &c.; so the ☽ in ♒ shews the secrets and diseases therein, &c. Hence he had great difficulty in making water, voided red gravel, and suffered great pain in those parts.

Whether the Disease would be curable or not?

The author of the disease being ♄, shewed it would be of

* This will be seen by the Table at the end of this chapter.

some continuance, for he is a slow ponderous planet; besides, the angles of the figure are all fixed, and the lord of the ascendant, ⊙, and ☽, are all in fixed signs. The lights are in □ aspect to each other from angles, and both in the terms of an evil planet; and the lord of the 6th in a fixed sign: all these shewed a long disease. The ☽ being in the 4th in aspect to ♄ in the 6th, and applying to □ of ⊙, who has dignities in the 6th, and the lord of the 4th in the 6th, and lord of the 8th in the 8th, the testimonies were strong for his death: *he died the 14th August following.*

Fig 13.

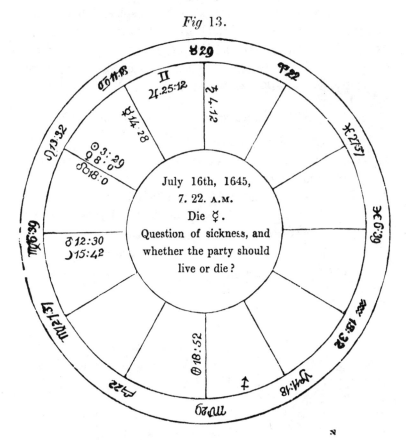

July 16th, 1645,
7. 22. A.M.
Die ☿.
Question of sickness, and whether the party should live or die?

QUESTION.—*What is the Disease? and will the Patient live or die ?*

The ascendant is ♍, and it is afflicted by the presence of ♂, who is partly lord of the 8th house, as great part of ♈ is already therein. Hence from the ascendant chiefly we must learn the cause and nature of the disease, and part afflicted. A fixed sign ♒ is on the 6th, afflicted by ♉, and ♄, lord of the 6th, is in ♉, an earthy sign, of the same nature as ♍, the ascendant. The ☽, a general significator in all diseases, is also in ♍ in ♂ with ♂. All these shewed the patient to be greatly afflicted with the spleen, cholic, and obstructions in his bowels, small fever, flatulence, and a failing weak pulse. And as the ☽ and ♂ are in the *ascendant*, the patient was perplexed with distempers in the head, slept unquietly, &c. (*All which was true.*)

Will the Patient live or die ?

All the significators promised death.

1st. ☉, light of time, was in close ▢ to ♄, lord of the 6th in fixed signs.

2d. The ascendant was extremely afflicted by presence of ♂, he being lord of nearly all the 8th house.

3d. The ☽ was afflicted by ♂ in the house of life.

4th. The ☽ separated from the ⚹ of ☿, lord of the ascendant, in signs of long ascension, and did transfer his light to ♃, lord of the 4th and 8th houses, denoting death and the grave.

N.B.—The patient died the 28th of the month, when ☿ came to the ▢ of ♄ and ♂ of ☉ in the figure. The ☽ came then to ☍ ☉, and had transited the cusp of the 6th house the day preceding, viz. ♒ 14°.

A TABLE

SHEWING WHAT PARTS OF MAN'S BODY EVERY PLANET SIGNIFIES IN THE TWELVE SIGNS.

SIGNS.	♄	♃	♂	☉	♀	☿	☽
♈	Breast Arms	Neck Throat Heart Bowels	Head Bowels Eyes	Thighs	Reins Feet	Secrets Legs	Head Knees
♉	Heart Breast Bowels	Neck Shoulders Arms Bowels	Throat Reins	Knees	Secret-Members Head	Thighs Feet	Throat Legs
♊	Heart Bowels	Breast Reins Secrets	Breast Arms Secrets	Legs Ancles	Throat Thighs	Head Knees	Shoulders Arms Thighs Feet
♋	Bowels Reins Secrets	Heart Secrets Thighs	Breast Feet	Feet	Arms Shoulders Knees	Eyes Throat Legs Knees	Head Breast Stomach
♌	Reins Secrets	Bowels Thighs Knees	Heart Bowels Knees	Head	Heart Breast Legs	Throat Arms Shoulders Feet	Arms Shoulders Bowels
♍	Thighs Secrets Feet	Reins Knees	Bowels Legs	Throat Neck	Stomach Heart Bowels Feet	Head Breast Heart	Arms Shoulders Bowels
♎	Knees Thighs	Head Eyes Secrets Legs	Reins Secrets Feet	Arms Shoulders	Head Intestines	Throat Heart Stomach Bowels	Breast Heart Reins Bowels
♏	Knees Legs	Thighs Feet	Head Arms Secrets Thighs	Breast Heart	Throat Reins Secrets	Arms Shoulders Back Bowels	Stomach Heart Bowels Secrets
♐	Legs Feet	Head Thighs Knees	Throat Hands Thighs Feet	Heart Bowels	Arms Shoulders Secrets Thighs	Breast Heart Reins Secrets	Back Bowels Thighs
♑	Head Feet	Eyes Neck Knees Legs	Arms Shoulders Knees Legs	Back Bowels	Breast Heart Thighs	Stomach Heart Secrets	Reins Thighs Knees
♒	Neck Head	Arms Shoulders Breast Feet	Breast Heart Legs	Reins Secrets	Heart Knees	Heart Bowels Thighs	Secrets Legs Ancles
♓	Arms Shoulders Neck	Head Breast Heart	Heart Bowels Ancles Feet	Secrets Thighs	Neck Throat Bowels Legs	Reins Secrets Thighs Knees	Thighs Feet

The DISEASES *each* PLANET *naturally signifies when it be-comes the afflictor, and is posited in any of the* TWELVE SIGNS.

DISEASES OF SATURN.

♄ in ♈ signifies rheum, melancholy, vapours, cold in the head, obstructions, stoppage in the stomach, pains in the teeth, deafness, &c.

♄ in ♉ signifies swelling in the neck and throat, king's evil, scurvy, hoarseness, melancholy, and chronic distempers about the neck and throat.

♄ in ♊ signifies infirmities incident to the arms and shoulders, consumption, black jaundice, and diseases proceeding from bad blood.

♄ in ♋ denotes phthisic, ulcerations in the lungs, obstructions and bruises in the breast, ague, scurvy, cancer, &c.

♄ in ♌ signifies the heart afflicted by grief or poison, consumption of the reins or inward parts, vapours, weakness, and pains in the back, &c.

♄ in ♍ shews the blood corrupted, obstructions in the bowels, costiveness, weakness in the thighs, melancholy, gripings, stone, &c.

♄ in ♎ shews the blood corrupted, back and kidneys distempered, strangury, consumptive pains in the knees and thighs, sciatica and gout.

♄ in ♏ denotes swellings or distempers of the secret parts, melancholy, piles, palsy, gout in the hands and feet.

♄ in ♐ signifies weakness in the hips and thighs, old aches and bruises in those parts, and sciatica or gout.

♄ in ♑ denotes the gout in the lower parts, pains and obstructions in the head, ague, &c.

♄ in ♒ signifies disorders in the head and teeth, defects in the ears, pains in the joints, bruises, swellings in the legs, and sometimes a sore throat.

♄ in ♓ gives defluxions of rheum, king's evil, consumption, all distempers of the feet and toes, such as the gout, and illness by colds.

DISEASES OF JUPITER.

♃ in ♈ produces distempers in the head, a quinsy or swelling in the throat, chiefly from ill blood in the veins of the head ; and causes strange dreams and imaginations.

♃ in ♉ brings distempers in the throat, wind in the blood, gripings in the bowels, and goutish humours in the hands and arms.

♃ in ♊.—A pleurisy, or some disorder of the reins.

♃ in ♋ gives the dropsy, the stomach offended, bad appetite, corrupt blood, scurvy, surfeits, &c.

♃ in ♌ indicates a fever, pleurisy, the heart ill affected.

♃ in ♍ indicates a consumption, obstructions of the lungs, melancholy, cold and dry liver.

♃ in ♎ shews the patient hath too much blood, whence arise obstructions, corrupt blood, fever, piles, tumours, inflammations, &c.

♃ in ♏ signifies the strangury, piles, the blood discharged with watery humours, whence arise dropsy, &c.

♃ in ♐ denotes some choleric distemper, arising from putrefaction of the blood ; a fever, pains and swellings about the knees, &c.

♃ in ♑.—The patient is afflicted with melancholy, obstructions in the throat, &c.

♃ in ♒.—The blood abounds too much, whence it is corrupted, and many diseases and flying pains afflict the body. It gives lumbago.

♃ in ♓.—The blood is too thin and waterish, which breeds dropsy.

DISEASES OF MARS.

♂ in ♈ signifies the patient is almost distracted with a violent pain in his head, rheum in the eyes, want of rest, &c.

♂ in ♉ denotes extreme pain in the throat and neck, king's evil, weakness in the loins, and the gravel or stone.

♂ in ♊ shews the blood is corrupted ; itch, breakings out, surfeit, fever, pains in the arms and shoulders, disorders in the secret parts, strangury, &c.

♂ in ♋ indicates pains in the breast and stomach, a dry cough, or a tumour in the thighs : accidents to the feet.

♂ in ♌ denotes affliction at the heart, choleric humours, gravel in the kidnies, pain in the knees, &c.

♂ in ♍ signifies choleric humours, obstructions in the bowels, bloody flux, worms in children, humours in the legs.

♂ in ♎ produces diseases in the reins and kidnies, stone or gravel, urine hot, lues, &c., as may be suspected.

♂ in ♏ shews a suspicion of some venereal distemper, or ulcer in the secret parts, pains in the bladder, pains in the head, overflowing of courses, &c.

♂ in ♐ produces pain or ulcers in the hips and thighs by humours settled in those parts, and an extreme heat in the mouth and throat.

♂ in ♑ denotes lameness in the knees, hands, or arms, or a flying gout.

♂ in ♒ signifies blood over-heated, pains in the legs, surfeit, or fever.

♂ in ♓ gives lameness in the feet, by corrupt humours settled there ; sometimes the heart is afflicted, &c.

DISEASES OF THE SUN.

☉ in ♈ produces sore eyes, megrims, head disturbed, fevers, &c.

⊙ in ♉ denotes tumours in the knees, quinsy or sore throat, breakings out and swellings in those parts.

⊙ in ♊.— Blood inflamed, pestilential fevers, breakings out in several parts of the body, scurvy, pains and weakness in the legs.

⊙ in ♋ shews the measles or small pox, a disordered stomach, hoarseness, dropsy or swelling in the feet.

⊙ in ♌ indicates violent pains in the head, madness, stone, pains in the back, plague, spotted fever.

⊙ in ♍ produces humours in the bowels, obstructions in the stomach, bloody flux, sore throat, or swellings in the neck.

⊙ in ♎.—Inflammation of the blood, pains in the arms and shoulders, stone and gravel, the venereal distemper, &c.

⊙ in ♏ indicates distempers in the secret parts, sharpness of urine, obstructions in the stomach, and female courses; also *phlegmatiæ dolens.*

⊙ in ♐. — The thighs are afflicted by hot humours; a fistula, fevers, swoonings, &c.

⊙ in ♑ signifies lameness about the knees, bowels disordered, and a fever.

⊙ in ♒.—The blood inflamed, breakings out, reins disordered, gravel, stone, strangury, &c.

⊙ in ♓.—The secret parts afflicted, strangury, and violent pains in those parts.

DISEASES OF VENUS.

♀ in ♈ indicates the disease is in the head from abundance of moist humours, lethargy, reins afflicted, and head disordered by cold.

♀ in ♉ signifies pain in the head or secret parts, swellings in the neck from moist humours in the head.

♀ in ♊ denotes a corrupted blood, king's evil, dropsy, and a flux of rheum

♀ in ♋ shews the stomach is much offended with **cold**, **raw**, undigested humours ; many times with a surfeit, **&c.**

♀ in ♌.—Some ill affection of the heart, love passion, **&c.**, pains in the legs, of bad consequence.

♀ in ♍ shews some distemper in the bowels, a flux, or the worms, mucus in the bowels.

♀ in ♎ denotes a gonorrhea or distemper in the reins, **or** surfeit by too plentiful eating or drinking, and windy disorders.

♀ in ♏ produces some venereal distemper, and pain in the private parts, &c.

♀ in ♐.—Hip gout, surfeits, cold and moist humours.

♀ in ♑ produces gout in the knees and thighs, and swellings in those parts.

♀ in ♒.—Pains and swellings in the legs or knees from a cold cause, and the heart afflicted.

♀ in ♓ indicates lameness in the feet, swellings in the legs, a flux, windy complaints, &c.

DISEASES OF MERCURY.

☿ in ♈ shews the disease lies in the head and brain, vertigo and spasms in the head, and sometimes disorders of the womb.

☿ in ♉ produces defects in the throat, swellings in the neck, hoarseness, and also pain in the feet.

☿ in ♊ signifies windiness in the blood, gouty pains in the head, arms, &c.

☿ in ♋ produces a cold stomach, gripings, windiness, distillation of rheum, lameness in the legs and *knees* from colds, &c.

☿ in ♌ indicates tremblings, melancholy, pains in the back, occasioned by colds caught in the feet.

☿ in ♍ imports much wind in the bowels, obstructions, pains in the head, short breath, and wind cholic.

☿ in ♎ shews stoppage of urine, obstructions, blood disordered ; breast, lungs, and reins afflicted.

☿ in ♏ denotes distempers in the secret parts, afflictions of the bowels, running pains in the arms and shoulders.

☿ in ♐ shews distempers in the reins, weakness in the back, stoppage at the stomach, coughs, swellings in the hips and thighs.

☿ in ♑ denotes stoppage of urine, goutish humours above the knees, pains in the back, melancholy, &c.

☿ in ♒ imports wind in the blood, running pains in different parts of the body, fluxes and disorders in the bowels.

☿ in ♓ signifies pains in the head, weakness in the legs and feet, a gonorrhea, or a distemper in the reins, &c.

DISEASES OF THE MOON.

☽ in ♈ signifies convulsions, defluxions of rheum from the head, lethargy, weakness in the eyes, and pains in the knees.

☽ in ♉ produces pains in the legs and feet, swellings, stoppage in and sore throat, &c.

☽ in ♊ denotes a wandering gout in the legs, arms, hands, and feet, surfeits, and great obstructions.

☽ in ♋ shews the stomach much afflicted, a surfeit, smallpox, convulsions, falling sickness, tympany, or dropsy.

☽ in ♌.—The heart afflicted, sore throat, quinsy, king's evil, &c.

☽ in ♍ signifies great pain and disorders in the bowels, melancholy blood, obstructions, weakness in the arms and shoulders.

☽ in ♎ denotes the reins are distempered, obstructions in the stomach, weakness in the back, whites in women, surfeits, pleurisy, &c.

☽ in ♏ shews the distemper is in the secrets, small-pox, dropsy, poison, the heart afflicted, swoonings, &c.

☽ in ♐ imports lameness or weakness in the thighs, dis·tempers in the bowels, &c.

☽ in ♑ signifies the stone, weak back, gout in the knees, whites in women, &c.

☽ in ♒ signifies hysterics, swellings, and pains in the legs and secret parts.

☽ in ♓ shews cold taken in the feet, and body disordered thereby; swellings in the legs, dropsies, and the body over-charged with moist humours.*

CHAPTER XXX.

THE SEVENTH HOUSE, AND ITS QUESTIONS.

This House signifies Marriage, Love Questions, Lawsuits and Controversies, Contracts, Wars, Duels, open Enemies, Bar-gains, Thefts, Fugitives, and all matters regarding Strangers.

THE questions to be judged by this house being more difficult than those of any other house, I have been more lengthy in delivering the opinions of the ancients as well as moderns thereon; and have written several aphorisms concerning its questions.

APHORISMS AND CONSIDERATIONS

FOR THE BETTER JUDGING ANY HORARY QUESTION, ESPECIALLY THOSE OF THE 7TH HOUSE.

1. See the question be radical and fit to be judged.
2. Be not confident of the judgment if either the first or

---

* This table is taken from the old Arab writers on astrology, wh flourished many centuries back: they used many terms inconsistent wit the modern nomenclature of diseases; but as the human frame is stil. the same, so are its diseases, though called by different names. Thus, *Mercury in Aquarius* is said to cause "wind in the blood," by which, we presume, was meant spasmodic action, arising from debility.

last degrees of a sign ascend. If few degrees ascend, the matter is not yet ripe for judgment: if the latter degrees, the matter of the question is elapsed, or the querent has been tampering with other artists, or despairs of success. Meddle not with it at that time.

3. If ♄, ♂, or ☋ be in the 10th house unfortunate, it will end in the discredit of the artist.

4. Judge not upon every trivial motion or light question, or when the querent has not wit to know what he would demand.

5. Observe well the strength and condition of ☽; for it is far better that the lord of the ascendant be unfortunate than the ☽.

6. The evil planets shew tardiness and difficulty in every question, unless ☽ and they receive each other in the signification.

7. The benefics, ♃ and ♀, never import evil but when ruling evil houses; and if they be significators without reception, even then they put forward the matter.

8. If ☽ be void of course, there is no great hope of the question, unless she be in ♋, ♉, ♐, or ♓.

9. Observe from what planet ☽ last separated; for it will shew what has already happened: if from a fortune, good; but from a malefic, evil; according to the nature of the house the planet rules and is in.

10. The application of ☽ shews the present condition of the matter, and what may be expected. If ☽ apply to a planet in his fall, it denotes trouble and delays.

11. If evil planets promise good, it will be imperfect or less than is expected, and come with much effort; and if they foreshew evil, it will be greater than may be feared.

12. If malefics threaten evil. observe whether ☉, ♃, or ♀

cast any good aspect to them, for then the evil will be mitigated.

13. If the fortunes promise good, but are weak, or behold not the ascendant, they perform but little without reception.

14. A planet peregrine, viz. having no essential dignities at all, is very malicious.

15. Confide not too much in a fortune, unless he be in his essential dignities.

16. In a figure where both fortunes and infortunes are equally weak and ill placed, venture not a judgment, but defer the party for another time.

17. In all questions where the significator of the thing is combust, or in ☍ to ☉, he can bring nothing to perfection.

18. If one infortune be joined to another, the good they promise will come to nothing ; but the evil they threaten will be more violent.

19. The lord of the ascendant out of his dignities, cadent, &c., shews the querent out of all hopes in the business.

20. A planet under the beams of ☉, (viz. within 12 degrees), has no fortitude ;* if within *sixteen minutes* of ☉, he is in cazimi or heart of ☉, and then he is very strong.

21. If the dispositor of the significator be *oriental,* and he either ♄, ♃, or ♂, the matter is sooner performed ; but if ♀ or ☿, later: the reverse, if they be *occidental.*

22. If the significator of the thing desired be in a *fixed* sign, it denotes stability, and that the thing shall continue, whether it be begun or is to be begun ; if he be in *common* signs, it shews the probability of the matter,

---

* We should judge that, if the planet dispose of ☉ by house, this rule does not hold. We have no faith in the doctrine of Cazimi.

ort not its conclusion ; and if in *moveable* signs, a
sudden resolution or concluding the matter one way
or other.   Hence we begin the foundations of buildings when the significators are fixed; short journeys
when moveable; but things wherein a mediocrity is
desirable, when they are in moveable signs.

23. The ☽ or lord of the ascendant, with ☋, brings damage,
according to the house they are in.   The ☊ is in like
manner beneficial.

24. If in any question you find ☽ afflicted, there is seldom
any good comes of the matter.

25. If ☽ or lord of the ascendant be in their fall, the querent
despairs of the matter, nor does he much care whether
it be performed or not.

26. Consider diligently the planet afflicting the significator
of the thing demanded, and what house he is lord of,
and where placed; from the nature of those houses
require the cause obstructing.

27. The most powerful affliction to the ☽ is when she is
combust, and if she applies to ☉ it is the worst.

28. If an infortune aspect your significator, and they be both
peregrine or retrograde, you may judge that the mischief threatened is almost inevitable.

29. Take especial notice whether any frustration or prohibition be before the perfect aspect of the significators ;
the planet which frustrates hinders the thing demanded.

30. In all questions of gain, look well to ⊕: the querent
will get by persons or things connected with the
house it is in; but if it be afflicted, he loses in the
same way.

31. In questions of marriage, an evil planet in the 7th shews
ill agreement in the married state.

32. If the lord of the 8th be unfortunate in the 8th, the querent will suffer by the death of some female; or, concerning debts due to him, by dead men.

33. In what house you find ♃ or ♀ well dignified, expect benefits by men or things signified by that house ; as if in the 3d, by kindred ; in the 4th, by your father or lands, &c. ; in the 5th, by play, pleasure, &c. ; and so of the others. And beware of slander or damage through that house where ☋ falls.

QUESTIONS CONCERNING MARRIAGE.

Whether a Man shall Marry ?

If a man ask this question, let the lord of the ascendant, ☽, and ♀, also planets in the ascendant, be his significators. Then if ☽ aspect favourably ☉, ♀, or lord of the 7th, or the lord of the 1st aspect the lord of the 7th, or be in the 7th, or the lord of the 7th be in the ascendant, or if most of these significators be in fruitful signs, or disposed of by ♀, the man shall marry.

Whether a Woman shall Marry ?

Follow the same rules as above, but, instead of ☽ and ♀, substitute ☉ and ♂. If ♂ have no aspect or familiarity with ☉, it is a strong testimony of the negative.

The Time of Marriage.

The degree of the application of ☽ to ☉ or ♀, or of ☉ to ♂, or the lords of the 1st and 7th to good aspect, cr to □ or ☍, if with strong mutual reception, or of the lord of the ascendant to the cusp of the ascendant, or the lord of the 7th to the cusp of the ascendant, must be noticed. And if the significators be swift, and the testimonies of marriage strong and numerous, moveable signs give days, weeks, or months, as the applying planet be angular, succeedent, or cadent; and common signs, in like way, give weeks, months, or years; and fixed signs give, in like manner, months or years.

Of Marriage with any particular Person who may be desired.

If the lord of the ascendant or ☽ (or if the querent be a woman, the ☉) be joined to the lord of the 7th in any of his dignities in the ascendant, 10th, or 11th, the querent shall obtain the party desired.

If both significators behold each other by ⚹ or △ out of the ascendant and 11th, or out of the 7th and 9th, or 7th and 5th, and no frustration or retrogradation of the chief significators happen before the good aspect be completed, the match will be perfected, if the *querent* please. For we always suppose a FREEDOM OF WILL to do or not to do. And if there be a □ or ☍ between the significators, without reception, the matter will come to nothing.

A □ aspect with reception will perfect the matter, but with some difficulty. If no reception be, there may be hopes, but no grounds to judge favourably.

When the lord of the ascendant is in the 7th, the querent loves best; and when the lord of the 7th is in the ascendant, the quesited loves best.

The match may be brought about, though there be no aspect between the significators, if there be any good translation of light; more especially if the planet who translates be a fortune, or be not retrograde, combust, or unfortunate, or afflicted by ♄ or ♂. The person signified may be known by the description of the planet, according to the sign he is in, and the way he is aspected; and the quality of the person, from the house he is lord of. A masculine diurnal planet shews a man, and a feminine nocturnal planet a female, or an effeminate man, and *vice versâ*.

Testimonies that the Marriage shall be hindered.

Observe the planet who receives the light of the significators. If he be a heavy planet, and have the □ or ☍ of a malefic, or be cadent, the intended match shall be broken off, though at present never so feasible.

Remark which party's significator is strongest; that party shall first marry after this dissolution.

If the significators apply by an evil aspect without reception, or if there be no good aspect between the luminaries, there will be no marriage; unless the lords of the ascendant and 7th be placed in each other's houses, and the other signs be very decided for the match.

If the evil ♄ be in the ascendant, he renders the querent cool, and but little inclined to marriage; unless he be very strong or well aspected. If he be in the 7th, he has the same effect on the quesited. He is generally an enemy to marriage, whereas ♀ assists marriage, and inclines the parties thereto.

What shall be the Cause of the Marriage being prevented?

Consider the evil planet who intercepts his rays between the significators, and hinders the marriage; and observe what house he is lord of, and where he is situated. If he be lord of the 2d, want of money will be objected to the querent, or he may fear to marry from lack of means.

The lord of the 3d denotes that it will be caused by the querent's kindred or neighbours, or by means of some short journey.

The lord of the 4th shews that his father will not agree,

ɔr it may (especially if a feminine planet) be the mother of the quesited ; or it may be for want of some settlement of houses or lands, &c.

The lord of the 5th causes obstacles by means of children, or by the querent having a character for loose living, &c.

The 6th denotes sickness in the querent, or opposition by some relation of his father, or by means of servants, or some private enemy of the quesited.

The lord of the 7th, or a planet therein, denotes a public enemy of the querent, or a lawsuit, or a rival.

The 8th denotes a lack of money on the part of the que- sited ; or, if other testimonies concur, it may be that the querent's death may intervene to prevent the match.

The 9th, in like manner, shews opposition by the relations of the quesited, or the interference of some lawyer or priest, or that the querent may go a long journey or voyage, and so the match be hindered.

The 10th and its lord shew the father of the quesited, or the mother of the querent, or some person having authority over the querent.

If it be the 11th house or its lord, then the friends of both parties dislike the match ; or those who first introduced the parties, or endeavoured to bring it about, will now try to dis- solve the connexion.

If it be by the lord of the 12th, or by a planet therein, there is some under-hand dealing or secret enmity to the querent. The affair shall be much retarded ; but the querent shall never know by whom ; or some private scandal will do much wrong, and quite break off the matter.

In the same manner that you may thus learn who will *oppose* the querent, you may ascertain who will *assist* him in his desires. And by varying the houses, you may know the persons who will aid or hinder the quesited.

To describe the Person and Qualities of the future Wife or Husband.

For the man, observe the planet the ☽ is nearest in aspect with and *applying ;* as if with ♀, say she is fair, slender, and pleasant. And according as that planet is found in any of the twelve signs, describe her person ; and as it is aspected and dignified, her qualities ; observing also the sign on the 7th house. And if there be any planets in the 7th, take that planet nearest the cusp ; unless ☽ aspect a planet there, then take that planet. For a woman, judge by the planet ☉ applies to, in like manner ; as if ☉ be in ✶ or △ to ♄, he is grave and laborious ; if ♃, honest ; if ♂, violent ; if ♀, fond of pleasure and agreeable ; if ☿, active and industrious ; and if ♅, strange and eccentric. If ☉ and ☽ are applying to □ or ☍, there will be contention and discord.

Whether the future Wife or Husband shall be rich or not ?

Observe the lord of the 8th and planets therein. If ☽ apply by good aspect to the lord of the 8th, or good planets be there, or the lord of the 8th have a good aspect to the querent's ⊕, or other significators of property, the future wife or husband will be rich. If evil planets be in the 8th, or its lord afflict the ☽ or ⊕, the querent will gain little by marriage. And if ♄ and ♂ be both in the 8th, he gains nothing ; and though the party may have property, the querent will be cheated of it, or lose it in some manner. The persons or means by which the property will be injured, may be discovered by observing what houses the afflicting planets are lords of for the persons, and what houses they are placed in for the means ; as ☿, lord of the 8th, being in the 9th, and throwing a □ to ⊕, might denote a lawsuit respecting the future wife or husband's property.

Whether the Marriage be legitimate or not ?

If the significators of either party be afflicted by ♄ or ♂, or joined to ☕, it denotes some dispute about the marriage ; and if other testimonies agree, a lawsuit may be the consequence.

How the Parties shall agree after Marriage ?

If the figure promise marriage, observe whether the lords of the ascendant and 7th are in good aspect ; or if the ☽ behold with good aspect the planet disposing of her by house or exaltation, and the luminaries be in good aspect, they will agree.

If the lords of the ascendant and 7th be in □ or ☍, or the ☽ be afflicted, and behold the ascendant by ill aspect, or ♄, ♂, or ☕, be in the ascendant, or 7th, they will live unhappily. If the ill planets, or ☕, be in the 1st, the querent is to blame ; and if it be ♂, is given to quarrel, or be loose in conduct, according to the sign ; and if they be in the 7th, it is the quesited. And judge the same way according as the significator of the 1st or 7th be afflicted. The ☽ in her fall, or □ or ☍ of ♄ or ♂, or any retrograde planet, and at the same time throwing any aspect to the ascendant, it is the man who brings on disputes, &c. If the ☉ do the same, under the same circumstances, it is the woman.

The lord of the 7th angular, and the more weighty planet, the quesited will strive for mastery ; and if neither the lord of the ascendant nor 7th be in angles, then note the weightier planet, for he points out the party who will rule. If ♀ be afflicted, it is worse for the man ; and if ☉, for the woman. The ☽ afflicted, is evil for both. The lights in evil aspec* shew discord.

The Cause of Contention.

If the afflicting planet be lord of the 3d, and be in the 1st
or 7th, he denotes quarrels, or injuries by neighbours or kindred.   If it be an *infortune* who afflicts, and he be in the
10th, it shews continual brawls.   If he be in the 4th, a divorce
or willingness thereto ; or some hindrance in the dowry or
fortune of the female.   Evil planets in the 10th or 4th lead
also to contention by means of the parents of the parties.   If
☽ behold the ascendant, and be unfortunate, it denotes brawling, separation, or dishonest living.   And if there be no application between the planet the ☽ separates from and that one
to which she applies, there will be continual contention.   If
☽ aspect evilly, or be in ♂ with ♄ or ♂, one of them shall
die shortly, or have some misfortune ; if in the 8th or 12th,
(and she void of course), they meet troubles, grief, and sickness ; and if in angles, long disagreements ; and probably
separation, if in a fixed sign.   If this be in the 10th, and a
masculine sign, the man is the chief sufferer ; if in the 4th,
and a feminine sign, the woman.

The Cause of Happiness.

The ☽ in ⚹ or △ of good planets, shews gifts or benefits
by friends ; if in □, by the dead.   If ☽ be in ♂ with good
planets, by their own conduct or industry.

Arabic Aphorisms not to be trusted to, unless the other Testimonies concur.

The woman who departs from or loses her husband when ☽
is in the last 13° of ♐, shall never return or marry.

The man who shall engage to marry when ☽ is in the first
12° of ♑, shall lose his betrothed before marriage, or die
within six months, or live in discord with her.

From what Part a Person shall Marry ?

If the lord of the 7th be in the 9th, the querent shall marry a stranger. If the lords of the 1st and 7th be in one quarter of heaven, or in one house or sign, the person will marry one near to their own residence. Consider the sign of the 7th, the sign and quarter of heaven the lord of the 7th is in ; and judge by the majority of testimonies from what direction the querent shall marry ; as if most of the testimonies be southern, the south, &c. Mix the sign and the quarter of heaven, preferring the former.

Which of the two shall be most honourable in Connexions, &c.

If the lord of the ascendant be angular, and the lord of the 7th succeedent, the querent is best connected, and *vice versâ*. In like manner you may judge of any two individuals. A more assured way is, by observing which of the two significators is the most powerful in dignities. You may combine the two systems.

Whether a Lady have a Lover besides the Querent ?

If there be any planet in the 7th, (if it be not lord of the 7th), she has one of the description of that planet. The lord of the 7th, or ☉ joined to ♂, she has a lover with whom she is familiar ; but, (unless other and very evil testimonies accord), not improperly. The lord of the 7th void of course, or with ☊, or if no planet be in the 7th, judge that she has none : and if the lord of the 7th aspect only the lord of the ascendant, judge the same.

If either the lord of the 7th, or the ☉ be joined to the lord of the triplicity then ascending, and ☉ separate from the lord of the ascendant, it seems that she has some friend that she loves besides the querent.

The lord of the 7th, or the ☉, or both, separating from any other planet but the lord of the ascendant, and he not separated above three degrees, the lady did love another, but she has now left him. If the lord of the 7th be with ☊, she is blameless; unless there be another planet in ♂ with them, and then she is not. And if it be ☋, she is faulty in her desires and affections; and if evil testimonies concur, such as aspects of ♂, or the ♂ be in ♏, it may be feared in acts also.

If the ☉, or lord of the 7th, be in ♂ with ♂, and ☊ be there, she loves a martial man, yet he cannot prevail on her entirely. If ☋ be there, she is sore pressed to comply. If they be near, or within very few degrees, the gentleman resides near her house; and if in the same degree, he is in the house, if it be a fixed sign; or frequently visits the house, if it be a moveable or common sign.

If ☉, or lord of the 7th, separate from ♂, she had formerly a lover, but now they have forsaken each other. If ☉ be lord of the 7th, and be in ♂ with ♂ or ♃ in any sign whatever, the lady has loved or does love a person described by ♂ or ♃ ; and he has rank as an officer, gentleman, or clergyman. And if there be mutual reception, they still love one another, and many acts of kindness pass between them.

If the ☉ or lord of the 7th be joined to ☿, the lover is a young clerk or merchant; lawyer or writer; a witty, nimble fellow. His age may be judged by the number of degrees ☿ is in the sign.

If the lord of the 7th be joined to ♀ with reception, (and it be a female who is inquired of,) then she cares little for the men; but is fond of female society, is rather free in her language, but not naturally vicious. If it be a male who is the quesited, he is found much in female company, and is partial to such an one as ♀ may describe, according to the sign she is in. If the aspect be ⚹ or △ and with mutual reception, the lady is partial to him; but if the ☽ or lord of the 7th dispose not of ♀, she cares not for him, unless the aspect be very close and in angles. And if the aspect be evil, there is no mutual regard, without there be very strong reception.

The lord of the 7th joined to ♄, she loves, (or did love if they separate), an elderly person, or farmer, &c.

The lord of the 7th joined to ☉, she loves some person of consequence, according to her rank in life; and if with mutual reception, he may do what he please with her. If they separate, or there be no reception, the feeling is passed away or was never mutual.

If other planets aspect ☉ and the lord of the 7th, especially ♄ or ☿, she has other admirers, &c.

If the lord of the 7th aspect ☽, or the ☽ be in the 7th, especially if they be then in aspect, or ♂ be in aspect with ☽, she is given to change and acts discreditably, yielding up her affections upon slight solicitation.

Generally, you may consider that if ♂ be in the 7th, unless he be in his own house, the lady has a lover. If ♄, she loves one, but there is no familiarity between them; if ♃ be there, she is honest; if ♀, she is giddy and merry, and is thought to be wanton, but is not; if ☿, she had a friend, but has not now; and if ☽, she has not yet, but will have more than one. If ☉ or ☊ be there, she is virtuous and honourable, and has no lover other than the querent. ☊ denotes discreditable desires at least.

Whether a Gentleman have a Lover besides the Querent?

You may judge this question exactly by the rules for judging of a lady, if you substitute the ☽ for the ☉ and ♀ for

♂. You may in like way judge of *friends* by taking the 11℞ for the 7th.

Whether a Damsel be virtuous or not ?

Behold the lord of the 7th, the cusp of the 7th, and the ☉; and if they be in fixed signs and well aspected, you may judge that she is correct. If ♂ be in ♌ and ♏ descend, she is suspected, but yet is honest. If ♏ descend and ♂ therein, it is suspicious; and if there be a moveable sign on the 7th, or the ☉ and ♂ be in common or moveable signs, and be ill aspected; and if ♂ and ♀ be in ill aspect, or the ☉ or ☽ behold ♂, and the evil stars aspect them from fixed signs, there is great reason to doubt. Yet if there be *any good aspect* to either the 7th or its lord, ♂, or ☉, it is not safe to judge the lady to be unchaste, though she may have been much tempted. The student will do well to avoid a positive judgment *unfavourable* on this head, unless *all* the testimonies are decided.

If there be great reason to doubt, then observe whether ☽ be in the last face of ♊, or in a moveable sign, and in the 5th house, and the lord of the 5th in the ascendant or 7th, and in a moveable sign, and either of them in aspect to ♂; or the lords of the 5th and 7th in ♂ in one sign. If all these, or nearly all, concur, you may be more confident that the lady is faulty.

Whether the Child conceived is the Child of him who is the reputed Father ?

Observe the lord of the ascendant, and the ☽, who signify the querent; then observe the sign of the 11th, and its lord, which signify the issue in conception. If these significators behold one another by ✶ or △, with reception or not, the conception is legitimate, viz., the child of its supposed father.

If they aspect each other by □ or ☍ with reception, and per-fect aspect: or the lord of the ascendant or ☾ be in the 5th, or the lord of the 5th in the ascendant, without the evil aspect of the infortunes, or if one of the fortunes behold the cusp of the 5th or its lord, then also is the child begotten by its reputed father. But if none of these things be, and ♄, ♂, or ☿ behold the 5th or lord thereof, there may be just sus-picion that the child is conceived in adultery, or is not the child of the querent.

Whether a Woman living from her Husband shall ever return to him, or be restored to Favour?

This question will equally resolve a doubt concerning a mistress or *person beloved.*

If the woman herself propose the question, consider the lord of the 7th, (for the 7th is ever given to the banished or expelled party;) and if the lord of the 7th behold the ascen-dant with a perfect aspect, and the lord of the ascendant be-hold the 7th, or its lord, without doubt she shall again come into favour. If the lord of the 7th do not behold the ascen-dant, but another planet, who is not afflicted, behold the as-cendant, the woman shall be received again through some per-son who shall interpose his friendship with the husband or friend. If none of these things be, observe ☽ and ♂; and if ☽ be above the earth, and ♂ behold the ascendant with ⚹ or △, she shall return quietly, and without much trouble.

If ☽ be under the earth and ♂ above, and behold the as-cendant with ⚹ or △, she shall return, but with trouble and delays, and with much publicity. If ☾ aspect the ascendant favourably, and be not afflicted, she shall return, but with solicitation. If ☽ decrease in light, but be not near the beams of ☉, and behold the ascendant, she will return easily and speedily.

If ♂ be retrograde, and hasten to aspect with ☾, she will of her own accord return ; but if ♂ and ☾, or the lords of the 1st and 7th, separate from good aspect, they have no mutual desire to return, nor will the lady much respect the gentleman for the future.

OF RUNAWAY SERVANTS, CATTLE STRAYED, AND THINGS LOST.

The significator of the thing missing is the ☾ ; wherefore if you find ☾ applying to the lord of the ascendant, or to the lord of the 12th, (being herself in the ascendant,) or to the lord of the house of the ☾, the thing missing shall be found again. But if ☾ apply to none of these, nor be in the ascendant or 2d, the thing lost shall not be found.* If the lord of the house of ☾ be in the 3d, or in ✶ to the ascendant, there is some hope of finding the thing again during that aspect with the degree ascending. Also, if he separate from the lord of the 6th, 8th, or 12th, and apply by any aspect to the cusp of the 2d, or behold the ☾, you may hope to find it. But if there be contrary indications between these, judge the reverse.

If the ☾ be aspected well by both fortunes, the thing lost is in the hands of some trusty person ; and if ☾ or one of the fortunes behold the ascendant, he will restore it to the owner.

The Place where the Thing lost is.

This is shewn by ☾, according to the sign she is in ; for if the sign be eastern, it is east ; and if west, it is western, &c. Observe also the place of ☾ in the figure ; for if she be in the ascendant, it is east, &c., but prefer the sign. If the lord of the house of ☾ be in human signs, (II, ♍, ♒, or the first

---

* This rule principally applies to cattle strayed.

half of ♐), it is in a place where men frequent. If in signs of small cattle, as ♈ or ♑, it is where they are found. If ☽ be in a fiery sign, it is where fire is; if in a watery sign, where water is, &c. If ☽ be in the same quarter as the lord of the ascendant, and there be not more than 30° between them, the thing lost is in the house of the owner, or about it; if they be above 30° and less than 70° apart, it is in the town where he resides; but if they be not in one quarter, it is far from the owner.

How the Thing was lost.

Observe from what planet the lord of the ascendant last separated. If from ♄, it was through forgetfulness of the owner; or through cold or illness which afflicted the loser, especially if ♄ be retrograde. If from ♃, it was through some abstinence, or ordering of laws, or by excess of care in managing affairs, or putting too much trust in the person by whom it was carried away or mislaid. If from ♂, or the lord of the ascendant be in the house of ♂, it was lost through fear or some sudden passion, provoking the loser to anger; or by fire, or by enmity, or upon some quarrel. If from ☉, by means of the king or some gentleman, or the master of the family, or by hunting or pastime. If from ♀, or in her house, by drinking, cards, &c., or making merry in a tavern, &c., or by singing or dallying with women. If from ☿, by writing, letters, messages, or going a message, &c. If from ☽, by too frequent use, or shewing the thing lost, or making it too common; or some messenger, widow, or servant lost the same.

If it be an Animal, and you would know whether it be stolen or not?

If you find the lord of the house of ☽ separating from any

planet, say that it went away of its own accord. If that lord be not separating, but another planet be separating from him, say that some person took it away. If the lord of the house of ☽ be in neither of these cases, look to the lord of the 2d house, and judge by him in the same way. And if you find no separation of either of these two lords, say that the animal still in or near its place, and is not gone away.

Whether it be dead?

Observe the ☽; and if you find her in application to the lord of the 8th house from her, say it is dead. But if you find no such testimony, observe her dispositor; and if you find him applying to the lord of the 8th house from the Moon, say likewise that it is dead, or will shortly die; but if in neither of these you find application, take the lord of the 8th house of the figure in the same way; and if neither ☽ nor her dispositor apply to it, then the animal is not dead.

Whether the Thing missing be stolen?

If the significator of the thief, (usually the lord of the 7th, unless there be any peregrine planet in an angle), be found in the ascendant, or disposing of the ☽, or ☽ disposing of him, or the lord of the ascendant be disposed of by him or dispose of him, or unless he apply to the ☽ or lord of the 1st or 2d, or ⊕, or its lord by ☌, □, or ☍, or some planet be in the ascendant, and be in □ or ☍ to the significator of the thief, the thing is *not* stolen. Generally any ill aspect of any evil planet, or the lord of the 7th to the ascendant or 2d house or their lords, or ☽ or ⊕, or their lords, denote that the thing is stolen.

Whether a Thing lost shall be found?

If ☽ apply to the lords of the ascendant or 2d, or to her

dispositor, it shall be found. ☽ in the ascendant, or her dispositor in ✶ or △ thereto, give hopes; the dispositor of ☽ separating from the lord of the 6th, 8th, or 12th, and applying to the lord of the ascendant or cusp of the 2d, give hopes also; and if ☽ be in aspect to her dispositor, it is good. But ☽ afflicted by the lords of the 6th, 8th, or 12th, it is in the hands of an evil person, who will not part with it; especially if an *infortune* afflict the ascendant or its lord. ☽ in △ to the ascendant, its lord or ☉, or in the ascendant, or ☉ there, unless in ♎ or ♒, it shall be found.

The Kind of Place a Thing lost is in?

If ☽ be in a human sign,* it is in a place where men fre-quent; and if in a brutal sign (♈, ♉, ♌, ♑, and the last half of ♐), the thing is where animals frequent. If ☽ be in fiery signs, it is where fire is or has been, or near a fire, or on hills or high ground; if in watery signs, where water is or has been;† if in airy signs, where many windows are, or open places, garrets, &c.; if in earthy signs, in an earthy place, where houses are built of mud, clay, &c., and in brick-fields. The ☽, or her dispositor, in a moveable sign, shews a place newly peopled, or a house newly built, or where there are hills and dales: if in a fixed sign, in a level plain country; if in a common sign, in a place of much water, according to the nature of the thing missing. Also ♊, ♍, ♐, ✶, shew, if it be not living things, within the house; but if cattle, &c., they shew ditches, pits, and among rushes, or in a market-

---

* The human signs are ♊, ♍, and ♒, also the first half of ♐. If the significator of any person or ☽ be in one of these signs, they are humane and civil in their manners.

† In this case ♋ generally denotes pure or running water; ♏ foul water, and filthy liquids, oils, dyes, &c.; and ✶ standing waters, spirituous liquors, wines, &c.

place.   ♉, ♌, ♏, ♒, shew that the things are laid low or
hid in the earth, or near walls, in hollow trees, &c.   ♈, ♋,
♎, ♑, shew high places, roofs, ceiling, &c., but watery signs
denote about the foundations of houses, or cellars, if water be
there.

Of Animals missing.

If the lord of the 6th be in the 6th, they are small animals ;
if the lord of the 12th be in the 12th, they are large.   If the
lord of the 6th be in the 12th, they are in pound ; and if in
a fiery sign, locked up.   If ☽ be in common signs, they are
in rushy grounds ; if in an angle, they are in enclosed ground ;
if in a succeedent, they are near enclosures ; if in a cadent
house, they are on commons.   If in watery signs or ♒, near
fish-ponds or other waters ; and if in the last moiety of ♑,
they are near ships, or on shipboard, or near some wood or
timber-yard.

Whether it shall be restored?

The ☽ aspecting ♃ or ♀, it is in the hands of an honest
man, who will restore it.   If ♃ or ♀ have any aspect to the
ascendant, or ☽ apply to the ascendant, it will be restored ;
and if ☽ be in the ascendant, it is restored without trouble
or pain.   The lord of the 7th, or 12th in the 12th house, the
fugitive is imprisoned.

If the ☽ be within 30° of the lord of the 1st, the thing is
with or near the loser ; if ☽ be more than 30° off the lord or
the 1st, it is far off.

If it be animals, and the lord of the 6th, (or if large cattle
the 12th,) be fortunate by the good aspects of ♀ or ♃, or
they be found in the 2d, 5th, or 11th, the animals will be had
again.   The same if the lord of the term in which ☽ is, or
the lord of the cusp of the 4th be with the lord of the as-

cendant, or the lord of the 6th or 12th be in △ to ☉ **out of angles.**

Of a Fugitive, and whether he shall be found or return?

The lord of the 7th in the ascendant, he will return of his own accord.* If ☽ separate from the lord of the ascendant, and be joined immediately to the lord or cusp of the 7th, news will shortly be brought of him. The lord of the 7th combust, he shall be found against his will. The ☽ afflicted by ♅, ♄, ♂, or ☍, or a retrograde planet, he shall be found or return, after much suffering. ☽ separating from ♃ or ♀, he shall quickly come back; and if she aspect her own house by ⚹ or △, he will return or shall be heard of within a very few days.

The lord of the 7th aspecting an infortune from the 7th, the querent will discover the quesited with some person, to whom he must give money before he can have him back. If the lord of the 7th be retrograde, it is a testimony of his return.

OF THEFTS.

The ascendant is for the querent, and its lord for him that has lost the goods; and it signifies the place from whence they were taken.

The 7th house and its lord, or the peregrine planet in an angle, signify the thief.

The 2d house, its lord, and the ☽, signify the things lost or stolen; and the 4th house, and its lord, shew the place where they are conveyed to, and then are.

The aspects of ☉ and ☽, the lords of the 1st and 2d, and

---

* If a servant, take the lord of the 6th in all these cases; and if the querent s child, the lord of the 5th, &c.

the dispositor of the ☽, by application to each other, shall shew whether they will be had again or not.

If the lord of the 2d and the ☽ be in the 7th, and the lord of the 7th behold them both by ⚹ or △ (though the aspect be several degrees distant), then are the goods taken away by some one, and not merely lost.

If ☽ be lady of the 2d, and going to ☌ of the lord of the 7th, then has the party mislain it ; and the thing is neither lost nor stolen.

If ☽ be lady of the ascendant, and in the 4th, and the lord of the 2d be in the 7th or 8th in ⚹ or △ of ☽, the thing is not stolen, but taken away in jest.

If ☽ be lady of the ascendant, and be in it, and ☉ lord of the 2d in the 10th, with the lord of the 7th, and the lord of the 7th □ ☽, then are the goods stolen and taken away. If ☽ be in the 3d, and in □ to the lord of the 7th, and the lord of the 2d be in the 7th, it was first taken in jest, but is now stolen, and will be hard to recover, unless ☉ and ☽ aspect the ascendant.

If ☽ be lady of the 5th, and in ♑, and ♀ lady of the 2d in the 10th, and ☽ in ☍ to the lord of the 7th, then has the party lost the goods as he went by the way, or left them in some place. If ☽ be in ♋ in the 8th, and the lord of the 2d in the 5th, and neither of them behold the lord of the 7th, and he be in the 7th, the goods are taken away in jest by the master of the house, and he will deny it. If ☽ be in the 4th in ☍ to its lord, and the lord of the 2d in the 12th in ⚹ to the lord of the 7th, then has somebody taken away the things in jest. If ☽ be in the house of the lord of the 7th, and be in the 12th, not beholding the lord of the 7th, and the lord of the 2d be in the 6th, then are the goods removed in jest ; and if, in this case, the lord of the 2d did last separate from the ruler of the ☽, they will scarcely be had again. If the ☽

separate from the lord of the 2d by □, they are taken away and stolen ; and the same, if the ☽, being lady of the 2d, separate from the lord of the house wherein she is.

If the lord of the ascendant separate from ♃, (he not being lord of the 7th, or peregrine in an angle), or from the lord of the 2d, the querent has lain it down and forgotten it, and so it was lost ; but, when both the lords of the 1st and 2d separate from ♃, this is surer. If (in such case) the lord of the 2d, or ♃, separate from the lord of the ascendant, then did the party lose the goods by the way as he went, or in some place where he was, or they fell out of his pocket accidentally, and they are neither found nor stolen. But if there be none of these separations, see if the peregrine planet, or lord of the 7th apply to ♃, or the lord of the 2d ; then, if they do, the goods are absolutely stolen. If the lord of the 2d, or ♃, apply to the significator of the thief, he came easily by them, and did not come with intent to steal ; but, seeing the thing unprotected, he was tempted to steal.

If the significator of the thief aspect the lord of the 1st or 2d, or the cusp of the 2d, or ⊕, or ☽, or their dispositor, or the planet in whose term ☽ is, or if he be in the ascendant, it is stolen ; but, if there be no *evil* aspect to any of these, it is not stolen.

Of the Age of the Thief.

Guido Bonatus says, that if the thief's significator be ☿, he is very young ; if ♀, rather older, but yet a young female ; ♂ shews him of full age ; ♃ of middle age, and ♄, elderly. If the ☉ be his significator, and be between the ascendant and 10th, he is young, and so increasing in age until he come to the angle of the earth. If the ☽ shew the thief, his age will correspond to her age ; and in all cases judge *also* by the position the thief's significator has reached in the sign where

P

he is found. If he be just entered the sign, quite young; if in the middle of the sign, of middle age; and if towards the end of the sign, elderly; and if ♄ aspect him any way, it adds to his age. Oriental planets denote also younger persons, and occidental planets elderly persons. You must consider all the testimonies before you judge the thief's age.

Whether the Thief be Male or Female?

The significator of the thief being masculine, and in a masculine sign, and the ☽ in a masculine sign, it is a male; *et e contrâ.* The angles of the figure masculine shew a man; and if feminine, a woman. If ♀ or the ☽ be the significator, or ☿, when aspecting them, it is a female; ♄, ♃, ♂, ☉, and ☿ aspecting them, a male.

Whether one Thief or more?

If the significator be in a fixed sign, it denotes one only; if he be in double-bodied signs, it denotes more than one, especially if there be more than one planet in the sign, and they peregrine. Also, when ☉ and ☽ are in angles, and in ☐ aspect, it shews more than one. If the significator be in ♋, ♏, or ♓, it is a testimony of there being more than one; the angles being moveable, the same. The ☽ in the ascendant, and in a double-bodied sign, shews more than one. And if the significator be in aspect with more than one planet, unless he be in a fixed sign, it shews plurality.

Of the Colour of the Thief's Clothes.

This must be judged in a general manner; and by the colours of the signs and houses of the significator, and the planets ruling them. Thus, ♄ is black; ♃ green, spotted, or ash; ♂ red; ☉ tawny, or saffron, or sandy; and if you mix the colours according to the signs and planets, &c., you will judge very nearly the general colour of the thief's clothes. Thus, ♄ and ♃, mixed, give dark green, or green spotted with black; ♄ and ♂, a dark reddish brown, or tawny; ♄ and ☉, a blackish orange, and shining; ♄ and ♀, a whitish grey; ♄ and ☿, a black blue; ♄ and ☽, a deep russet, or grey; ♃ and ♂, a tawny, light spotted; ♃ and ☉, a deep, shining red; ♃ and ♀, a greenish grey; ♃ and ☿, a spotted green; ♃ and ☽, a high-coloured green; ♂ and ☉, a deep red, or scarlet; ♂ and ♀, light red, or crimson; ♂ and ☿, a tawny red, or brick colour; ♂ and ☽, a light red, glistening.

You must observe, that if the signifier be ♄, in his own house, ♑, and not in close aspect with any other planet, the thief will be dressed all in *black;* because both sign and planet rule that colour. But if he were in the 1st house, which rules *white,* he would have some *white* about his person. Also, if it were ♂, who rules *red,* and he were found in ♏, which rules *brown,* he would denote a rusty, dirty, reddish brown; but if he were in ♌, which rules *red and green,* and ♃ were in aspect, there would be much *green,* as well as *red,* about the dress; and so of the others.

The relation the Thief bears to the Owner.

The lord of the 7th, or significator of the thief, being in the ascendant, it is one well known to the querent, or one who frequents his house; and is in no way suspected.

If the significator of the thief be in the 2d, it is one of the household, or an acquaintance; but if in a feminine sign, it may be the querent's wife or maid-servant; and it is in the loser's power, and may be recovered by money.

If he be in the 3d, it is one of his near kindred or neighbours; or some messenger, or other person, often in his sight.

If in the 4th, it is his father, or some elderly person, or one who resides in the house. &c., of his father; or he is a labourer or farm-servant.

If in the fifth, it is his son or daughter, or one of the near relations of his brother or sister, or near neighbour; or one of the household of his father, or his kept mistress, or some one connected with taverns, theatres, &c.

If he be in the 6th, it is a servant, or the querent's father's relation; or it is some person in bad health.

If he be in the 7th, it may be his own wife or lover, or some female who has been suspected of having connexion with the querent: or it is some person with whom he deals publicly, or one who is his open enemy.

If in the 8th, it is a stranger; yet it is likely to be one who is, or has been, at times employed about the house, such as an occasional gardener, or charwoman, washerwoman, &c.

If in the 9th, it is some traveller or vagrant, or some person employed about churches, &c.; or a person in connexion with some jailor, or master of a workhouse, &c.

If in the 10th, it is a person of respectable circumstances, or some master tradesman, &c.; one not necessitated to turn thief; and, generally, a person who lodged in the house, or visited it frequently when the thing was taken.

If in the 11th, a friend, or one who is trusted, and has done the querent some service; or one connected with a neighbouring clergyman, or the household of the querent's mother.

If in the 12th house, it is a stranger, or some poor, common thief or beggar; a person in miserable circumstances, who partly lives by thieving or thief taking.

Other Particulars of the Thief.

If the thief's significator be in the end of a sign, or apply ing to a planet in the 3d or 9th, he is going off; and if it be a superior planet, and leaving a sign, he is undoubtedly leaving his house or lodgings, &c.

If his significator be in an angle, he is still in the town; if succeedent, he is not far off; but if cadent, he is far gone.

If it be in an angle, he is in a house; and if ☽ be in an angle, in his own house, &c.; if in a succeedent, in a field or enclosure; and if ☽ be succeedent, it is his own, or where he resides; and if in a cadent house, he is on a common or open place, and if ☽ be cadent, it belongs to the town, &c. where he lives.

If the lord of the ascendant and the significator of the thief be together, the thief is with the querent. And if the thief's significator be in the ascendant, the thief will be at the querent's house before the querent. But if the significator be in the 7th, he is hid at home, and dare not be seen. The direction in which the thief lives may be judged by the sign and quarter in which the significator is.

The ☽ denotes also the door of the thief's house. If she be in a fixed sign, the house has but one door; if in a moveable sign, the door is high above the earth, and it is probable that there is another smaller door. If ♄ aspect the sign of the ☽, the door has been broken, and often repaired, or is old or black. If ♂ aspect it, the gate or door has some mark of fire. If ♄ and ♂ both have a friendly aspect to the sign the ☽ is in, the door is iron, or is very strong. If ☽ be afflicted, it is broken or injured; and if ☽ be decreasing, and near ☉, the gate, &c. opens on the back premises, and there is no front door to the street; if she increase, and is near ☉, it is low down, and there is a step to descend in entering. But if ☽ be in a moveable sign, there are steps up to it.

Whether the Goods are in the Hands of the Thief?

If the thief's significator be in aspect to, and disposed of by another planet, they are not in his hands; otherwise they are.

The Place where the Goods are.

The nature of the place is judged by the lord of the 4th house. If he be in a moveable sign, it is in a place high above the ground; in a fixed sign, in the earth; and in a common sign, it is under the eaves of a house, &c.* And you must judge also by the quality of the sign; as ♈ shews a place where small cattle are, as sheep, hogs, &c. ♌ shews a place of animals that bite, as dogs, foxes, &c.; ♐ a place of animals that are ridden, as horses, mules, &c., and their stables. ♉, ♍, and ♑ shew a place of large cattle, as ♉ oxen, kine, &c.; ♍ and ♑ shew camels, mules, asses, &c., ♍ also shews barns where corn is kept, and a place about the earth. ♑ denotes goats, hogs, &c.; ♊ shews a wall or partition in a house; ♎ a high part, or near a closet or little house; ♒ shews near a door, above another door or gate in a high part; ♏ shews a place of unclean water; ♓ a place always moist. But if the ☽ be in the same sign with the lord of the 4th, judge by her more than him.

In what Part of a House Things lost, stolen, or concealed may be.

If the thing lost be in the house, (whether stolen or not), behold the lord of the 4th, (or, if a planet be in the 4th, take him in preference.)

If it be ♄, it is in a dark or secret place; and if he be in

---

* We should pay more attention to the nature of the sign, as fiery earthy, &c.; and judge as in the rules for things mislaid.

aspect with ♂, or in the house of ♂, it is in or abou some dirty place, where people seldom go, a privy, &c.

If ♃, a place of wood, bushes, &c.

If ♂, a kitchen or place where fire is kept; if aspected by ☿, a shop.

If ☉, the hall, dining-room, or chief room where the master frequents.

If ♀, a bed, or among bed-clothes, or where females much frequent. In this case ♎ would shew the top of the bed.

If ☿, a place of books, pictures, carving, &c.; and if ♍, where corn is.

If ☽, it is in a pit, cistern, or washing place.

Description of the House or Place where the Things are that are lost, &c.

The ☉ describes the house, and also its front entrance. If he be in an airy sign, it is high, &c., and its colour may be known by the sign and house he is in. The ☽ describes the cellar, pump, or place holding the water; as, if she be in ♒, it is a cistern, high above the ground, &c.; if ♏, a low pit or pond; if ♍, a deep well. ♀ shews the place of mirth, female apartments, &c. ☋ denotes the stairs or ladder to climb by, &c. ☋ describes the place the wood is in, or the animals are kept. ☿ denotes the room, &c.; if in a common sign, it is a cupboard, or small room within another; if in a fixed sign, it shews a house having no cellar, or a single chamber. If ♃, ♀, or both, be in the 10th, the door has a fair appearance, and opening; if ♄ be in the 10th, the door is near some ditch, pit, or deep place; if ♂ be there, there is a fire-place near the door, or place for killing animals; if ☿ be there, near the door is a place where tools or instruments are kept; if ☉ be there, then there is some seat or porch near the door; and if ☽ be in the 10th, there is near the entrance a door to go under ground, a trap or cellar door, or some other convenience in very common use.*

The Nature of the Thing stolen.

This is judged by the lord of the 2d house. ♄ shews lead, iron, things of a black or dark blue colour, wool, black garments, heavy things, earthy materials, agricultural implements, carts, &c. ♃ oil, honey, silk, fruit, men's clothes, merchandize, horses, &c. ♂ arms, pepper, brass, red clothes, red wine, and red things ; generally sharp-pointed, cutting, and hot things, horses for war, &c., and all warlike engines or instruments. ☉ gold, brass, yellow clothes, diamonds, and things of value. ♀ women's dresses, or ornaments, such as rings, ear-rings, &c., white cloth, and white wine. ☿ shews money, paper, books, pictures, and party-coloured dresses, &c., and scientific instruments, writing-desks, &c. The ☽ all common commodities, such as crockery, &c. cattle, poultry, and also silver.

Whether the Goods shall be recovered or not.

The ☽ in the 7th, aspecting the lord of the 7th with a △ ; a fortune strong in the ascendant ; ♃ in the 2d direct ; in ☽ the 10th in a △ to a planet in the 2d ; ☽ in the 2d in △ to the lord of the 2d ; ☉ and ☽ going to △, or ☉ and ☽ aspecting the cusp of the 2d with a △ ; or the lord of the 2d in the ascendant or 4th, well aspected by application ; ☽ in the 2d, going to ☐ of ☉ in the 12th, in signs of short ascension : *all these are signs of its recovery.*

Also, if the lords of the term and house of the ☽ be both

* These minute particulars may be found useful in many other questions, such as where fugitives, &c. are ; and they might be of use in discovering criminals.

increasing in light and motion,* and free from affliction, it shall be recovered, and be uninjured.

Generally, if there be a diminution of their light and motion, the thing is already partly destroyed. If there be good aspects to the lords or cusps of the ascendant, or 2d, or to ⊕ or its lord, by planets in angles, it will soon be recovered.

The lord of the 8th in the ascendant, or with its lord, shews recovery; the lord of the 7th in the 8th, denies it: ♄, ♂, or ☊ in the ascendant, or 2d, shew dividing and loss of the thing.

The lord of the 2d in the ascendant shews recovery; and the lord of the 1st in the 2d the same, after long search. If the 2d or its lord be afflicted, all the things lost shall not be recovered. If both luminaries be under the earth, it is a strong testimony against recovery.

If both ☉ and ☽ aspect the ascendant, the thing cannot be lost, but will shortly be discovered.

Of the Time of the Thing being recovered.

Observe the *application* of the planets that signify recovery, and determine the number of days, weeks, or months, as they may be in moveable, common, or fixed signs, in angles, succeedents, or cadents. And if the signifiers are swift in motion, it hastens the recovery; if slow, it retards.

Of the Thief's Person.

In addition to the planet's general description in the sign he is in, observe the aspects he has, and take all these into consideration. Moreover, if the significator be oriental, and in ♌, ♍, or ♐, the person is *large;* if occidental, and in ♋, ♏, or ♓, the body is *smaller*. If the planet have *south*

---

* This means, going faster than they were the previous day.

latitude, he is nimble; if in *north* latitude, slow in his motions. If going out of one sign into another, he is weak and feeble.*

* ♄ shews one of a pale, swarthy, dark complexion; hard, rough skin; hairy body; small, leering eyes; jaundiced look; lean, crooked, or ill made; beetle browed; thin beard; thick, negro lips; bow-legged, or one who knocks his knees or ancles one against the other, and shuffles in his gait. He has a down look, his eyes always on the earth; is seldom free from cough and bad breath. He is crafty, revengeful, and malicious; dirty, a great eater, covetous, and seldom rich.

♃ denotes a full face, white and red mixed; full eyes; good make, light beard, but this depends chiefly on the sign; thick hair, good teeth, but some defect in the two front teeth; moderately curling hair. If in a watery sign, fat and plump; in an earthy sign, large make: in an airy sign, strong—a person who bears a good moral character.

♂ denotes a full face, red or sunburnt; a sharp, fierce countenance; eyes fiery and ferocious, with rather a yellow tinge; hair and beard reddish; but this depends on the sign, unless he be with fixed stars of his own nature, such as *Aldebaran, the Lion's Heart, &c.* In earthy signs it is a sad brown; in watery, lighter or flaxen; in airy, curling or crisping; in fiery, strong and wiry. He is strong, broad shouldered, proud, scornful, drunken, and debauched; with a mark or scar, generally in the face.

☉ denotes a round full face; sanguine complexion; short chin; curling hair; fair, comely, sometimes swarthy or bronzed; bold, ambitious, vain, slow of speech; outwardly decent, but secretly vicious and lascivious.

♀ gives a fair, round face; full or large eyes; red, plump lips, the lower larger than the upper; black eyelids, smooth brown hair; person well-shaped and handsome; rather short than tall; face pleasing, with smiles and dimples.

☿ middling complexion; darkish hair, or a sad brown; long face; high forehead; black or grey eyes; thin beard and whiskers, often hardly any; slender, small legs; one quick in walking, and full of talk and business.

☽ a round face, more white than red; in watery signs, freckled; and ♓ ♏ ♋, and in no aspect to ♂ or ☉, very pale and white, or wan—a person generally short and full; and one who is dull and heavy, and also very vulgar and ill-mannered.

N.B. The above descriptions are partly taken from *Wilson's Astrological Dictionary;* a very useful work for the young student.

Signs of the Thief being taken.

If the lord of the 7th (or thief's significator) be in the 1st or 7th, in ♂ with the lord of the ascendant, or a retrograde planet. If the ☽ separate from the thief's significator, and apply to ♂ of the lord of the 1st; or go from ♂ of the lord of the 1st to him. Or if ☉ and ☽ be in ♂ with him; or if he be going to combustion, or be in ♂ with an infortune in the 7th. He is captured if ☽ be in the 7th, applying to □ of ♂, the ☉, or ☿; ☽ separating from □ of ♄ or ☿, and applying to □ of ☉, or separating from ♂ ♄, and going to □ ☿; or in the 8th, in ☍ ♂, or in the 7th, going to the lord of the 8th.

The Thief escapes.

If his significator be in aspect with a fortune; if he be in aspect to ♃ or ♀, they being in the 11th, he escapes by friends; if in the 3d, by strangers, or by law quibbles, &c.

Of Battle, War, Duels, Prize Fights, or other Contentions.

The lord of the ascendant, planets therein, and ☽, are for the querent or challenger, or him who attacks; the 7th house, its lord and planets therein, for the adversary. Behold whose significators are most angular, best dignified and aspected, and expect victory for that party. If evil planets be in the ascendant, and fortunes in the 7th, the adversary shall overcome, and *vice versâ :* also the lord of the 7th, in the ascendant, betokens victory to the querent, and *vice versâ.*

Whether any one shall return safe from War, or any dangerous Voyage, &c.

The lord of the ascendant, strong, well aspected, and his

dispositor a good planet; good planets in the ascendant, or aspecting its cusp, are all good testimonies; and the reverse are evil.   If the lord of the 7th, and the 7th house, be fortunate, (though the first be not,) the party returns, though not without great crosses and hinderances; *et. e contra.*   Observe how ☽ is disposed; for her application to the good planets is fortunate; *and the contrary.*   Evil planets in the 8th are signs of fear and death; ♄ shews bruises and hurts by falls, &c., and losses; ♂ denotes wounds by weapons; ☊, injuries and disgrace.

If an evil planet be with the lord of the ascendant, and a good one in the ascendant, he will suffer great loss or be sorely wounded, but not die.

♄ in the 1st, or with its lord, shews loss to the querent by one whom he will meet; ♄ in the 1st, and an evil planet with its lord, he shall be wounded by wood or stone; ♂ shews wounds by fire or iron, and if ☊ be in the ascendant, and ♄ afflict its lord, he shall receive a wound, and be nearly killed. It is evil if ☉ be with the lord of the 7th, or be in the 8th.

The lord of the ascendant in the 8th, or with its lord, or the lord of the 8th in the ascendant, denotes the querent's death.   And the lord of the 7th in the second, or with its lord, shews the death of the adversary.

If the lord of the 7th be strong, and have good aspects from the 10th, or its lord, the querent will gain honour.   And if the cusp of the 2d and its lord, and ⊕ or its lord, be fortunate, then he gains money by the war, &c.

In the same manner as the 8th house and its lord shew death, the 12th and its lord denote imprisonment.

And if the question concern the general result of a war or expedition, it must be judged on the same principles.

Of Partnership.

If good planets be in the 1st and 7th, the partnership shall be and do well. And if the lord of the 7th be strong, and in fixed signs, it shall endure. If the two lords agree in aspects, and by mutual reception, the partners will accord well together. But if they disagree, the fault will be with that party who has ♅, ♄, ♂, or ☋ in their house.

The significators of substance will shew the means of each party; and as they may be about to receive good or ill aspects, will they thrive or lose by the concern. The 8th, its lord, and planets there, are for the quesited's property.

If ☽ separate from one fortune, and apply to the other, they will neither of them gain much by the concern. If she leave a good planet and apply to an ill, they begin well but end ill : and if she separate from one evil planet, and apply to another, they begin with complaining, continue with jealousy, and end with lawsuits. An evil planet, or ☋ in the 2d, the querent gains but little, will be cheated, or get into debt: if they be in the 8th, judge this of the quesited. And if the lord of the 7th or 8th, □ or ☍ ⊕, the querent may hope but little gain from his partner, who will embezzle the common stock, &c.

Of removing from Place to Place.

The lord of the ascendant and planets therein stronger than the 7th, and planets there, it is better to remain. If there be a benefic in the 7th or ☋, and especially if ☽ separate from an infortune, remove ; an evil planet there, or the lord of the 1st or ☽ leaving a benefic, remain.

The 8th house shews the property of the querent in the place he desires to remove to: if evil planets be there, it is better to remain. (*See also n. 141*)

Of Lawsuits, and their Success.

The lord of the ascendant or ☽ joined to the lord of the 7th, or in ⚹ or △, with reception mutual, the parties will easily agree together, and make up the quarrel. But if one dispose of the other, and the reception be not mutual, they will agree without a lawsuit, but not without the interceding of friends. If they be in good aspect without, or in evil aspect with, reception, they will accord, after one effort at law. That party shall be most ready to agree whose significator is disposed of by the other. If they hasten to a mutual good aspect, and the lord of the 9th or 10th interpose an evil aspect, they will be led to dispute by a lawyer or by the judge. If there be any translation of light by the ☽, or other planet, between the two significators, it denotes that they will be reconciled by a third person, described by that planet.

Observe whether the lord of the ascendant or 7th be strongest or most powerful, and best aspected ; for that one shall gain the day. If they compound, the first motion thereto comes from the lighter planet, who is disposed of by the other. If the lord of the ascendant be in the 7th, the adversary will overcome, and *vice versâ*. If either lord of the 1st or 7th be retrograde, he shews that the party does not believe that he has right on his side ; nor will he stand to it very stoutly.

If the lord of the 10th, which denotes the *judge*, be direct, he will proceed fairly, and endeavour to settle the cause speedily. But if he be retrograde, the judge will not act fairly according to law, nor strive to terminate the cause. If the lord of the 10th throw an evil aspect to either significator, the judge will be against that party.

If ☉ or ☽ be in the ascendant, or aspect its lord, or be in either of his houses, it is a good testimony for the querent ;

and if, on the contrary, the lord of the 7th be so situated, it is in favour of the quesited. If the lord of the 10th receive both significators, the judge will settle the matter before it comes to full trial.

If the lord of the 10th be in the 10th, in his own house, the judge will do justice, and decide the case with honour to himself, unless the lord of the 10th be ♄. If the lord of the 10th be only in his own term, or triplicity, the judge will determine the cause, but he is indifferent about it. If a planet having no dignities, or not in reception with the lord of the 10th, be in the 10th, the parties will not be satisfied with that judge or court. If ♄ be judge, he will not decide aright; and if ♃, ♀, ☉, ☿, or ☽ be in any aspect to him but ☍, there will be an ill report against him, of which he will clear himself; but if it be ☍, he will have a hard report against him, which will long continue. And if ♂ ☍ to ♄, the judge will be sorely defamed; and if also ☉ ☐ ♄, he may be disgraced.

In deciding as to the result, observe well the lord of the 4th, and how he aspects the significators, or the lords of their substance; also the *application* of the ☽. If both significators aspect one planet, some person will intercede between them. If the ascendant and 7th be in fixed signs, both parties are resolutely bent on the suit; if common signs, they will continue it long also, and remove the cause out of one court into another; and if moveable signs, they are not very determined, and will soon bring it to an end.

That party who is weakest, and most afflicted by the infortunes, shall receive most prejudice by the contention.

Of making Purchases or Sales.

If ☽ be joined with the lord of the 7th, the querent may make the purchase. The lighter planet of the two houses

(1st and 7th) will be the occasion of the sale.   Judge the nature of the commodity by the house by which it is governed ;
as the 4th for a house, the 12th for large cattle, the 9th for
books, &c., the 10th for merchandize.

If infortunes be in the 7th, be cautious of the seller ; he
will try to trick the purchaser.   The fourth house will shew
the final result : but if ☽ be void of course, there may be
many meetings, &c., but scarcely any bargain concluded.

*Whether a City, Town, Castle, &c. besieged, shall be taken
or not.*

The ascendant and its lord are for the querent and for the
besiegers ; the 4th signifies the place besieged or to be besieged, and the lord of the 4th the governor ; the 5th and
planets therein the ammunition, soldiers, &c. in the place.

If you find the lord of the first strong and fortunate, or
joined to the lord of the 4th in the ascendant, or with the ☽
or lord of the 10th, or any where but in the 6th, 8th, or 12th,
and the lord of the 1st dispose of the lord of the 4th ; or if
☽ dispose him, and be not disposed of by him, it is an argument that the place shall be taken.   Or if the lord of the 4th
be in such houses as behold not the 4th, and be with infortunes, and weak, it will be taken, and the governor may be
wounded.   If infortunes be in the 4th, without some strong
aspect of the fortunes, it will be taken.   If ☋ be in the 4th,
it will be taken, and some parties will try to betray it, or
some principal work or fort therein : the sign will shew which
part of the town, &c.   In this case the governor does not expect to preserve it.

If the lord of the 4th be in the 4th, strong and not afflicted.
neither retrograde nor combust, nor besieged of the infortunes, or if the lord of the 7th be there, *free from all impediments*, or if ♃, ♀, or ☊ be therein, and no reception be-

tween the lords of the 1st and 4th, then shall not the city, &c. be taken ; and if there be both a fortune and infortune in the 4th, it shall not be taken, if the fortune be the nearest to the cusp, or first transit that degree ; and this more certainly, if the lord of the ascendant be weak or unfortunate, especially if a light planet. But if the lord of the ascendant be strong, or fortune therein, and the ☽ behold the cusp of the 4th, it shall be surprised or surrendered. An infortune in the 2d, or its lord, &c. afflicted, the querent lacks means to pursue the siege with vigour.

Of Commanders in Armies : and whether they shall be victorious or not.

If there be an infortune in the ascendant, it shews that the querent has no great justice on his part, or cause of quarrel. And if an infortune ☐ the ascendant, the party shewn by it (viz. that for which the querent asks) will not manage their affairs well or discreetly. If a good planet be in the ascendant, or aspect it by ⚹ or △, it shews a good cause, and that it will be well managed.

An evil star in the 2d, and having no dignities therein, or aspecting its cusp by ☐ aspect, denotes that either there will be no war, or that the querent will gain nothing by it ; a benefic testifies the reverse. If ♃ (or ♂ well dignified) be in the 3d, the querent's party will have good warlike stores, &c., and will consist of good, brave soldiers ; but if ♂ be there, ill dignified, they will be bad characters, and ill disciplined.

If an infortune be in the 4th, the campaign will be held in a difficult country. If the sign describe a hilly country, it will offer obstacles by woods and bad roads ; and if it shew a moist country, it will be unfit for military occupations, by

Q

reason of rivers, marshes, &c.; and so the army can do no good service.

If ♂ be in the 5th, well dignified, or a fortune aspect it, the army on the querent's side will be good soldiers, and well behaved; but ♄ there, or ☍, denotes the contrary.

If a fortune or ☌ be in the 6th, the ammunition train, artillery, &c. will be good; if ♂ be there, the horses will be fierce, wild and unbroken. If ♄ be there (without dignities, they will be unserviceable, slow, and worn out.

A fortune in the 7th, the arms and instruments of war will be plentiful and serviceable. If an infortune be there, or afflicting it by evil aspect, they will be the reverse. In the former case, the enemy will be brave and no fool, and will fight fair; in the latter case, the enemy will fight rather by craft and treachery, than fair manhood.

A fortune in the 8th, shews that there will not be many men slain on the querent's side; nor any very important battle be fought. If ♄ be there, there will be much plundering and destruction, and many prisoners be taken; also much death by sickness and want, &c. If ♂ be there, then expect much bloodshed.

A fortune in or aspecting the 9th, the enemy is well situated, and will strive to gain by false reports, alarms, &c.; he is politic. If an infortune, he will wear himself out by marching, and will be often deceived by false intelligence; and if a fortune be in the 3d at the same time, the querent's side will gain by this conduct of the enemy.

A fortune in the 10th, or aspecting its cusp by ⚹ or △, shews that the commanding officer is expert and capable. But if ♄, ☍, or ♂, (unfortunate), be there, or afflict the 10th house by □, the commander on the querent's side will be extremely incapable and unworthy, and meet only disgrace.

A fortune or ☊ in the 11th, shews the officers are clever, and understand their duty, and will well support the commander; but an infortune, or ☍, the reverse.

If a fortune (or ♂ well dignified) be in the 12th, it denotes that the enemy is well prepared, and will defend themselves well. An infortune there, shews that they are weak and will disagree among themselves, and fear their own forces. If ☍ be in the 12th, the querent may expect treachery; and if the lord of the 12th be there, and have any dignities in the ascendant, the querent's side will suffer by desertion.

Whether the two Armies will Fight or not.

Observe the ascendant and its lord, the ☽ and lord of the 7th, if they be ☌ in any angle they will fight. If the lords of the 1st and 7th be not in ☌, but are in ☐ or ☍ from angles, they will engage; or if there be any planet which transfers the light of one to the other by ☐ or ☍, there will be a fight, if there be no reception between them. But if there be none of these, and the heavier planet receive the lighter, there will be no serious engagement.

Whether the Querent have any Adversaries or open Enemies.

If the question regard not any relation, take the 7th house for any open enemy, if any person be specially considered; but if it be simply as to enemies in general, look to the 12th house. If it be as to some individual enemy, see whether the lord of the 7th, or planet therein, throw a ☐ or ☍ to the lord of the ascendant, or ☽; this denotes that the quesited is envious or inimical. If the aspect apply, the enmity will increase; and if the enemy's significator dispose of the querent's without reception mutual, the querent will suffer by him: the manner how may be learned by the house he is in. If the aspect be past, the injury is done, and the enmity is dying away, unless the querent's significator, or ☽, be about to receive another ill aspect.

If the quesited's significator be placed in the 12th, or in any good aspect with any planet which is in ☐ or ☍ to the ☽, or lord of the ascendant, without reception, there is enmity to the querent.

If the question be general, the lord of the 12th and planets therein must be taken; and they shew private enemies to the querent, unless a benefic planet be in the 12th, and throw a ✶, or △, to the querent's significators. If there be many planets in the 7th, it shews many open enemies; and if in the 12th, many secret foes. The ☐ shews envy and malice, which may be reconciled; the ☍, if without reception, denotes irreconcilable enemies. If an evil planet in the 12th throw a good aspect to the querent's significator, it shews that there is some person who under pretence of friendship wishes to injure the querent. The same if the lord of the 11th be in the 12th. The house the lord of the 12th is in, will describe what person will injure the querent.

Fig. 14.

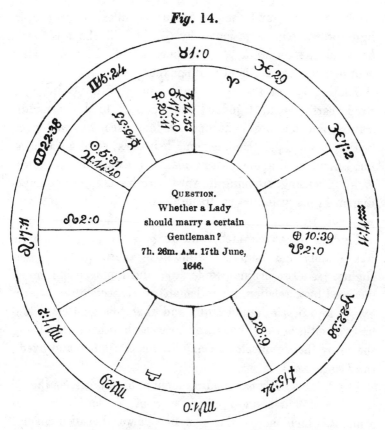

QUESTION.
Whether a Lady
should marry a certain
Gentleman?
7h. 26m. A.M. 17th June,
1646.

JUDGMENT ON THE FIGURE ABOVE.

State of the Querent's case.—A gentleman had been a long
time an earnest suitor unto her for marriage; but she had
continually slighted, and at last had given him a positive
denial; after which she sorely repented her conduct, and
wished she had her former opportunity. She was in this
state when she propounded her question to me.

The ascendant and ☉ are for the querent; ♄, lord of the
7th, and ☽, are for the gentleman. The querent was mode-

rately tall, of round face, sanguine complexion, grey eyes, light brown hair, occasioned by ☉, lord of the ascendant, being in the terms of ♂, and she was of cheerful modest countenance, comely, and well spoken.

Finding ♄, in the south angle, in ♂ with ♂ in ♉, a fixed, earthy sign, I judged the quesited to be of middle stature, not tall, nor handsome; a long face, not well composed; a wan, pale complexion; hair dark, or of a sad chesnut colour, curling and crisp; his eyes fixed, always downlooking, musing, stooping forward with his head, some impediment in his walking, as treading awry, &c. (*All this was confessed.*)

Finding ♄ so elevated, and in ♂ ♂, I judged that he was gloomy and angry, discontented, scorning his former slights, (as all saturnine people do); and I judged him much incensed by a relation, a gentleman of respectability, shewn by ♂, lord of *his* 3d and 10th, and that this gentleman and he lived either in one house, or near each other; this being shewn by the significator's being in his 4th angle and fixed; (*and so it was.*)

I said the gentleman had no inclination for her, as the ☽ was void of course, and applied to ☍ of ☉, lord of the ascendant, which shewed that she herself was her own enemy. She then confessed the truth, and implored my advice how, consistent with honour, she might, if possible, bring it on again; and she appearing in great distress, I began to consider what hopes she had in the figure. I found ☉ applying to ⚹ of ♄; this argued her desire and affection towards the quesited: but as there was no reception it gave little hopes. Finding reception between ♃ and ☽, and ☉ and ☽, and also that ☽ disposed of ♄ in her exaltation, and ♃ in her house, and that ♃ was very near a ⚹ of ♄, *applying,* and not separating; and also that ♃ was in his exaltation, he being a

fortune, and ever assisting nature and the afflicted, and that
he was able to take off the malice of ♄; I was confident,
from the exactness of the aspect, that the quesited was inti-
mately acquainted with a person of rank and worth, (such as
♃ represented), whom I exactly described, and the lady very
well knew. I directed her to apply to him, and acquaint
him with the full extent of her folly, and I assured her that
in him she would find all honour and secrecy; and I doubted
not but, by God's blessing, he would again revive the business, and bring her to her heart's content. But finding that
⊙ and ♄ came to ⚹ aspect on the 27th of the month, I
advised to hasten all before that aspect was over; and as on
the 19th of June ♄ and ♃ came to a ⚹, I told her that the
gentleman should first move the quesited on that day near
noon. My counsel was followed, and by that gentleman's
means the match was brought on again, and completed within
twenty days, to the content of the sorrowful (but to me unthankful) lady, &c.

I acquainted this lady, that shortly before her lover had
been offered a match, and that the lady was well descended,
of good fortune, and described by ♀; but that she need not
fear his marrying her, as some officer or gentleman, who had
been in the army, shewn by ♂, would prevent that. She
well knew both the parties, and confessed that such a matter
had been.

Had the query been, *who should live longest?* I should
have judged the female, because ⊙ is going to ♂ ♃, and ♂
afflicts ♄.

If, whether the quesited were rich? I should say he had
a good estate, as ♃, lord of his 2d, was direct, swift, and in
his exaltation, &c.

If, would they agree? I should say they would, as ⊙ and
♄ are applying to ⚹; yet ♄ with ♂ shews a man who looks

to have authority, one choleric as well as melancholy, **jealous** without a cause, &c. ; yet the ✶ of ♃ mitigates his ill **manners** by means of education.

If, will the querent be honest ? I answer, her significator ☉ is no way afflicted by ♂ ; her ascendant is *fixed*, and there is reception between ♃ and ☽, which are arguments of a **virtuous woman.***

In this manner you may examine any figure for discovery of what is necessary, &c.

* We should rely much on her significator ☉ being in ♂ with ♃.

Fig. 15.

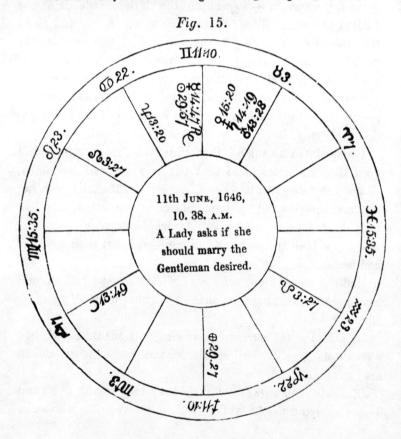

11th JUNE, 1646,
10. 38. A.M.
A Lady asks if she
should marry the
Gentleman desired.

JUDGMENT ON THE ABOVE QUESTION.

The querent was of tall stature, ruddy complexion, sober, discreet, and well spoken, &c. The quesited was very tall, slender, lean, and of a long visage, with black hair. His tallness I attribute to ♃ being in the terms of ☿, and the cusp of the 7th being also in his terms. Indeed, a significator being in the terms of any planet, does vary the party from his natural constitution ; so that he will retain a tincture from that planet, according as he is dignified.* The darkness of his hair I attribute to the aspect of ♄ to ♃, and ☽ being in the term of ♃.

☿ is here the querent's significator, and being retrograde, and under the beams of ☉, shewed that she was in distress and fear that the quesited would not have her. And she had some reason for it ; for ♃ was in his exaltation, and near the ✳ of ♀, an argument that the man stood upon high terms, and had been tampering with another : yet, as both significators were in *semi-sextile* aspect, and in good houses, I gathered hope that there were some mutual sparks of love. And when I found ☽ separating from □ of ♃, and hastening to △ of ☿, thus conveying the light of the quesited's significator to the lord of the ascendant, which he received willingly by his retrograde movement, I was confident that the match would be suddenly brought about by a person described by ☽ ; who did, indeed, though with a little difficulty, produce the marriage to the content of both parties.

---

* We should rather consider that ☿ in ♊ aspecting the cusp of the 7th ; and the ☽, the *man's* general significator, being in ♎ and aspectin ♃, shewed his tallness. ♊ and ♎ are tall signs.

Fig. 16.

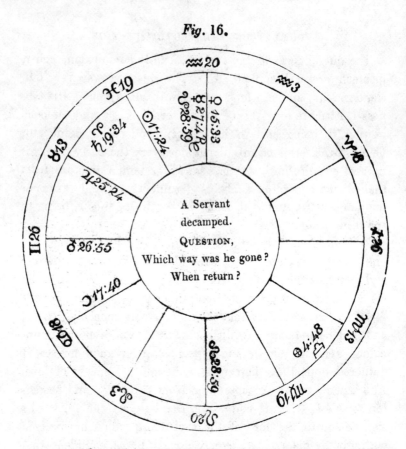

JUDGMENT UPON THE ABOVE FIGURE.

The ascendant, ☿ in ♒, and ♂ in ♊, taken together, signified and described the querent, (the servant's master). He was short of stature, corpulent, of good complexion, and ruddy, fresh colour. His fatness I attribute to the north latitude of ☿, which was one degree; also the ascendant was in the terms of ♂, and face of ☉, who was in partile △ to ☽ in a moist sign, which shews a full body, and phlegmatic.

The servant was shewn by ♂ (lord of the 6th) and ♏.

He was a well-set short fellow, large joints, broad and full face, dark brown hair, his teeth irregular, complexion obscure and sunburnt, yet his skin clear; his age about nineteen.

I observed that he went away from his master the preceding Sunday, when ☽ was in ♊, a western sign, where ♂ now was; and that ☿, the common significator of servants, was in ♒, a western sign, but south quarter of heaven.

I judged, therefore, that he went westward at first, and that at the time of the question he was west from the querent's house; and this I judged, because ♂ was angular, otherwise I should have judged by ☽. As ♂ and ☿, lord of the ascendant, were hastening to a △ out of angles, I judged that in a day or two he should have his servant again.

Upon the Friday following he came home, and said he had been at Kingston upon Thames; which, if true, he was nearly west, but a little south; and near a great water, (viz. the Thames), as the ☽ in ♋ might signify.

Fig. 17.

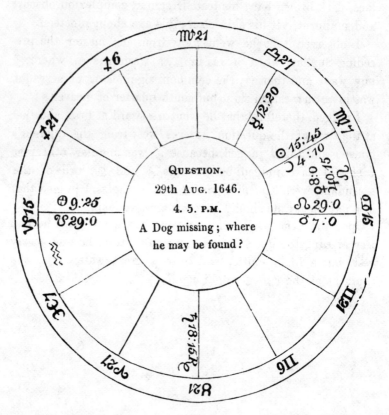

JUDGMENT UPON THE ABOVE FIGURE.

The queries to me were, *What part of the city they should search?* and, *should he be found?*

The querent was described by the sign ascending, and *Cauda* (☋) therein; and, indeed, he was *saturnine,* and vitiated both in body and mind; that is, he was a little deformed in body, of small stature, and extremely covetous in disposition, &c. The sign of the 6th signifies a dog, as it would have done a sheep, hog, &c., or any small cattle.

The sign ♊ is west and by south, the quarter of heaven westerly ; ☿, the dog's significator, is in ♎, a western sign, and is in a south-western quarter of heaven ; the ☽ is in ♍, a south-west sign, verging to the west angle. The plurality of testimonies shewed that the dog ought to be *west* from where the owner lived, which was at Temple-bar ; therefore I judged that the dog was about Long Acre, or upper part of Drury Lane. As ☿ was in a sign of the same triplicity with ♊, which signifies London, and applied to △ of the cusp of the 6th, I judged that the dog was not out of the lines of communication, but in the same quarter ; of which I was more satisfied by the △ of ☉ to ♄. ☿ being in an airy sign, I said the dog was in some garret or upper room ; and, as ☽ was under the beams of ☉, and ☿, ☽, and ☉ were in the 8th house, that he was kept privately, or in great secrecy. But as ☉, on the following Monday, formed a △ to ♄, lord of the ascendant, and ☽ formed a △ to ♂, who has dignities in the ascendant, I intimated that he should then have news of his dog ; and this proved true ; for a gentleman of the querent's acquaintance, coming accidentally to see a friend in Long Acre, found the dog chained up under a table, and knowing him to belong to the querent, sent him home about ten o'clock on the Monday morning, to my very great credit.

Usually I find that all fugitives go by the ☽ ; and as she varies her sign, they waver and shift their flight, declining more to east, west, north, or south. But you must judge by the significator or the ☽, according to which is strongest ; or if both be equally strong, take that which best describes the fugitive, with regard also to that one which is nearest in aspect to the cusp of the house from whence signification is taken. That is, if the fugitive be a servant or small animal the 6th ; if a large animal, the 12th ; if a son or daughter, the 5th ; and if a wife, the 7th, &c.

Fig. 18.

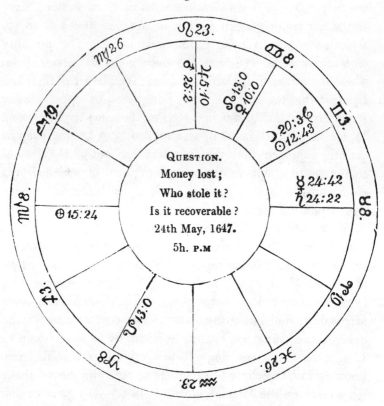

QUESTION.
Money lost;
Who stole it?
Is it recoverable?
24th May, 1647.
5h. P.M

JUDGMENT ON THE ABOVE FIGURE.

Here ♍ ascends, and partly describes the querent's person; ♂, his mind and disposition; ♂ in □ to ☿ and ♄,
shewed him ill-conditioned, arrogant, proud, wasteful, &c.
As ♂ is in 25° 2′ of ♌, he has entered his own *terms*, and is
in his own *face*, I therefore refused him for the thief's significator.   In the next place, ♄, though in the west angle, (the
house of theft), is in his own *term* and *face*; I also passed
him by.   But finding ☿ in an angle, having no essential dignity, and in partile ♂ of ♄, and □ of ♂, I took him to

signify the thief.   But whether he described a male or female was the question.   The angles are part masculine, part feminine ;   no certain judgment could, therefore, be formed from thence.   The ☽ was in a masculine sign, applying to a masculine planet, (♂), and ☿ was in ♂ with ♄ , and □ to ♂, both masculine planets ;   I judged, therefore, that the sex was male.

As ☿ ever signifies youth, and as ☽ was so near the ☉, separating, I said he was a youth, of some 15 or 16.   I described him of reasonable stature, thin visaged, hanging eyebrows, with some scar or blemish in his face, because ♂ casts his □ to ☿ ;   bad eyesight, as ☿ is with evil fixed stars, *(the Pleiades,)* of the nature of ♂ and ☽ ;   dark hair, because of his closeness to ♄ ;   a scurvy countenance, and one formerly accused of theft and knavery.

The youth's significator being in ♂ with ♄ , lord of the 3d and 4th houses, I judged him the child of some neighbour ; and as ☽ is in ♊, and ☿ in ♉ in the 7th, I said he dwelt either opposite to the querent, or a little south-west. The ⊕ being in the ascendant, and disposed of by ♂ , lord of the ascendant in the 10th, and as ☽ applied to his ⚹, and was within about four degrees of the aspect, I judged he should not only hear of, but have his money again within four days. He believed not one word I said, but would need persuade me that a woman servant, shewn by ♂ , was one thief, and ♄ another ; but I stood firm to the art, and would not consent to this, as both ♄ and ♂ were essentially dignified. The event proved me right, both as to the person and the return of the money, which was within three days after.

Fig. 19.

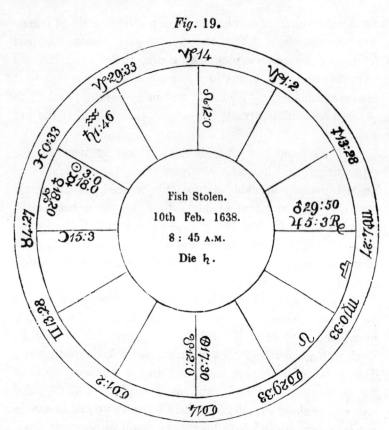

EXPLANATION OF THE ABOVE FIGURE.

Living in the country in 1637, I had bought at London some fish for my provision in Lent; it came down by the barge to Walton. On Saturday, the 10th February, one of the watermen, instead of bringing my fish home, acquainted me that their warehouse was robbed last night, and my fish stolen. I took the exact time I first heard the report, and erected this figure accordingly; endeavouring to give myself satisfaction as to what became of my goods, and, if possible, to recover part or all of them.

Judgment.

I first observed that there was no peregrine planet in an angle but ♃, whom I found on the cusp of the 7th house. I considered the signification of ♃ in ♏ a moist sign, and the significator of my goods, ☿ in ♓, a moist sign; and that ⊕ was in ♋, a moist sign. Discretion, together with art, led me to think he who had my goods must be a person whose profession, or calling, was to live upon the water; and that they were in some low room, in a moist place, because ⊕ was in ♋, and ☽ was in ♉, an earthy sign, and under the earth.

I was confident I should hear of my goods again, as ☿, lord of the 2d, was applied to by ⚹ of ☽, who was lady of ⊕, and yet without hope of recovering them, as ☿ was in his fall, and detriment; but as he was in his own terms, and had a △ to ⊕, there were hopes of regaining some of my goods.

There being no waterman in Walton described by ♄ in ♏. I examined what fisherman there was of that complexion: and as ♂, lord of the 7th, was leaving ♏, his own sign, and entering another, I inquired if any fisherman of the nature of ♂ and ♃ had lately sold any land, or was leaving his own house and going to another; such a one I discovered, who lived near the Thames side, a mere fisherman, but a jovial fellow, though much suspected of thievery. He was of good stature, thick, and full-bodied, fair complexion, and red or yellowish hair.

I procured a warrant from a justice of peace, and reserved it privately until Sunday, the 18th of the month; and then, with a constable and the bargeman, I searched only that one house of the suspected fisherman. I found part of my fish in water, part eaten, part not consumed; **all confessed**. I

R

asked the woman for seven *Portugal onions* which I had lost also; but she, not knowing what they were, had made pottage with them. I freely remitted the remainder of my fish, though the hireling priest of Walton affirmed that I had satisfaction for it. But he never hurt himself with a lie.

Thus you see, that the peregrine planet in an angle describes the thief; and that either ☉ or ☽ in the ascendant gives assured hopes of discovering who it was. The ☽ applying to the lord of the 2d, argues recovery; if they both be essentially dignified, *complete*; but if accidentally fortified, *partial*. If both be peregrine, and they apply, there will be a discovery, but no recovery.

Fig. 20.

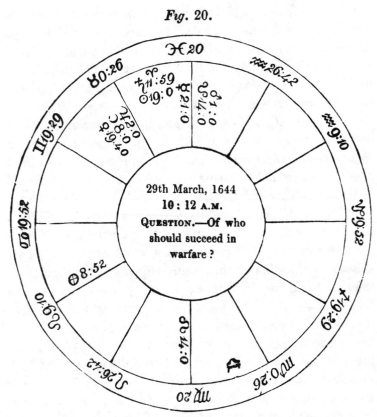

A Figure erected to know whether Sir WILLIAM WALLER *or Sir* RALPH HOPTON *should overcome ; they being supposed to be engaged near Alsford* ♀ *29th March,* 1644.

JUDGMENT ON THE ABOVE FIGURE.

The ascendant is for our army, the ☽, ♃, and ♀, for our generals, viz. Sir William Waller, and Major-General Browne, a valiant and prudent citizen of London, who may justly claim a large share of honour in that day's service. Sir Ralph Hopton is signified by ♄, lord of the 7th; his army oy ♑ in the descending part of heaven which is usually

given to the friends and assistants of the enemy.   There are
only ♂ and ☋ in the 9th; so it appears that Sir Ralph had
no supplies ready to attend that day's success, &c.   From
the ☽, having principal signification of us and our army,
being in her exaltation with ♃, I concluded all was and
would be well on our side, and that the victory would be ours.
From her separation from ♃, I said, I verily conceived that we
had already taken some ammunition from them, or performed
some service against them.   This I was confirmed in by ☉, lord
of our substance and assistants, being posited in the 10th house,
in the very degree of his exaltation; (the 19th).   And though
I thought by the proximity of ♄ to ☉ we should not gain
the whole, or have a perfect victory, without diminution of
some part of it; yet I was confident we should obtain a considerable proportion of their ammunition, and have a victory,
the only thing inquired after; for the ☽ applied to ♀, and
then to a ⚹ of ☿, he being angular.   I told the *querent*
that within eleven or twelve hours after the question we should
have perfect news, and it satisfactory.   For, considering that
the fight was within fifty miles of London, I ordered my time
with discretion, not allowing days for the time, but *hours;*
and this because ☽ is distant from ♀ 11°, but is withal swift
in motion, and increasing in light.   These were also signs of
our success, and the enemies' defeat.   It appeared, by a letter
from the army on that same Friday, that our generals took
on the previous day 120 commanders and gentlemen, 560
common soldiers, and much ammunition.   Thus the enemy
was worsted, as appeared by ♄, (the Lord Hopton's significator), being *sub radiis,* in his fall in no aspect to any planet,
wholly peregrine, and unfortunate, and aspecting the cusp of
the 7th by □.   All this argued that he would bring loss to
his army, and dishonour to himself by the fight, &c.

Fig. 21.

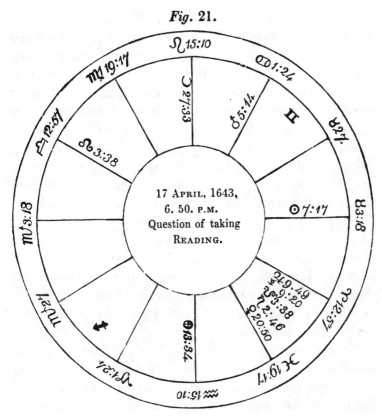

17 APRIL, 1643,
6. 50. P.M.
Question of taking
READING.

QUESTION.—*Whether his Excellency* ROBERT *Earl of* ESSEX *should take* READING, *having then surrounded it with his Army ?*

JUDGMENT ON THE ABOVE FIGURE.

The General Essex is here shewn by ♂, lord of ♏, and his Majesty by ☉, lord of the 10th, the forces that were to relieve Reading by ♀ in ♓, and ☉ in ♉ ; also the town by ♒, the sign on the 4th; the governor, Sir Arthur Acton, (reputed an able soldier), by the lord of the 4th, ♄ ; and their ammunition and provision by ♃, lord of the 5th, and by ♀ located therein.

The significator of his Excellency ♂ is well fortified, and afflicted in no way but by being in his fall. This figure manifests that it is of great importance in questions of warfare to have ♂ friendly to the querent. The ☽ separated from *nothing*, and was void of course; and, indeed, there was little hope of its being gained in the time it was. She applied to ⚹ of ♂ from signs of long ascension, which was equivalent to a ▢ ; which argued that his Excellency would have much difficulty and some fighting ere he could get it. But as ♂ and ☽ were in reception, viz. ♂ in her house, and she in his terms and face, and near *Cor* ♌, and in the house of honour, I judged that his Excellency would obtain and take Reading, and gain honour thereby. Finding ☉, his Majesty's significator, in the 7th in a fixed sign, I said that he would send forces to relieve the town, and oppose all he could ; but that he would not prevail, as ♂ was better fortified than ☉. The King did come in person, and was beaten back at Causham Bridge.

Finding that ♒ was not afflicted, I judged the town strong, and able to hold out ; and ♀ being in the 5th, that they wanted not ammunition. Having well weighed all things, and that ♄ , lord of the 4th, signifying the Governor, was in his fall with ☍, and that ☿ and ♃ were not far from ☍, I said, (and sent somebody word), that the most certain way, and which would assuredly occasion the surrender of the town, was to set division among the principal officers, and incense them against their chief officer, and that about eight days from the time of the question his Excellency would be master of the town ; yet rather by composition than by blood. This because ☉ and ♂ were separated from their ⚹ aspect, and ♂ was also separated from the ▢ of ♄ ; as also because the ☽ applied so directly to ⚹ of the lord of the ascendant, without any frustration, &c.

The town was delivered for the Parliament's use on the 27th April, three days after the time I said; but it is observable that they began to treat on the very Monday before, just eight days after the figure was set.

The Governor was hurt in the head, as ♄ in ♈ with ☍ shews; nor did they want provisions, &c., as ♀ in the 5th signifies.*

Fig. 22.

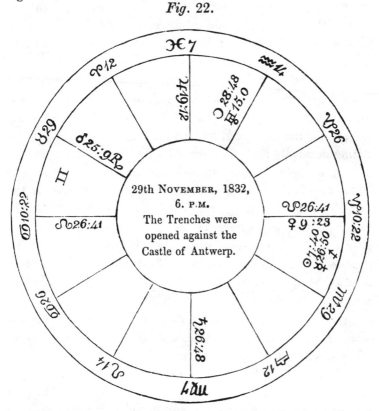

29th NOVEMBER, 1832, 6. P.M. The Trenches were opened against the Castle of Antwerp.

* The well-known instance of a military siege, the capture of the Castle of Antwerp, being so applicable to this question, and the time of its commencement by the opening of the trenches being so well authenticated, we are induced to offer to the student's notice a figure re erected for that time.

JUDGMENT ON THE PRECEDING FIGURE.

This figure is erected for the latitude and longitude of Antwerp, and is an exact representation of the heavens at the time the French troops opened ground, (or began the siege), before the citadel of Antwerp. By it the student will perceive that the rules laid down by our author, being founded in truth and nature, are infallible ; and that they hold equally true in the 19th as they did in the 17th century. They must eventually put the sceptic to silence, and convince the world of the truth of planetary influence.

The ascendant and its lady, the ☽, are for the besiegers, the 7th and its lord for the besieged, the 4th is for the town, and its lord for the governor. The 10th is the house of honour for the besiegers, and we find ♃ potent therein, denoting decidedly that they should gain honour by the siege. The ☊ in the ascendant shewed success to the French, and ☋ in the 7th the reverse to their enemies. The lord of the 4th, ☿, is in his detriment, cadent, and in exact ☐ to the evil ♄, denoting disgrace to the governor, who is thereby shewn to be extremely obstinate, as, indeed, he was. The malefic in the 4th denoted that the place should be taken, and, as ☽ was in close ☐ to ♂, it would be by much loss of men and bloodshed on the part of the besiegers. The ☽ is in the *terms* of ♂, and he in her *exaltation* and *triplicity*, which reception denotes courageous conduct on the part of the besiegers ; and although the ☽ is in ☐ to ♂, yet, there being mutual reception, it shews success in a martial exploit ; but with much difficulty, because of the ☐ aspect. The garrison were denoted by the 5th, and its ruler ♀ ; and as ♀ is in the 6th, (the 12th from the enemies' ascendant), it shewed that all the enemies' party would be made prisoners, which was the case.

The citadel capitulated when a breach had been effected; and they surrendered to the French on the 23d December following; when the ☽, the besiegers' significator, crossed the cusp of the 7th house; thus entering the 7th just as the besiegers entered the place itself. It deserves notice that on the day ☿ fell retrograde, and ☽ crossed the cusp of the 5th (Dec. 15th), the besiegers carried the horn work.

The student will observe, that the lord of the 7th was peregrine, having no essential dignity whatever; and that the ☽, besides her aspect and her mutual reception with ♂, the chief significator of warfare, is in her own face, and disposes of ♄ by triplicity. Hence the besiegers are decidedly the strongest party, and should, by the rules of the science, certainly prevail.

The student may rely that the figure of the heavens at the first moment of commencing any enterprise whatever, will infallibly point out, to those who really understand astrology, its final result.

CHAPTER XXXI.

OF THE EIGHTH HOUSE, AND ITS QUESTIONS:

THESE ARE DEATH, DOWRY, THE WIFE'S SUBSTANCE, &c.

QUERY.—*Whether an absent Person be dead or alive?*

Take care to learn whether the *quesited* be any relation to the *querent*: if so, look to the house signifying that relation; and if not, look to the 7th for the quesited's significator. If the lord of the quesited's ascendant be in the 4th or the 8th, either from his own house or in the figure, it is one argument that the party is dead. If, also, his significator be in the

12th, or his own 12th in □ or ☍ to a malefic, or if ☽ **or** ☉
be unfortunate in like way, you have strong testimony that he
is deceased.

If the significator of the absent be strong, and in a good
house, and separated from a fortune, he is not dead. If he
be afflicted, and was lately in ☍ or □ of an evil planet, I
judge that he has been in trouble or misfortune, according to
the nature of the house from whence afflicted ; but not dead,
unless the lord of the 8th afflict him also, and the lights be
afflicted.

Of the Death of the Querent?

If any one ask concerning the probable length of his life,
or when he may probably die, observe the ascendant, its lord,
and ☽ ; also, the lord of the 8th, an unfortunate planet in
the 8th, and that planet to whom the lord of the 1st or ☽ be
joined by ☌, □, or ☍ ; and you may determine the death
of the querent, according to the number of degrees between
the significator and the aspect of the afflicting planet. If
the lord of the ascendant be in ☌ with the lord of the 8th
in an angle, it notes so many years ; for in this question
angles do not accelerate death, but show that life and nature
are strong. If in a succeedent house, months ; though if
the sign be *fixed*, it gives half years, half months. In a
cadent house, weeks. But you must always consider whether
the significators are extremely afflicted ; if not, the querent
may live longer, and only be *near* death at the time threatened. The lord of the ascendant is more to be considered in
this case than the ☽ ; and, therefore, his ☌ with the lord of
the 8th or ☉ is to be most feared.

Observe that the ☽ being strong even, yet if the lord of
the ascendant be afflicted extremely, she does not denote
health or life, but only success in his affairs, &c. **Aspects**

by separation are not to be considered, but only those by *application.**

What manner of Death the Querent shall die?

This judgment is chiefly shewn by the lord of the 8th, if in the 8th, or any planet therein or nearest to its cusp, and having dignities in the 8th house ; or from the planet which afflicts the lord of the ascendant, and has dignities in the 8th. If it be either ♃ or ♀, or that they be in the 8th house, or aspect its cusp by ⚹ or △, they shew a natural death by such diseases as they shew in the sign they are in, and the part of man's body it governs. If evil planets be there, they shew violent deaths, or fevers, and long and painful illnesses ; and if the figure be violent, it may be by accidents, &c. The ☍ with the significator of death is very evil ; and if it be ♄, (and ♀ assist by her □, &c.), it shews fear of poison. The lord of the 1st and 8th being the same planet, shews that the querent brings on his own death by imprudence, &c.

Whether the Wife's Fortune will be great, or easily obtained, or whether the Person inquired of be rich or not?

The cusp of the 8th, in terms of ♃ or ♀, gives good hopes of wealth, or if ♃ or ♀ be therein. If they be essentially strong, and free from combustion, &c., they denote much wealth ; but though well dignified, if they be combust, slow, or retrograde, they shew trouble in procuring the fortune, &c. The lord of the 8th in the 8th, and strong, and no way afflicted, gives good hopes of some estate or legacy to fall to the quesited ; this is more sure if either the lord of

* If the fatal ♂ or aspect fall in the term of ♃ or ♀, or exactly in their ⚹ or △, there is much less fear of death.

the 4th or 10th be in good aspect with the lord of the 8th
from angles.   If ⊕ be in the 8th, and in ♌, or ♒, or any
of the houses of ♃ or ♀, or they in good aspect to ⊕, the
quesited's fortune is good.   The dispositor of ⊕ in good
aspect to it, or ♃ and ♀, shew the same thing.   If all these
happen, the quesited is very rich.

If ♄ or ♂ be in the 8th and peregrine, the party is poor,
or there will be contention about the property.   The lord of
the 8th combust, shews slow performance, and little ability
of what is promised ; and if ☍ be in the 8th, and no planet
there, fraud is intended, or more will be promised than can
be performed.

The lord of the 8th in the 2d, or in ⚹ or △ to its lord,
the querent shall have what is promised; in □, with difficulty; in ☍, with much wrangling; if without reception,
never.   But weigh well what the particular figure promises
besides these general rules.

Whether the Querent shall suffer by a particular Thing of which he is in fear?

If you find the ☽ afflicted, or the lord of the ascendant
unfortunate and falling from an angle, or especially if he be
in the 12th, and the ☽ with him, there is ground for his
fear ; and he may expect to be accused, &c. of much of which
he is not guilty.   If the lord of the 1st ascends into the 11th
or 10th, or be joined to a fortune, he shall not be injured.
If he apply to infortunes, the thing threatened is true ; but if
to a fortune, and not at the same time to an infortune, it is
false or ungrounded.   The ☽ in △ to ☉ discovers all suddenly.   The ☽ cadent, and applying to a cadent planet, the
supposed danger will be nothing, or come to nothing in the
end.

Fig. 23.

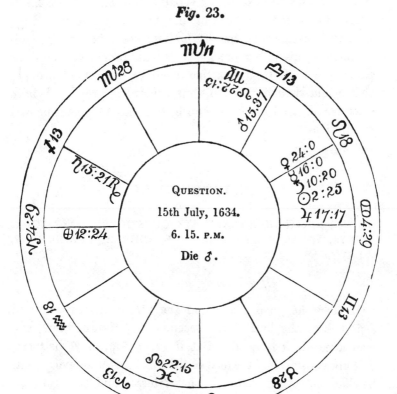

QUESTION.—SHALL THE QUERENT RECEIVE THE PORTION
PROMISED?

Judgment.—The querent's significator retrograde in the
12th, shewed he had been in despair of it, which he confessed.
The female is signified by ♃ and ☽; ♃ in his exaltation,
and ☽ in ♌, a fixed sign, argue that she thinks well of herself, is confident, &c., yet modest and virtuous.   The ☽ being
near ☉, she had a scar near her right eye.

Finding ☉ lord of the quesited's 2d in his own house, and

♀ in her 2d, and also that ☽ separated from ☉, and transferring his light to ♄, lord of the ascendant and 2d and ⊕,
I assured the querent that he had no cause to fear the non-
payment of his wife's portion; that all promised would be
paid; and that, to his farther comfort, she would prove a
chaste and virtuous woman, but somewhat proud. I have
since heard, from his own mouth, that this judgment proved
exactly true.

CHAPTER XXXII.

OF THE NINTH HOUSE AND ITS QUESTIONS. LONG JOUR. NEYS, VOYAGES, ARTS, SCIENCE, CHURCH PREFERMENT, LAW, &c.

Of a Voyage, and its Issue.

If there be good planets in the 9th, or its cusp be well
aspected, or the lord of the ascendant or 10th be there, and
well affected, it is good. But if ♅, ♄, ♂, or ☗ be there,
it is always evil. If the lord of the 9th be with an evil planet,
he shall not speed well. ♄ shews losses and sickness; ♂
shews danger by thieves or pirates: and ☗ much the same
as ♂, but more of cozening and cheating. The house of
substance from the 9th is the 10th. Fortunes there shew
wealth; infortunes loss. If benefics be in the 9th, a good
voyage; if malefics, many hardships, &c.

What Wind and Weather the Querent will experience.

The lord of the ascendant with good planets, and they
strong and in friendly aspect, and the lords of the 1st and
9th in △ out of ♊, ♎, or ♒, shew fair weather and favourable winds. The significators in ☍, out of fixed signs, shew

detention by foul winds; and if near violent fixed stars, storms and contrary winds will drive him back.

Of a long Journey, and its Issue.

If a fortune be in the ascendant, say he will have good success before he sets out, or in the commencement of his journey; if it be in the 10th, then he will have success on the journey; if in the 7th, at the place to which he goes; and if in the 4th, it will be on his return, and when he is come home. In this case ♃ gives benefits by clerical persons, judges, magistrates, or gentlemen, according to the querent's situation in life and the house ♃ rules, and the nature of the ruler of ♃. As if it be ☉, by a king, or nobleman, or person in power; if ♄, it will be by old people, or ancient matters, or farmers, &c. Let him apply to such a person in his affairs as ♄ describes, according to the sign he is in and the aspects he receives. If it be ♀, it will be by women, pleasure, sport, &c.; or by dealing in linen, silks, jewels, spices, &c. If ☿, by writing or merchandize, letters of introduction, &c. If ☽, by some female, probably a widow, or by a sailor, or by carrying news, &c., or by play.

Of the Length of the Journey, &c.

The lord of the 9th, or planet therein, or ☽ in moveable signs, swift and oriental, shew a short time absent. If they be in fixed signs, slow and occidental, it shews a long and tedious journey and absence. If they be in common signs, they shew change of mind, and a varying of his journey, going to other places, &c. According as the ☽ is assisted or afflicted, judge results to happen. As, for example, if ☽ be in the 6th, or in ☍ to its lord, it shews sickness or impediments from servants. The lord of the 4th, and the 4th house, denote the final issue.

Of the Return, &c., of a Person who is gone a long Journey

The lord of the ascendant in the ascendant or midheaven, or aspected by planets therein, shows that he is thinking of returning. But if he be in the 7th or 4th, his return is prolonged ; and he is not thinking of leaving the place he went to. The lord of the ascendant in the 3d or 9th, applying to a planet in the ascendant, he is on his journey homeward. The same may be judged if he be in the 8th or 2d, and apply to a planet in the 10th ; but in this case observe also the ☽ , and whether she aspect the ascendant, or a planet therein. If the lord of the ascendant or ☽ apply to a retrograde planet, or the lord of the ascendant be himself a retrograde, and behold the ascendant, he is coming ; but if his significator be afflicted, it shews some hinderance which makes him tarry. The dispositor of the ☽ afflicted, shews hinderance also.

If you find ☿ or the ☽ in the ascendant or midheaven, judge that letters or some news shall come shortly from the party ; for ☿ is the significator of letters, and the ☽ of news. If they separate from a fortune, it denotes good news ; and if from an infortune, the contrary.

The planet from whom the lord of the ascendant of the quesited is separated, is the significator of the state and condition in which he lately was ; the planet to whom he applies, of the state in which he now is ; and the planet to whom he afterwards applies is the significator of him to whom he intends to come.

If the quesited's significator be going out of one sign into another, judge that he went out of the place he was in, and entered another, or that he has undertaken another journey. Observe in which of those signs he was stronger, better aspected and received, &c. ; and so judge of his corresponding condition.

Observe, that combustion in all questions of one absent,

shews some great evil; such as imprisonment, &c. ; and if it
be in the house of death, or ☉ be lord of the house of death,
it generally denotes death.

Ever consider for whom the question is asked, and take his
proper significator. The lord of the 7th for a husband (or
for any one who is no relation), the lord of the 3d a brother,
5th a son, &c.; and note how the fortunes are placed; if
strong in the figure, well aspecting the significator of the
quesited, or in his house, judge health and prosperity; and
the reverse by infortunes.

OF PROFIT BY, OR PROFICIENCY IN, ANY SCIENCE, &C.

The ascendant, its lord, and the ☽, are for the querent;
and the 9th, its lord, or planet therein (if more than one, the
nearest to the cusp), for the science.

See whether the lord of the 9th be fortunate or not,
oriental, angular, &c. ; and whether he behold the lord of the
ascendant with ⚹ or △. If he be a fortune, and aspect the
lord of the ascendant, the man has scientific knowledge, and
will gain thereby ; the more so if there be reception. If the
aspect be □ or ☍, the man has talent, but shall do no good
by it. If an infortune aspect either the lord of the ascendant or 9th, the man has wearied himself, but to no purpose,
for he will never attain the knowledge he desires. If infortunes be in the 9th, or its lord afflicted, the party has but
little scientific knowledge.

The ☽ must also be observed with the lord of the 9th ;
for if they both apply to fortunes, the man is scientific ; if to
infortunes, the contrary.

If the question be put regarding another person, you must
in this case give the ascendant for the quesited.*

* We do not agree with our author on this point; for unless the
quesited has given his *consent* to the question, we think he should have
the same significators as in any other question; the 7th, 5th, 3d, &c.

S

EXAMPLE.

The author having given no good example regarding this question, the reader is here presented with a figure, which will no doubt prove interesting.

The editor being in company with two other artists, a general desire was expressed to know the future destiny of astrology, and the following figure was erected.

Fig. 24.

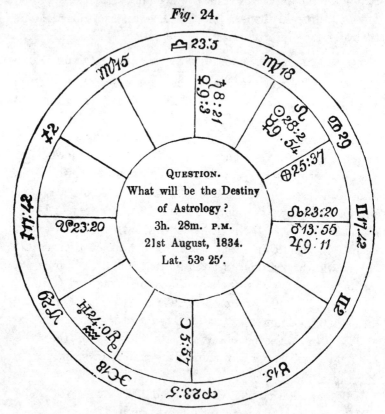

JUDGMENT ON THE ABOVE FIGURE.

The first thing to be observed in this figure is that ☿, the atural significator of science, is lord of the 9th, and is, therefore, the significator of the science of astrology. He is found cadent, and almost peregrine, having no essential dignity but his term, by which may be seen the present enfeebled state of the science ; but as ☿ has passed through four degrees of his term in a *fixed* sign, this points out, that for four years it has been in some measure more in credit than previously. And this is the case, as it is about four years since the Editor's publications began to call attention to the science. And as ☿ has just passed a ⚹ of ♃, who describes the person asking the question, it is shewn that the science has been much benefited by such a person, about nine months before, because ☿ is past the ⚹ of ♃ by 43', which shews about nine months, taking a degree for a year. And the fact is, that the *Grammar of Astrology* was published about nine months before the time of the question.

The ☍ in the ascendant shews the difficulties the Editor has had to encounter, and the contumely he has had to meet in bringing the science forward again.

The presence of ♄ in the 9th, denotes the discredit in which the science is generally held ; and being in ♂ with ♀, it shews that injury has been done to it by elderly females, who pretend to practise divining, &c., but who are held in great contempt by the public, as may be seen by the ☽ (the general significator of the public) being in ☍ to both ♀ and ♄, from the house of enemies to the science.

The next aspect formed by ☿, is the ⚹ of ♂, who being lord of the 11th house of the figure, and placed on the cusp of the 11th from the ninth, denotes *friends*. This shews, that in about four years from the time of the question, the science will gain many friends among persons denoted by ♂ in ♊, such as writers of public spirit, booksellers, &c. ; and there is no doubt that about that time it will suddenly and rapidly gain ground in public opinion. The next aspect formed by ☿, is the ☍ of ♅, from which he is distant 14°; this may shew that some *sudden* mischief may be done to the interests of the science by means of female agents, as ♀ is in exact sesquiquadrate aspect to ♅. But as ♅ is retrograde, and not angular, this will not be very important. The ☉ is in the 12th from the 9th, and denotes secret enmity to the science by men in power, the ☉ being in ♌; and as he disposes of ☿, it shews that the hand of power at present keeps it down. As ☿ is 18° from ☉, I judge that, about the year 1852, some important honour will be done to the science; probably by the present penal laws being repealed, which forbid the acceptance of any remuneration for practising it. As ☿ has 20° to pass before he reaches ♍, his own dignities, and as ♄ will then have entered ♊, and be disposed of by ☿, I judge that about 20 years hence the science will be publicly honoured; and as ☿ has afterwards 18° to pass in a common sign (signifying months), I conceive that about 18 months after that, when ☿ crosses the cusp of the 9th house in this figure (about the year 1856), the science will rapidly rise in public estimation, and be publicly studied in colleges, &c.

The ☉ enters ♍ after two years, as he is two degrees off, which will cause the ruling powers to relax something of their severity against the science; and as he then has 18°, (equal to 18 months, being in a common sign,) to go before he passes the cusp, there will be some person of rank who will assist the science at that time; viz. three years and a half from the time of the question, or the year 1838.

The ☽ must now be considered; she is hastening to ☍ of two planets in the 9th, which shews that there is yet much opposition to be expected to the science by the public, and especially by rash and violent people, which ☽ in the house of ♂ always denotes. But after the influence of the ☍ of ♄

and ♀ is passed away, the ☽ meets nothing but favourable aspects. It is very remarkable that the ☽ is aspected by every one of the planets before she passes through ♈. The first aspect she forms after ☍ of ♄ and ♀ is ⚹ of ♃, which denotes popularity for the works of the Editor, connected with the science. The next is △ of ☿, which shews an increase of students, and public discussion. The next is ⚹ of ♂, denoting increase of powerful friends, who will boldly advocate the cause of the science. The ⚹ of ♅ is of little import; but the △ of ☉ being the last aspect she forms before leaving the sign, decidedly shews that at last the science will receive the highest patronage, and be publicly honoured; and as ☉ is in ♌, a fixed sign, this will be **permanent**. Finally, the cusp of the 4th is in the term as well as house of ♂, and is ruled by ☉, by triplicity, and face; and ☉ casts a △ thereto; ♂, lord of the 4th, is in ☌ with ♃, in ⚹ to ☿ and ☽, and △ to ♄ **and** ♀; and he rules the ☽ by house and face, and the ☉ **by face**. All these are decided testimonies, that in the end the cause of truth shall triumph, and the reality and utility of the science be permanently established. ☿ in a fixed sign, and so powerfully aspected by ♄, ♃, ♂, (lord of the 4th, the house denoting the end of the matter) ♀ and ☽, is another strong evidence that AS-TROLOGY IS DESTINED TO FLOURISH WHILE THE WORLD ENDURES!

N.B. It is remarkable that ☿ had just passed the ⚹ of ♀, lady of the 2d (or house of property), from the 9th, and lady also of the 10th in the figure, and 9th (house of law) from the 9th. This shewed the benefit resulting to astrology, by the repeal of the law which taxed Almanacs, and which greatly injured the science. It is also remarkable, that ♃ was exactly passing over the 2d degree of ♊, the cusp of the 10th (house of honour) from the 9th, about the 7th

February, 1835, when the last sheet of the former edition of this work went through the press; and at the same time ♄ was in ♎ 23° 6', having just quitted the 9th house, where he had injured the interests of the science.

Fig. 25.

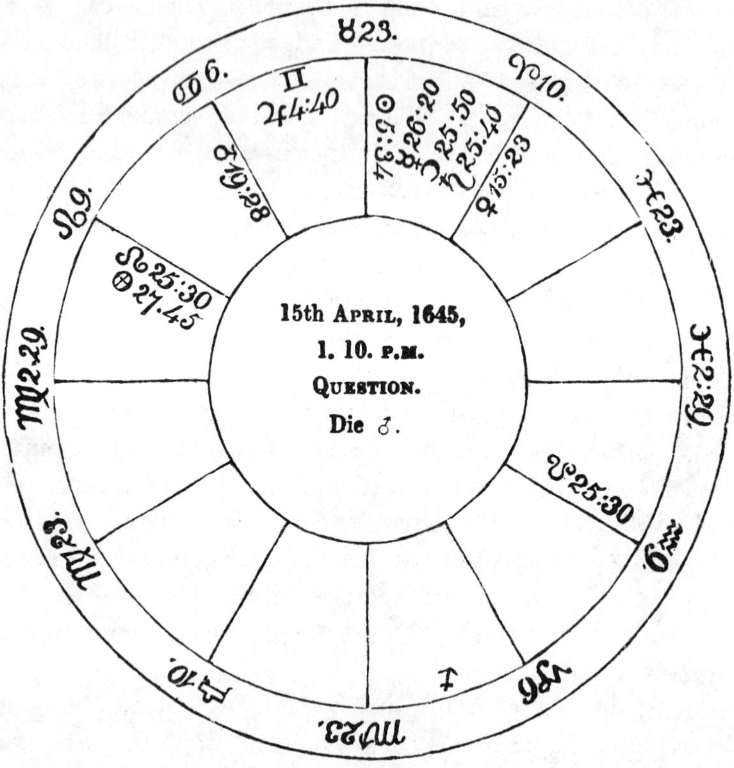

A WOMAN ASKS OF HER HUSBAND, WHO IS AT SEA; IF ALIVE? WHEN RETURN?

Judgment. — The lord of the ascendant, ☿, shews the querent. He being with ☽ and ♄ in ♈, which rules the face, she was extremely disfigured in the face by small pock, had weak eyes, &c., and was full of grief and sorrow for her husband, occasioned by ♄ afflicting ☿. She had also a lisp, and spoke ill; for ♄ in a bestial sign afflicting ☿, causes impediments in speech, especially if also ☽ be afflicted.

♃ signified the quesited, who being in the 10th, and lately separated from ⚹ of ♀, now in the 9th, and lady of the 3d, it shewed that he had been lately some voyage south-east. And as ♃ was no way afflicted and swift in motion, as well as angular, I judged the man was alive and in health. But as ☿ who disposes of ♃, is lord of his 8th (viz. the 2d house), and as ☽ is so exceedingly afflicted by ☿ and ♄, I said he had been in much danger and peril of his life by treachery and plots of his adversaries; for ☿ is lord of the 7th from his ascendant, and ♄ of his 12th.

Moreover, ♃ is accidentally but not essentially fortified, and is in his detriment, and near *Oculus* ♉, a violent fixed star; intimating that the man had endured many sudden and violent chances.

Finding ♃ more fortified than ☽, she almost entering ♉, a southern sign, and ♃ in Ⅱ, a western sign, and south quarter, I judged that the quesited was in the south-west of England, in some harbour, as ♃ was angular.

When She should hear of Him, or see Him?

The ☽ separates from ♄, and applies to ☿, the querent's significator; shewing that after much expectation, &c., she should hear of him, and in about three days, as ☽ is so near ☿, and in a moveable sign, (*and so she did*). But as ☿ is in a moveable sign, and ☽ afflicted by him and ♄, the news she heard was false, for she heard that he was in town; but it was not so. Considering that ☿ and ♃ hastened to a ♂ in Ⅱ, ☿ being therein very potent, and that this was about the 5th May following, I judged that she would about that time have certain news of her husband, if he did not then come home. The second week in May she did hear from him, but he did not come home till July. He had been several voyages in the west, was taken prisoner by the king's forces, and, at the time of the question, was in Barnstaple.

Fig. 26.

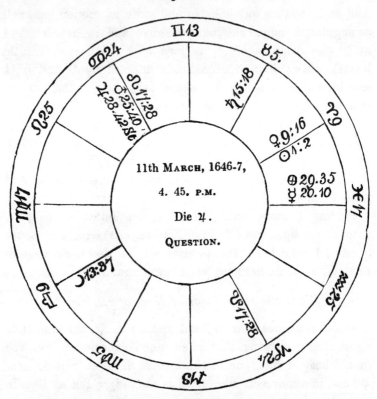

QUESTION.—WHETHER PRESBYTERY SHALL STAND?

Judgment.—The angles of the figure are not fixed, but the cusp of the 9th, from which this judgment is to be deduced, is ♉, a fixed and stable sign ; and we must also judge from

♄ therein in the terms of ♃, who is the general significator of religious matters.   ♃ is now stationary, and is leaving his exaltation, and is impeded by ♂ ; after leaving ♋, he enters the fixed sign ♌, and is in the terms of ♄. We find ♀, who rules the 9th, in her detriment, and in the 12th house from her own, the 9th.   She has twenty-one degrees to pass through in the 8th house before she get into her own sign ♉, and where she would be fixed.   But before she reaches ♉, she meets the □ of ♃, (shewing that the gentry of England will oppose it), and then of ♂, (lord of the ascendant of England, ♈), hence the whole commonalty of the kingdom will disapprove of it), and all three planets at the time of the aspect in the term of ♄.

There is not a single planet fixed, except ♄, nor essentially dignified, except ♃ ; the ☽ entering *via combusta*, ♂ and ♀ in their fall, ♀ in her detriment, and ♃ impeded by ♂. The ☽ separates from ♀ in the 8th, and then goes to □ of ♂ and ♃. From these configurations we shall form our judgment, THAT POSTERITY MAY SEE THAT THERE IS SOME VERITY IN ASTROLOGY.

The position of ♄ in the 9th, who is naturally of a severe, surly, rigid, and harsh temper, may argue that Presbytery will oe too strict, sullen, and dogged for the English constitutions ; little gentle or compliant with the nature of the community. And that there shall spring up among themselves many strange opinions and distractions even, concerning this very Presbytery ; that they shall grow excessively covetous, contentious, and desirous of more than belongs to them ; worldly, envious, and malicious one against the other ; that among them some juniors, represented by ♀,* shall be light in

---

* The reason of this is, that ♀ in the house of ♂ shews persons given to pleasure.

judgment, wavering, and decline the strictness of their discipline ; and that the elders, represented by ♄, shall not be respected on account of their excessive rigidness, nor shall their orthodox opinions be consented to.

Observe, that ♄ is peregrine, and supported by no favourable aspect of either fortune ; there is reception between ☽ and him, but no aspect : ☿, lord of the 10th, signifying authority, is fast separating from ♄, as if the gentry or supreme of the kingdom do already decline from the severity of the austere Presbyterian clergy, fearing thraldom rather than freedom to ensue from their power.

Three whole years from hence shall not pass, ere authority itself, or some Divine Providence, will inform our judgment with a way in discipline or government either nearer to the former purity of the primitive times, or better beloved of the whole kingdom of England ; or authority shall in this space of time moderate many things now strongly desired. For some time we shall not discover what shall be established, out all shall be even as when there was no king in Israel ; a confusion among us shall yet awhile remain. The soldiery then, or some men of fiery spirits, will arise, and keep back their contribution from the clergy, and will deny obedience or submission to this thing called Presbytery. It will then come to be handled by the magistracy, and the grand authority of the kingdom. Also, by the plurality of the clergy, or men of sound judgment, it will be contradicted, disputed against, disapproved ; and these shall make it manifest that this very Presbytery, now maintained, is not the same that the commonwealth of England will entertain as a standing rule to live under.

From what I find by this figure, I conclude *that Presbytery shall not stand here in England.**

---

* We have given this judgment at great length, as its complete fulfil-

Fig. 27.

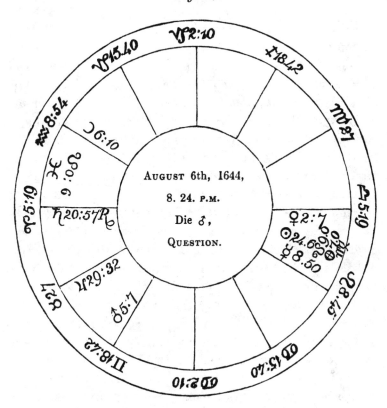

QUESTION.—WHETHER THE QUERENT SHOULD OBTAIN
THE PARSONAGE DESIRED?

Judgment.—In the first place, I find ♂ between ♃, lord
of the 9th, and ♂, lord of the ascendant, but separating.

ment, by the re-establishment of the Episcopal church, being a matter of
history, is a decisive proof of the truth of the science, and of its ability to
decide the most important questions both public and private The student
will readily perceive that the prediction of the downfall of the Presbyterian
church, as far as regards England, is made according to the strictest rules
of the doctrines laid down by our author.

2dly. Neither the ☽, nor lord of the ascendant, in the 9th. 3dly. There is no planet translating the light of ♃ to ♂. 4thly. There is no reception between ♃ and ♂. 5thly. ♄ is impedited in the ascendant, and by his presence afflicts the querent, and causes him to despair of success. 6thly, The ☽ separates from a △ of ♂, and applies to ☍ of ☿, lord of the 3d; which intimated that some neighbour of the querent, either with a letter, words, or cross information, would wholly destroy the querent's hopes; and that mercurial men, viz. scholars or divines, would be his enemies: and as I found ♀ in ♎, opposing the ascendant, I judged that some female would inform against him, or prejudice him in his suit.

From all this I persuaded him against proceeding any further in the matter; but the parson being covetous, would proceed, and did: and when he thought to have success, behold a scurvy letter, revealing some unpleasant truths concerning a female, dashed the good man's hopes, *et exit.*

The querent was ♄ and ♂ exactly, had wit and volubility of tongue; and as ☿ and ☽ were in ☍, he under the earth, she in the 12th, he could never discover which of his neighbours it was that thus injured him; nor would he ask me. If he had, it must have been ♄, lord of the 12th, viz. some farmer or dealer in cattle, a sickly, repining character, living north-east, about fifteen furlongs, from him.

CHAPTER XXXIII

THE TENTH HOUSE AND ITS QUESTIONS.—VIZ. OFFICE, DIGNITY, PREFERMENT, GOVERNMENT, TRADE, OR PROFESSION, &c.

THE usual significators are for the querent; and the 10th house, its lord, and the ☉, for the place, preferment, &c., inquired after.

If the lord of the ascendant or ☽ be both joined by good aspect to the ☉, or by ☌ or good aspect to the lord of the 10th, and this planet behold the 10th, or be therein, the querent shall gain the thing sought for, if he use proper endeavours.

Or if none of the significators be joined to the lord of the 10th, yet if the lord of the ascendant or ☽ be in the 10th, unafflicted, he shall gain it; and also, if the lord of the 10th be in the ascendant; and very easily, if the two lords be going to a good aspect.

The lord of the 10th joined to ♃ or ♀, and in the ascendant, he gains the office, &c., easily; if joined to ♄ or ♂, and either of them in the ascendant, but well dignified, it will be gained, but with difficulty.

The lord of the 10th receiving ☽, or the lord of the 1st, denotes success. And if there be translation of light from the lord of the ascendant to the lord of the 10th, it denotes that it will be gained by means of such a person as the planet translating the light describes.

If the lord of the ascendant apply to ☌ of the lord of the 10th, and there happen no previous abscission by any other planet before the ☌ be complete, the querent will gain his desire, but he must labour hard for it.

If any planet be in ⚹ or △ to the lord of the 10th, or the

☉, let the querent make application to such persons as they describe; for they may greatly befriend the querent by means of their influence.

If the promising planet in any case be in an angle, the matter will be readily completed; if in a succeedent, but slowly; and if in a cadent, the affair goes backward at times; but may, at last, be performed, if the planet be otherwise well dignified.

If an evil planet behold ☽ or the ascendant by ☐ or ☍, without reception mutual, he hinders the querent by means of that person who is to solicit the cause, &c. for him.

The best sign of all is, when the two lords be joined together, and the ☽ separate from the lord of the 10th, and apply to the lord of the ascendant; but it she apply to either, it is good.

If the lord of the ascendant apply to good aspect of the lord of the 4th, it denotes success; but if the lord of the 4th be joined also to the lord of the 10th, the matter shall be effected, but only after much delay and vexation.

Whether a Person shall remain in the Office he holds, or not?

Observe whether the lords of the 1st and 10th be in ♂, or any aspect; and note whether the more ponderous planet of the two be in any angle but the 4th; if so, he shall not be removed. But if the heavy planet be in the 4th, or approaching it from the 5th, he will leave his office. Yet, if there be reception between the two lords, he shall recover it again; and if the reception be mutual, he returns speedily, and with more honour than before.

You may judge the same if the lord of the ascendant be joined to a planet in the 3d or 9th, or to their lords, and after separation be joined to a planet in any angle, except the 4th.

But if the two lords (of the 1st and 10th) separate from each other, then he returns no more to his office, but loses it entirely.

If the lord of the ascendant, or 10th, or the ☽, are disposed of by any planet in an angle, (except the 4th), and that planet be slow in motion, he shall not be removed until that planet be combust or retrograde, or leave the sign he is in; but much about that time he will be removed, unless some powerful aspects intervene.

If the ☽ be joined to the lord of the 10th, and he in the 10th, the officer or governor, &c., shall not be removed.

If the lord of the ascendant, or ☽, be joined to the lord of the 10th, and he more weighty than either of them, and in the 10th, 11th, or 5th houses, free from impediment, though he behold not the 10th, the officer shall be transferred to some other place or office; but if he behold the 10th, he shall remain where he is.

If the ☽ be joined to any planet not in his essential dignities, though with reception, (unless it be ♃ or ♀ by ✶ or △), the querent shall leave his employment, office, &c. If either the lord of the 4th, or ☽, be in the 4th, and ♈, ♋, ♎, or ♑, be on its cusp, he will leave it; and this is more certain if ☽ be then joined to the lord of the 4th, and he peregrine. The same may be feared if ☽ be in ♑, and afflicted, or if she be void of course, and the lord of the ascendant be afflicted.

Whether a King expelled his Kingdom, or an Officer having lost his Place, shall be restored?

The ascendant and its lord are for the querent, be he king, duke, or gentleman, &c. Observe, that if the lord of the 1st be in ♂ with the lord of the 10th, and the more ponderous planet behold the 10th house, then the king or ruler, &c. shall be restored.

If the planet do not behold the 10th house, observe whether ☽ be joined to any planet in the ascendant, or 10th, which also will denote his restoration. If ☽ be in ♈, ♋, ♎, or ♑, he returns the sooner. If the lord of the 10th be joined to a planet in the 10th, or the ☉, (but not by ♂ to ☉), it denotes the same. The lord of the 10th a lighter planet than the lord of the 4th, and separated from him, argues the same.

If the lord of the 10th be lighter than the lord of the ascendant, and be joined to him, he shall return to his office, &c. So also, if ☽ be joined to the lord of the 10th, and behold the 10th house, unless disposed of by a peregrine planet under the earth.

The lord of the 1st aspected and received by a planet not afflicted, he returns; if not received, he will not.

The ☽ joined to a planet in the 9th, (it not being a fortune), shews that the king, &c. recedes from his kingdom, &c. If it be a fortune, and in ♈, ♉, ♋, ♌, ♎, ♑, ♒, he will return; and if it be in ♊, ♍, ♐, or ♓, he obtains office, power, &c. in another place.

The lord of the 10th, or ☽, being afflicted by ♂ of an infortune in any angle, the king, &c. shall never be restored.*

Of the Profession, Trade, or Employment of which any one is capable.

Consider the lords of the ascendant and 10th, and the

* This rule will answer the question of the re-election of any Member of Parliament for any place he has formerly represented; as well as the restoration of any minister, &c. to power, or the return of any individual to any office or employment.

cusps of those houses, the ☽, and also the places of ♂ **and** ♀ ; for these two planets are the significators of trade or employment. Observe which of the two (♂ or ♀) is the most powerful, and note the sign he may be in ; also consider the four angles, and any planet in them. If they be in fiery signs, or the majority of them, (viz. ♂, ♀, the planet in an angle, and the cusps of angles, especially the 10th), and ♂ have any dignity in the place of the lord of the 10th, or the ☉, say the querent will make a good tradesman, &c. in any business where *fire* is used, or of its nature ; and if the lord of the 10th be in his exaltation, he will do well in serving the king, or any high nobleman, &c.

If the significator of the employment, (usually the lord of the 10th, or a planet, especially ♂ or ♀, in the 10th, near the cusp), be in ♈, *weak*, he will make a good cattle-dealer, groom, farrier, grazier, &c. ; if *strong*, a coachmaker, veterinary surgeon, &c., where he has to do with horses or great cattle, in a respectable way.

If the significator be in ♉, then husbandry will best suit him ; or gardening, corn-dealing, grazing, &c. ; or if ♀ be the significator, such things as appertain to women's affairs, a soap-boiler, fuller of cloth, scourer, &c.

If the significator be in ♊, he will make a writer, clerk, bailiff, &c., or a surveyor, painter, astronomer, astrologer, geometer, schoolmaster, &c.

If he be in ♋, he will be fitted for a variety of occupations ; but he will be likely to go to sea, or to deal in liquids, such as wines, beer, &c. ; and he will be fond of political distinction.

If he be in ♌, he will make a good horse-jockey or coachman ; a smith, watchmaker, glassblower, huntsman, or cowdoctor ; or to do with any trade which uses fire.

If in ♍, he will make a good secretary to a person in

power, a schoolmaster, accountant, stationer, printer; he will be an excellent politician, or be a good astrologer, &c.

If in ♎, he will be a good poet or orator; singer, or musician; silkman, or linendraper, &c.

If in ♏, he may prove a good surgeon, apothecary, or physician; or a brazier, founder, brewer, vintner, waterman, or malster.

If in ♐, he will do very well to make a clergyman, to study chemistry, to buy and sell cattle, or to be a cook or butcher.

If he be in ♑, he will prove a good chandler, victualler, farrier, farmer, dealer in wool, lead, or farming commodities.

If he be in ♒, he will make an excellent ship-carpenter; and if any planet aspect him out of a watery sign, he may prove a good sailor or ship-master, or a painter and ornamenter of ships, or a merchant.

If he be in ♓, he makes a good jester, singer, player, &c., or brewer, or fishmonger; but generally the genius is dull, and the party given to sottishness.

As fiery signs shew workers at the fire, whether goldsmiths, &c., or bakers, &c., so earthy signs shew occupations connected with the earth, as potters, ditchers, brickmakers, gardeners, &c.; airy signs import singers, gamekeepers, actors, &c.; and watery, sailors, fishermen, watermen, laundresses waiters in taverns, &c.

Fig. 28.

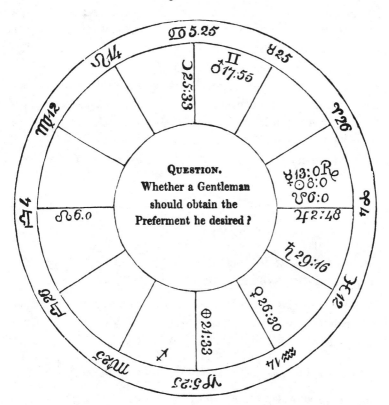

JUDGMENT ON THE ABOVE FIGURE.

The ascendant and ♀ are for the querent, the 10th house for the office or preferment he expected.

Finding ☽ strong in the 10th, was one argument that he should succeed. In the next place ☽, applied to △ of ♄, who has exaltation in the ascendant, and who receives ♀ by house, and is received by her again by exaltation. The ☽ applying to △ of the lord of the 4th (♄), argued that in the *end* he should obtain the office : but as ☉ was in the 7th in ☍ to the ascendant, with ☋, and was lord of the 11th, I judged that he employed as a friend a *solar* man, who was false, and did rather envy than feel friendly to him. I concluded, that with some difficulty he would obtain the office, notwithstanding the opposition a pretended friend offered; and so it came to pass within three weeks, and he then discovered that his friend was false; who had a great scar in his face, his hair of a blackish colour, shewn by ☉ being so near ☋. The separation of ☽ from □ of ☿, argued that he had delivered many petitions about it, hitherto without any success.

CHAPTER XXXIV.

OF THE ELEVENTH HOUSE, AND ITS QUESTIONS, VIZ. OF FRIENDS, HOPES, PROPERTY OF THE KING, &c.

IF the lord of this house be strong, fortunate, and well aspected, it foreshews the obtaining the thing hoped for; also the love and concord of friends, &c., if that be the question.

Whether any one shall have the Thing hoped for ?

Observe whether there be any good aspect or reception between the lord of the ascendant and 11th, or translation of light, or that the lord of the ascendant be in the 11th, or the lord of the 11th in the ascendant. All or any of these give reason to expect it. But if there be none of these, note the ☽, and if she be not well qualified with the lord of the 11th, nor any benefic, or ☋ in the 11th, judge the contrary.

The lord of the 11th in an angle, received by the lord of the ascendant, you may judge in the affirmative.

If the receiver of the ☽ be in a common sign, judge that he shall have but part of the thing hoped for. If in a moveable sign, he shall have but a little, a mere sign of the thing ; but if the receiver be in a fixed sign, he shall have the whole or complete thing. Yet, if the receiver of ☽ be unfortunate, the matter shall get some injury or hurt, &c. after he is in possession of it.

If there be mutual reception between the receiver of the ☽ and the ☽, he shall obtain the thing, and more than he looked for. And if the lord of the ascendant be also received, he shall obtain whatsoever he hoped for, that is feasible or possible.

If the querent's significator or ☽ apply to a fortune, not cadent, he may expect the thing desired.

N.B. if the querent *name* the thing hoped for, then judge of it by its own proper house, &c. ; as, if it be money the 2d, if it be children the 5th, &c.

Of the Sincerity of Friends.*

Good planets in the 11th, or ☊ there, or good aspects between the lords of the 11th and ascendant, denote the friends of the querent to be sincere ; and if they throw good aspects to the cusp of the 2d house, its lord, or ⊕, it denotes gain thereby. Evil planets, and evil aspects in like manner, denote false friends and losses. The lord of the 12th in the 11th, denotes a secret enemy under the guise of friendship. ☿ in the 11th, shews wavering, unsteady friends, unless he be in a fixed sign.

* These rules are not found in our author.

CHAPTER XXXV.

OF THE TWELFTH HOUSE, AND ITS QUESTIONS, VIZ. OF IM-
PRISONMENT, GREAT CATTLE, PRIVATE ENEMIES, BANISHED
MEN, &c.

IF a question be asked regarding secret enemies, who are not
named, observe the lord of the 12th, and planets therein, how
they aspect the lord of the ascendant, and from what houses,
&c.   If the lord of the 12th behold the lord of the ascendant
from the 6th, 8th, or 12th, or from the 4th, 7th. or 10th.
then there are some who privately wish ill to the querent.

To know who a private Enemy is.

Observe how the lord of the 12th is affected, and whether
he be with good or evil planets, and how he behold the lord
of the ascendant.   If he be in the 6th, or joined to its lord,
it shews the secret enemy is afflicted with some secret disease
or malady ; if the lord of the 6th be in the 12th, he is also
sickly.   If the lord of the 12th be in the 10th, or with its
lord, he is in favour with the king or some person of rank ;
and if he be strong, it will not be well for the querent to
meddle with him, especially if he aspect the lord of the ascendant or ☽ by □ or ☍.   If the lord of the 12th be with
the lord of the 4th or 8th, or in those houses, he is sickly or
near dying, or is repining, and very miserable.   Consider and
judge farther, as in former cases directed.

Whether a Person committed to Prison shall be discharged ?

First learn your ascendant exactly, by knowing what relation the quesited bears to the querent.   If ☽ be swift in
motion, it denotes a short stay in prison ; · if she aspect a

planet ın the 3d or 9th by ✶ or △, or by □, if with reception), he shall soon leave the prison; the same, if she aspect the lord of the 3d or 9th, and be not in an angle. As you judge by ☽, judge also by the lord of the ascendant. But these aspects must be by application.

The lords of the angles being in angles, is an ill testimony; and so much the worse if the lord of the ascendant be in the 4th, or if either he or the lord of the 12th dispose of each other. It is still worse if the lord of the ascendant be disposed of by a planet in an angle, especially a malefic; and worst of all if that malefic be in the 4th; and if he be the lord of the 8th, he may expect to die in prison. The ☽ disposed of by the lord of the 12th, or any malefic, is a sign of a long stay; and it is still worse, if her dispositor be in an angle, and especially in the 4th. If, however, the disposing planet be in a moveable sign, or swift in motion, it shortens the time; but a retrograde planet shews a long detention. If the lord of the ascendant, or ☽, be combust, it shews a long imprisonment.

The ☽ and ☿ in moveable signs, when ☿ is lord of the ascendant, shews speedy enlargement, especially if they aspect a fortune. If ♃ ascend, or be in ♂ with ☽, or ♀ be in the ascendant in ♂ with ☽, or ☿ be in ♂ with ♃, and aspect the ☽, or ☽ apply to ♃ or ♀, he will be discharged. The dispositor of ☽ with a fortune denotes the same.

Whether a Prisoner of War shall escape or be exchanged, &c.

If the lord of the ascendant separate from the lord of the 4th, and apply to a fortune; or if the lord of the ascendant be cadent, or leaving an angle, he shall escape. Also if he separate from combustion, or ☽ get from under the beams of ☉.

If at the time of being taken, or of the question, a fixed

sign ascend, or the ☽, or lord of the ascendant, be in a fixed sign, or in ♓, it denotes long imprisonment. The same if a fixed sign be on the 12th, or its lord be angular, and in a fixed sign. The ☽, or lord of the 1st, in ♉ or ♌, and in ☍ to ♂, shews danger of being slain by the sword, or by quarrelling; if in ☍ to ♄, it shews irons or severe punishments. (If it be an ordinary prisoner, these may shew sickness, want, and ill treatment, or accident, &c.)

An infortune in ♒, shews a long imprisonment. If the lord of the ascendant be in his fall or detriment, and the ☽ in ♒, the same; also the ☽, or lord of the 1st, in the 8th or 12th. If ☽ apply to a fortune, and the lord of the ascendant and the cusp of the ascendant be fortunate, it denotes liberation.

Note.— ♀ is better than ♃ in this question, especially if in aspect to ☿ or ☽. If ☽ be with ♄, and ♃ behold them by ☐, and ♂ by △, it denotes that, after a long confinement and suffering, he shall break prison and escape.

If a felon, &c., be imprisoned when ☉ ascends or rules the ascendant, he shall escape (the ancients declare) within a month; if ♀, within 40 days; if ☿, he has long imprisonment; if ☽, his state will depend on and change according as she has applications with other planets; if ♄, he has long confinement; if ♃, short; and if ♂, he shall be ill-treated, beaten, put into irons, &c.

Fig. 29.

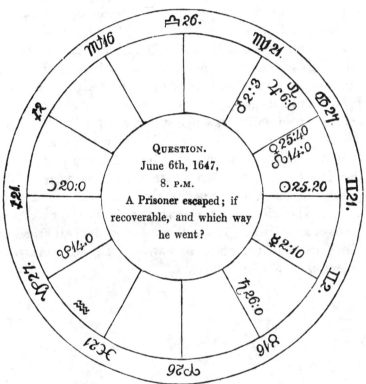

QUESTION.
June 6th, 1647,
8. P.M.
A Prisoner escaped; if
recoverable, and which way
he went?

JUDGMENT ON THE ABOVE QUESTION.

The prisoner's person is described by ♐, the cusp of the
12th, and by ♃ in ♌. The way he went, and intended to
go, is here shewn by the cusp of the 12th ♐, and by ♌,
where ♃ is, and by the sign and quarter of heaven wherein
we find ☽.

All of them considered, they signify, unanimously, that the
prisoner would go eastward, or full east, (*and so he did*).
The closeness of ☽ to the ascendant shewed that he was not

yet out of town, or, at least, that he would not be far from town. And as ♃ was in the 8th, I judged that he lay obscure for awhile, viz. a night; but that then he would go away, (*which he did*).

I confidently affirmed, that he should be taken again by some man of authority; for ☽ separated from △ of ♃, his significator, and applied to ☍ of ☉, both in angles. It never fails, but that if the ☽, or the significator of a fugitive, be afflicted by an unfortunate planet in the 7th house, that fugitive, or prisoner, is again taken. In the next place, I found ♃ and ☿ in ✶, ☿ in his own house, and applying to ♃; therefore I judged that the querent should have news of the prisoner by letter, or by some young man, within six or seven days, or when the significators came to ✶ aspect; which was six days afterwards. The truth is, that on the next Friday he had a letter to tell where he was, and on the Sunday he apprehended him by authority.

Fig. 30.

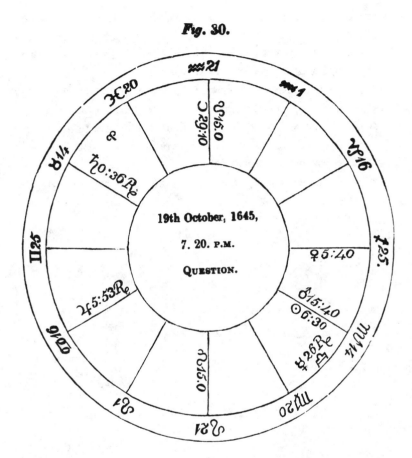

19th October, 1645,

7. 20. P.M.

QUESTION.

QUESTION.—A LADY ASKS WHEN HER HUSBAND, WHO IS
IMPRISONED, SHALL BE DELIVERED?

Judgment.—The lady's husband is signified by ♃ lord of
the 7th; he is in ♋ retrograde, and had the day before been
in △ to ☉. The ☽ applies to ✶ of ♄ retrograde, then to △
of ♃, with a most forcible reception. From hence I made
not many words, but told the lady she need not trouble herself to make friends to apply to his majesty, for that I was

assured that either he was, or would be, within three days, discharged from his imprisonment by means of a *solar* man, a commander who would release him and furnish him with what was necessary for his convenience.

The truth is, he was released, and the garrison where he was prisoner taken the day before the question was asked, (when ☉ was in △ to his significator), by an honest parliamentary colonel, who plentifully relieved him with money, and all convenient necessaries. ♃ in his exaltation, retrograde, *in a moveable sign,* and in △ to ☉, shewed short imprisonment; the more so, as ☉ is lord of the 4th, and the △ so perfect.

Fig. 31.

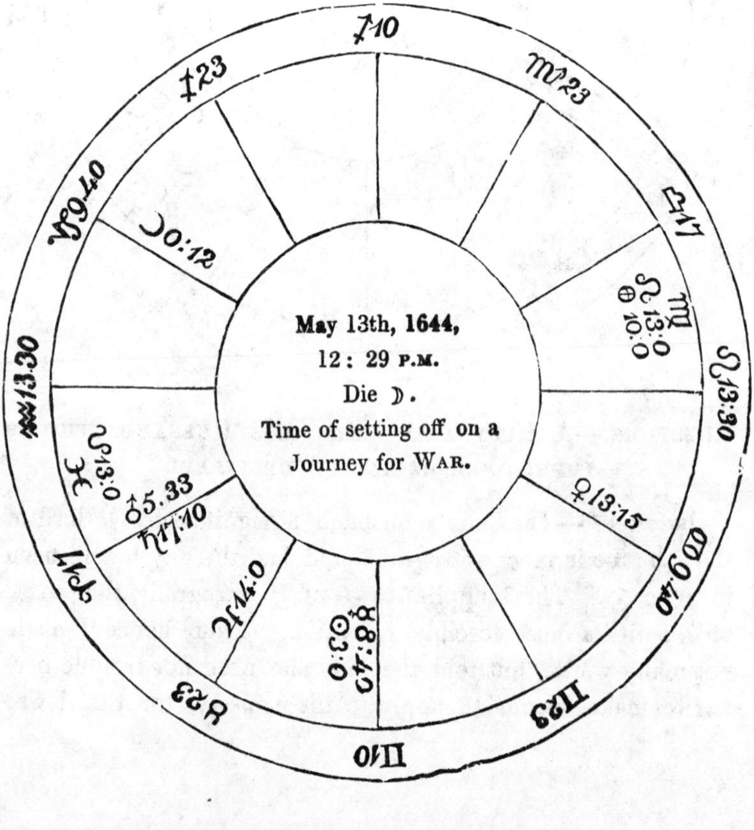

May 13th, **1644,**
12: 29 P.M.
Die ☽.
Time of setting off on a
Journey for WAR.

The Time of His Excellency ROBERT *Earl of* ESSEX *last setting forth into the West of England.*

Here ♒, the ascending sign, well represents his form of body, for it was comely, &c. ♄, ☿, and ♀, his mind, they having all dignities in the ascendant. ♃ has also much to do with his qualities, being lord of ♓, an intercepted sign in the ascendant.

I first considered that the ☽ separated from a △ of ♄, and applied to a □ of ♂, lord of his house of substance, assistants, &c., and also of the 9th, his house of journeys. This intimated he should have but slender success, and lose much by his present march. Finding ☍ in the ascendant, I judged that he would be betrayed in his councils; and seeing ♄, lord of his ascendant, peregrine, and in his fall in the 2d, the ☽ in her detriment, and ⊕ disposed of by ☿, lord of his 7th, signifying his enemies, and that ♃, the general significator of wealth, casts a □ to the ascending degree, I gave this judgment:—that his Excellency must expect no success from this employment; that he would have no honour by the journey; that he would be extremely crossed by men of great power here at London, who pretended great friendship to him; (♃, lord of the 10th and 11th, being in □ to his ascendant), that he would be betrayed wholly, and be in danger to lose all; that, in short, I was extremely sorry he had chosen so unlucky a time to set forth, &c. &c.

The issue was thus, (for I write to posterity): he prospered in the beginning, and daily men of good quality and authority jeered at me, and derided my prediction. I was quite content to be abused, provided that he might have had success. But observe, that on the 8th September following, came sad news, that on the 2d of September this worthy man had surrendered all his ammunition to his majesty, having only quarter for his soldiers; with some other articles, which were dishonourably performed, to the eternal shame of the royal party.

Fig. 32.

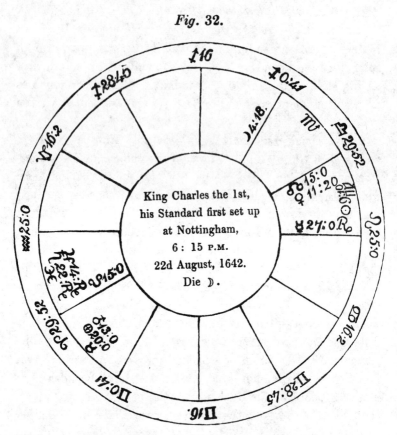

King Charles the 1st,
his Standard first set up
at Nottingham,
6 : 15 P.M.
22d August, 1642.
Die ☽.

JUDGMENT ON THE ABOVE FIGURE.

The above remarkable era in the life of King Charles the First affords a striking illustration of the truth of the rules of the science as laid down by our author.

The King is here represented by the ascendant, the ☽, and the lord of the ascendant, because *he* began the WAR, as it were, by this act.*

* "The King had lain most part at York, or rambled into some other counties near adjacent, until August, and done little to any purpose.

Here we find ♄ peregrine, and retrograde in the ascendant, a decided testimony of ill success; the ☋ is also ascending, a sign of evil and treachery to the King. His second house is afflicted by ♂, who is in his detriment, and disposed of by ☿, the significator of his adversaries. The King's ⊕ is afflicted by ♂ of ♂, and by □ of ☿, having only the ⚹ of ♃, who is retrograde, and in ☍ to ☉, the joint significator of his foes. Then we find the ascendant in ☍ to ☿, the significator of the enemy; and also the ☽ in □ to the ☉, cadent and peregrine. Each one of his significators is afflicted, and ♃, the lord of the 11th, his house of hopes, and of the 10th, the house of honour, and dispositor of ☽, is afflicted by the ☍ of ☉, by being retrograde, and by being within orbs of a ♂ of ♄, lord of the 12th, the house of disgrace and misfortune.

Now as regards the adversary, we find ☉ and ☿ both ruling the 7th, and placed therein in mutual reception, ☉ being in the house of ☿, and ☿ in the house of ☉. The ☋ is also in the 7th, and ♀ lady of their 2d, or house of substance and means, assistants, &c., is strong in her own house ♎, angular, and no way afflicted.

The general significator of *war*, ♂, is in his detriment, and is disposed of by ♀, a benefic in the 7th. The lord of the adversaries 10th, or house of honour, is ☿, and he is in reception mutual with the ☉, angular, and no way impedited,

For the several counties were generally nothing inclinable to his purpose; in most whereof, and in every county he came in, he rather received petty affronts than support. Yet at last he came to Nottingham, and there set up his STANDARD, (with a full resolution for war), the 22d August, 1642, under this constellation; having some few horse with him, but in great expectation of more aid from the Welsh, &c., whom he thought most doted on monarchy."—*Monarchy or no Monarchy*, p. 112.

except being retrograde; and he is in the term of ♂, and ♂ is in his term; another mutual reception.

All these things were decided testimonies that his Majesty should fail in all his endeavours, and eventually be ruined. The lord of the 12th being also lord of the ascendant, shewed that he had been himself his greatest enemy, and the cause of his misfortunes. The lord of the 12th, (house of imprisonment) being in the ascendant, shewed that he should be imprisoned; the more so from his being in ♓. And history tells us how truly the "signs of heaven" spoke on this occasion; for "all the remainder of his life, after this August 22d, 1642, was a mere labyrinth of sorrow; a continued and daily misfortune."

The student will perceive that his death was plainly foreshewn by the ☽ applying to ⚹ of ♀, lady of the 8th, or house of death, from signs of long ascension; in which a ⚹, it is said, has the same effect as a □ in other signs. The ☽ moreover is with *Antares*, a violent fixed star, (now in about 7° 30′ ♐) which is said to denote a *violent death;* which is farther shewn by the □ of ☽ to ☉, the latter being in an angle. The lord of the 4th being in ☍ to the ascendant, was also a token of his death; and perhaps ♏ being in the 8th, and ♂, its ruler, approaching *Caput Algol*, which is said to denote *beheading*, might intimate that; but all such minute points must be left to posterity to decide, when the science will be better understood.

The hour of the King's death was 4h. 4m. P.M., 30th January, 1648-9, when the heavens were as represented in the following figure. The student will see that ♄, lord of the ascendant in this figure, had exactly gained the □ aspect of the ☉ at that time, being in ♊ 9° 25′; and that ☉ was just transiting the ascendant of this figure; and that the cusp of the 10th (which denoted the King) is there the place of ♄

in this figure. The ☽ is in the 29th degree of ♑, a ☐ aspect to the cusp of the 8th, in this also ; and ♃, part lord of the ascendant here, is in ♂ with the place of ♀, lady of the 8th. All these coincidences must be considered by the genuine searcher after truth as strong evidences of the truth of planetary influence, as evinced in *horary astrology*. The consequences and final result of the mad attempt of this unhappy King to make war upon the nation were here plainly depicted ; and it is for the opponents of astrology to shew, that these things are merely accidental coincidence, or the fruit of *chance*, the deity they so fondly worship.

Fig. 33

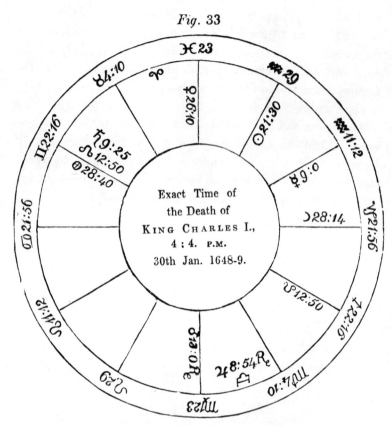

OBSERVATIONS ON THE ABOVE FIGURE.

King Charles I. was born at *Dumfernline*, in Scotland, about fifteen miles from Edinburgh, on the 19th November, 1600; at which time ☉ was in 9° of ♐. Hence, at the period of his death, ♄ was exactly in ☍ to the place of ☉ at his birth, and ♂ nearly in □ to that place.

The ☍ of ♄ to ☉ will ever be found to bring trouble, sorrow, disgrace, and often death, to the native. It will be seen that at the time of the King's setting up his standard at **Nottingham**, the ☉ was exactly transiting the □ of his own place at birth ; a decided cause of failure, discredit, &c. But although we mention these circumstances, we would remind the student that such transits can have but little effect unless evil directions be operating at the time ; which, there can be no doubt, was the case in the nativity of the unfortunate and ill-advised King Charles the First.

If we regard this figure as that of the exact commencement of the COMMONWEALTH, we shall find that it will point out the result of that change in the government, as it would of any other thing which might then have commenced.

The ☽ is lady of the ascendant, and she is in her detriment and peregrine ; hence the commonwealth was not *successful;* her being in a moveable sign, and moveable signs on the ascendant and 7th, and such signs intercepted in the other two angles, shewed that it would not be *permanent.* The lord of the 4th being also lord of the 12th, shewed that it would come to an end by means of the exertions of its *secret* enemies ; and as ♄ is also lord of the 7th, and rules the ☽, it shewed that its *enemies* would overthrow it at length. The end of it was clearly pointed out to be when ☽ came to ♂ of the lord of the 4th, ☿, and to the △ in signs of short ascension of the lord of the 8th, ♄, who is very powerful, as being in reception with ☿, and △ with ♃, and ruling both ☉ and ☽, and being also with ☋. If we calculate from the place of the ☽ to the △ of ♄, we shall find eleven degrees and a quarter, which would be equivalent to *eleven years and a quarter;* which, it is well known, was THE EXACT DURATION OF THE COMMONWEALEH.

APHORISMS, BY ZADKIEL.

1st. In all cases of hearing rumours or reports, receiving letters or messages, &c., if you erect a figure for the exact minute of hearing or reading the news, &c., the lord of the 3d in good aspect with the cusp of the 7th, or a planet in the 7th, shews that the news is *true*, and that you are not deceived; if he be in evil aspect, either semi-square, □, sesquiquadrate, or ☍, the news is *false*.

2d. Whenever any person applies to another on any business whatever, either by letter, message, or personally, the 1st house represents him who is the first mover in the matter, who either goes or sends to the other, and the 7th represents the person applied to. Therefore, when a person reads a report in a newspaper, or elsewhere, the 7th shews that person, because the report, &c. comes. as it were, to him.

3d. If you apply to a person for goods of any kind, and they are promised, the application of the lord of the 2d to the lord of the 8th, or a planet therein, shews the time when they will be received.

4th. If you receive a bill of exchange, the figure for that time will shew whether it will be paid. If ⊕ receive a good aspect of the lord of the 1st, it will be paid; but if ⊕ receive any evil aspect of the lord of the 1st, it will not be paid. *Probatum est.*

The ⊕ always denotes *money*, whether in cash or bills; but *property*, whether in goods or lands, houses, &c., is always shewn by the lord of the 2d, or a planet therein.

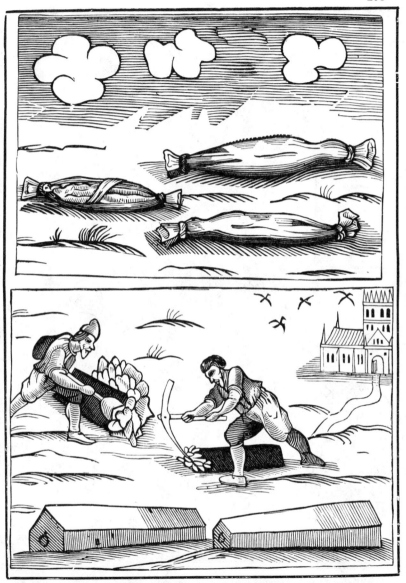

Fac-Simile *of the* Hieroglyphic *of the* GREAT PLAGUE *in* 1665, *published by* W. LILLY, *in the* Year 1651.

FAC-SIMILE *of the* ASTROLOGICAL HIEROGLYPHIC *of the* GREAT FIRE *in*
LONDON, SEPTEMBER 2d, 1666, *published by* W. LILLY, *in the* YEAR
1651.

APPENDIX.

EXPLANATION OF THE HIEROGLYPHICS.

The first of these curious cuts, which have been exactly copied from our author's tract, entitled " *Monarchy or no Monarchy in England,*" is intended to represent a great mortality, in which the vast number of deaths should so far exceed the supply of coffins, that the dead must needs be buried in their shrouds, or merely stitched up in sheets, &c., as therein rudely represented.—The second cut is an *Astrological* Hieroglyphic, as may be understood by the horoscope being introduced therein ; and the two children or twins are intended to represent the sign *Gemini*, which, in astrology, is known to rule London ; and the twins are, therefore, intended to denote that city. Their falling headlong into the fire, describes the extensive injury to be done to London by that element fifteen years afterwards. The manner in which this was foreseen by the author has been explained in our remarks on his life.

These two Hieroglyphics, even if there had been only these, whereas there were several others equally pointing out future events, published with them, would ever remain undeniable monuments of our author's skill, and of the substantial truth of the science of astro-ogy.

DESCRIPTION OF PERSONS ACCORDING AS THE SIGNIFICATOR MAY BE FOUND IN EACH OF THE TWELVE SIGNS.

SATURN *in the Twelve Signs.*

♄ *in* ♈

Gives a ruddy complexion, a spare, rawboned person, full-faced, dark hair, not much beard, addicted to boasting, resolute, quarrelsome, and very ill-natured.

♄ *in* ♉

Gives a person in no wise comely, but a heavy, lumpish, awkward appearance, dark hair, middle stature, not well made, rough in carriage, sordid, vicious, &c.

♄ *in* ♊

Represents a person of rather tall stature, dark, sanguine complexion, oval visage, dark brown or black hair, ingenious but unpolished, perverse, and generally unfortunate in most of his undertakings.

♄ *in* ♋

Denotes a person of middle stature, rather short than tall, sickly and feeble, meagre face, dark hair, languid eyes; the body sometimes crooked; jealous, malicious, and deceitful in his dealings.

♄ *in* ♌

Gives a person of moderate large stature, broad, round shoulders, wide chest, lightish hair, large boned, surly aspect, eyes sunk, apt to stoop. Qualities tolerably good, generous but passionate; not over valiant or courageous when put to the test.

♄ *in* ♍

Represents a person of a tall, spare body, swarthy, dark or black hair, and it plentiful; a long head, solid countenance; generally unfortunate; inclined to melancholy, retaining anger; a projector of many curious matters to little purpose; studious, subtle, reserved; inclined to pilfering and indirect dealings.

♄ *in* ♎

Describes a person above the middle stature, comely brown hair, oval face, large nose and forehead, clear complexion; one opinionated of himself, prodigal of expense. They are given to debate and controversy, and seldom leave any wealth at their death.

♄ *in* ♏

Represents a person of a mean stature, squat, thick, trussed body, broad shoulders, black or dark hair, which is usually short and thick; quarrelsome, mischievous; one who will undertake violent and dangerous actions, though to his own detriment.

♄ *in* ♐

Gives a large body, brown hair, good make, tolerable complexion; obliging disposition, not covetous, moderately frugal, rarely profuse, but somewhat choleric. One who will not bear an affront, yet willing to do good to all; a lover of his friend, and merciful to an enemy.

♄ *in* ♑

Personates a lean, raw-boned body, dark or black hair, middle stature, dark complexion, small leering eyes, long visage, and a stooping awkward posture in walking. One who is peevish, discontented, melancholy, covetous, of few words, fearful, retains anger, and is of great gravity.

♄ *in* ♒

Gives a reasonable full-bodied person, a large head and face, rather inclined to corpulency, middle stature, sad brown hair, a clear complexion, a sober, graceful deportment. Affable, courteous disposition; of an excellent, searching fancy, and generally very proficient in what they undertake in arts or sciences; a person of a pregnant genius, yet subject to be conceited.

♄ *in* ♓

Describes a middle-statured person, pale complexion, sad or dark black hair, a large head and full eye; sometimes the teeth are distorted. A person not very comely. Active to do mischief, malicious and given to contention and dissimulation. An uncertain, fickle person in every thing; though often presenting a good outside, yet fraudulent and deceitful in the end. They are not loquacious, but deliberative, and do evil with malice aforethought. They are said to improve as they grow aged.

N.B. ♄ always gives bad teeth; and in this sign they are generally discoloured and rotten.

JUPITER *in the Twelve Signs.*

♃ *in* ♈

Describes a middle stature, but not stout, rather lean than corpulent, a quick and penetrating eye, a high nose, oval visage, with generally pimples or a peculiar redness in the face. They are of a free, noble, and generous disposition; very obliging, polite, and complaisant, especially to their friends.

♃ *in* ♉

Gives a middle stature, stout, well-set body, but, though

compact, not handsome; hair brown, rough, and curling. Complexion swarthy; and frequently the skin looks shining or oily. The disposition reasonably good, judgment sound, deportment good, behaviour free and charitable; fond of the female sex, and very humane and compassionate to the distressed.

♃ *in* ♊

Represents a well-made, compact body, plump, yet above the middle stature; sanguine complexion, though rather dusky; brown hair, and full, expressive eyes. The deportment graceful, affable, courteous, gentle, mild, obliging, and good-natured. An admirer of the female sex, and a lover of learning. But if ♃ be near *Occulus Taurus*, (in ♊ 6° 15', with 2° 36' south lat.) he will be addicted to women. And if near *Aldebaran*, (in ♊ 7° 30', with 5° 29' south lat.) he will be rash and unstable, inimical to himself, and disagreeable to others. If with the *Bull's North Horn*, in ♊ 20° 20', with 5° 22' north lat., he will be rash and violent.

♃ *in* ♋

Gives a person of middle stature, a pale, sickly, and unwholesome complexion; oval face; hair, dark brown; body rather plump, but disproportioned. A busy, loquacious character, very conceited, and apt to intermeddle with other people's concerns. A lover of women, and fond of the water, whereon he is usually fortunate. Unless ♂ throw a good aspect to ♃, he is not courageous.

♃ *in* ♌

Represents a strong, and well-proportioned, tall body; the hair is a light or yellowish brown, and curling; complexion, ruddy; eye, full and fiery; person, rather handsome. The disposition is noble-minded, courageous, and magnanimous, but lofty, and proud, and ambitious; one who delights in warlike actions, is a terror to his enemies, and who scorns to bend to them; fond of contending for honours, &c., and full of daring and enterprise.

♃ in ♍

Gives a person of a reasonably full stature, well built, and what may be termed handsome; sad brown or black hair, ruddy complexion, but not clear or fair. One who is choleric, and given to boasting; studious, yet covetous, and by his rashness often meeting serious losses; he is not easily imposed or wrought upon by any person.

♃ in ♎

Renders the body complete and elegant, a handsome form, and inviting face; upright, tall stature, rather slender; clear complexion, a full eye, oval face, light brown hair, subject to have pimples or a rash in the face. Disposition and temper, mild; behaviour, winning, and obliging to all; partial to exercise and recreation; much esteemed, and honoured.

♃ in ♏

Gives a middle stature, stout, compact body; dark, coarse hair, fleshy and full face; muddy, dull complexion. Manners, proud and lofty; one who is ambitious, and desires to bear rule over his equals, resolute, covetous, ill-natured, and selfish; very subtle and crafty, therefore to be very warily dealt with

♃ in ♐

Gives a fine, tall, upright body, good form and make, oval face, ruddy complexion, brown chestnut-coloured hair, full beard and whiskers; but the hair falls off early in life, especially about the temples; a good eye, and much expression

m the face. The mind is just and noble ; disposition courteous, humane, affable, and agreeable ; manners, polite and
accomplished. One fond of horses and hunting.

♃ in ♑

Describes a small stature, pale complexion, thin face, little
head, not much beard, weakly person, dark brown hair, said
to be darker than the beard. The mind is ingenious, but
peevish, inactive, helpless, indolent.

♃ in ♒

Personates a middle stature, well set, brown hair, clear
complexion, rather corpulent, compact make ; and one of a
cheerful, obliging disposition, hurtful to none ; well conducted, and moderate in recreations ; just and merciful, good-
humoured, industrious, communicative, inclined to be scientific, and but little given to extravagance.

♃ in ♓

Describes a person of middle stature, obscure complexion,
plump, fleshy body, lightish-brown hair. Disposition harmless, studious, and possessed of excellent talents and good
acquirements ; friendly, kind, and inoffensive. They delight
in good company, and to be upon the water, where if ☽
throw not an evil aspect to ♃, they are found to be fortunate.

N.B. ♃ usually gives good teeth, and frequently an appa-
rent mark in the fore-teeth. In an airy sign, he gives broad
fore-teeth ; in a fiery sign, crooked ; in earthy they are discoloured ; and in a watery sign, the teeth decay suddenly,
and grow black and rotten, especially if he be in ♂ with ☋,
or in any evil aspect of ♄ or ♂, If he be in a watery sign,
in □, or ☍, ☿, the party has some defect in his delivery or
speech. ♃ in an airy sign, the body is more strong ˄nd cor-

pulent; in a fiery sign more square made, and strong; in an earthy, a well-composed body, and in a watery, more fat and comely.

MARS *in the Twelve Signs.*

♂ *in* ♈

Represents a middle-statured person, well-set, large boned; swarthy complexion, light hair, and curling, frequently red; austere countenance, and, if ♂ be oriental, ruddy, and smooth; bold and undaunted, confident, choleric, and proud; fond of war and dispute; one who often gains by those means

♂ *in* ♉

Gives a middle stature, well set, rather short; dusky complexion, dark or black hair, which is rough and coarse; broad face, wide mouth; he will generally have some scar or other mark in the face, which is often ruddy, but never fair. He is gluttonous, debauched, given to drinking and wenching; also a gambler, and very quarrelsome, treacherous, and ill-natured. He is generally unfortunate, but, if ♂ be near the Pleiades, remarkably so.

♂ *in* ♊

Gives a tall person, with black or dark brown hair, (though if ♂ be in the first seven degrees of ♊, the terms of ☿, it will be light), sanguine complexion, and well proportioned body. He is restless and unsettled, but ingenious; unfortunate in most things, living in a mean way, generally shifting here and there, leaving his debts unpaid, and exercising his wits for a livelihood; in short, a *chevalier d'industrie,* or mere swindler. But good aspects of ☉, ♃, or ♀, will mitigate this evil judgment.

♂ in ♋

Describes a short figure, and a bad complexion, **without** much hair, and it brown; the body is generally ill made, and crooked. The temper is sour and bad; one who is given to sottishness; a mean, servile, unfortunate creature; usually he is employed in some low business, being incapable of better.

♂ in ♌

Shews a well-proportioned body, rather tall; light brown hair, oval face, sanguine or sunburnt complexion, large eyes, stout limbs, and a brisk, cheerful aspect. A lover of women, given to boasting; fond of robust sports, as hunting, riding, shooting, &c., and ready for warlike occupation at any time. He dresses well, and is a favourite with the ladies, but it is generally to his prejudice.

♂ in ♍

Produces a middle-sized body, and well made and proportioned; black hair or very dark brown; the first seven degrees give lighter hair than the rest of the sign, being the terms of ☿; the complexion is swarthy or darkish, and generally some scar, marks, or blemish in the face. A hasty, proud, revengeful, and spiteful mind; one who retains an injury, is hard to please, conceited, and generally very unfortunate in all he undertakes.

♂ in ♎

Gives a neat made, rather tall person; his face oval; complexion sanguine, and hair light brown, and soft, but, if in the last six degrees, his own term, it is more wiry and reddish. The disposition is brisk and cheerful, but fond of boasting, and very conceited; one who is fond of dress, effeminate in appearance, much attached to women, by whom he is also much beloved, and frequently ruined.

♂ *in* ♏

Produces a well-set form of middle stature, rather corpulent; swarthy complexion, black curling hair, broad and plain face. The temper is very unsociable, and rash; they are generally revengeful, ungrateful, quarrelsome, and wicked; yet of good genius and ready apprehension, excelling in mystery, &c.

♂ *in* ♐

Denotes a tall person, with a well-proportioned body, compact and well-made, sanguine complexion, oval visage; a quick, penetrating eye; the mind is cheerful, merry, and jovial; but disposition hasty and passionate, high-minded, and lofty, courageous, loquacious, and fond of applause; on the whole, a good character.

♂ *in* ♑

Represents a mean or small stature, thin, lean body, little head, thin face, bad complexion, being sallow and obscure; black, lank hair. An ingenious mind, witty, shrewd, and penetrating; generally fortunate, and successful in his undertakings.

♂ *in* ♒

Gives a well-composed body, rather corpulent, and inclined to be tall (though frequently not above the middle size), fair or clear complexion; sandy hair; a turbulent disposition, and addicted to controversy, &c.; not very fortunate in general.

♂ *in* ♓

Represents a mean stature, rather short and fleshy; a bad complexion, far from handsome; a debauched look; light brown hair; sottish and stupid; a great lover of women (if in his own terms or those of ☿, sly and artful), deceitful, idle, and worthless; not friendly to any one.

N.B. If ♂ be in ☌, □, or ☍ of ♄, or with ☊, the disposition is very evil, especially if they be in angles; when the person he describes is very fierce and violent. He is the giver of courage and resolution, which, if he be weak and afflicted, are very deficient. If ♂ be in fiery signs, he is hasty and choleric; and there is generally observed to be a falling in of the cheeks, and a lightness of feature, with an angry look; in earthy signs, a sullen, dogged temper; in airy signs, more free and obliging; in watery, sottish, dull, and stupid, unless he be well aspected by ♃, ☉, or ☽.

The Sun *in the Twelve Signs.*

☉ *in* ♈

Describes a good stature, strong and well-made; a good complexion, though not very clear; light hair, flaxen or yellowish, and large eyes. The man is noble, valiant, and courageous; delighting in warlike actions and enterprise; he gains victory, is famous, and a terror to his enemies, &c.

☉ *in* ♉

Gives a short, well set, rather ugly person; dusky complexion, brown hair, large broad face, wide mouth, and great nose. A confident, proud, and bold man, fond of opposition, proud of his physical strength, and one who generally is victorious.

☉ *in* ♊

Represents a well-proportioned body, above the middle stature, sanguine complexion, brown hair. He is affable, courteous, and kind; not very fortunate, as he is so meek and mild-tempered, that he is contr lled and imr osed on by others.

☉ *in* ♋

Gives a mean, ill-formed body, deformed in the face, with
a very unhealthy aspect ; the hair brown. A harmless, cheerful person, but indolent, and not fond of employment ; one
who spends his time in sports and pastimes, dancing, &c.,
and is greatly addicted to women.

☉ *in* ♌

Gives a strong, well-proportioned body, and a very portly
person ; sanguine complexion, light brown or yellowish hair,
a full face, and large staring eyes, very prominent ; there is
generally a mark or scar on the face.　A very just, upright,
and honourable man, who scorns to do any meanness ; punc-
tual, faithful to his friends, and magnanimous even to his
enemies ; in short, a right royal disposition ; a very ambitious man withal, fond of rule and authority, and given to
war and dominion, conquest, &c.

☉ *in* ♍

Makes a person something tall of stature, and slender, but
very well proportioned, good complexion, dark hair, and
much of it, but not black ; the mind ingenious, cheerful, and
fond of honest recreations, especially agreeable, convivial
parties, &c.

☉ *in* ♎

Produces an upright, tall, and slender body, full eyes, oval
face, ruddy complexion, light hair, and frequently a rash or
pimples in the face.　The mind is honourable, and disposition good ; but the party is always unfortunate, especially in
all matters of war or ambition.

☉ *in* ♏

Gives a remarkably square-built, full, fleshy person, broad
face, cloudy complexion, dun or sunburnt ; brown hair. The

mind ingenious, but the temper rugged and overbearing; manners disagreeable, disposition ambitious; one who will not admit of an equal; they are fortunate upon the seas, or as surgeons, physicians, &c.

⊙ in ♐

Makes a tall, handsome, well-proportioned body, oval face, sanguine complexion, or rather olive-brown or sun-burnt; light brown hair, but in the first eight degrees of the sign it is darker; one who is very lofty and proud-spirited, aiming at great things, austere and severe, and one who performs some honourable exploits, and often becomes ennobled, or receives titles, honorary distinctions, &c.

⊙ in ♑

Represents a mean stature, ill-made, spare, thin body, oval face, sickly complexion; brown, soft hair, not curling, and if in the first six degrees of the sign, it is light brown; the party is just and honourable in his principles, a tolerably fair temper and gains love and friendship by his agreeable conversation; one who is very hasty at times, and much given to woman.

⊙ in ♒

Describes a person of middle stature, well-made, corpulent body, round full face, clear complexion, and light brown hair (in the term of ♄ it is dark brown). The disposition tolerably good, free from malice or deceit, but yet vain, proud, desirous of bearing rule, and ostentatious.

⊙ in ♓

Gives a stature rather short, body plump and fleshy, a round full face, and indifferent complexion; light brown hair; in the first eight degrees of the sign it is flaxen, and

X

very soft : the party is extremely partial to female society,
very effeminate, fond of pleasures, &c., and though harmless
to others, ruins himself by extravagance, debauchery, gaming,
intemperance, feasting, &c.

Venus *in the Twelve Signs.*

♀ *in* ♈

Describes a middle stature, rather tall and slender, light
hair, (if in the term of ♃, dark), good complexion, a pensive
aspect, and usually a mark or scar in the face, (often marked
more or less with small-pox, according as ♀ may be afflicted
or not). They are generally unfortunate both to themselves
and others, unless ♀ have a ✳ or △ of ♃.

♀ in ♉

Gives a handsome person, though the stature is not great
the body is extremely well made, plump, but not gross ; and
if ♀ be well aspected, they are very handsome ; the complexion is ruddy, but not fair ; generally females are handsome brunettes, and have much the form and figure of the
Venus de Medicis. The hair is generally brown, and, if ♀
be in her own term, it is very soft and luxuriant ; if in the
term of ♃, it is a shining black. The eyes are generally
black, and very expressive. The temper is mild and winning,
the disposition kind, humane, obliging, &c. They generally
gain much respect from those with whom they converse, and
are fortunate.

♀ *in* ♊

Gives one above the middle height, slender, upright, and
well-made body. The complexion clear and fair, with soft
brown hair ; frequently brown or hazel eyes. They are good-
humoured, loving, liberal, just and charitable ; and rarely
guilty of any thing dishonourable.

♀ *in* ♋

Represents a short person, a fleshy body, round, pale, and sickly face, with light hair; and if the ☽ be with ♀, and they in the ascendant, the face will be quite white and wan, and the hair very light coloured; but if ♀ be in the term of ♂, the hair may be reddish, and a tinge of colour appear in the cheeks. They have generally small grey or greenish eyes. The disposition is idle and dull; they are fond of low company and vicious pleasures and pursuits; if it be a female of the poorer classes, she is a frequenter of spirit shops, &c. They are very fickle and timid, put the best side outwards, and seem to be in earnest when they are not; ever mutable and inconstant.

♀ *in* ♌

Gives a person reasonably tall of stature, well-composed body, clear complexion, round face, full eye, freckled and fair skin, hair reddish, or if in the term of ♀, it may be flaxen. They are petulant and passionate, soon angry, and soon pleased again; free, generous, sociable, and good-humoured, but rather proud, and frequently indisposed, though not seriously.

♀ *in* ♍

Shews a tall, well-proportioned figure, oval face, dark hair, or, if in her own term, sad brown, and a dusky complexion. They are ingenious, eloquent, active, and clever, of an aspiring turn, but rarely successful in their pursuits; generally unfortunate.

♀ *in* ♎

Describes an upright, tall, elegant person, extremely well made, with a genteel carriage. The face is oval, and rather beautiful, having pleasing smiles and beautiful dimples; but they are frequently freckled; the hair is brown and soft, bu rather grows long than plentiful. They are kind, affectionate, and very obliging; and generally well-beloved by all with whom they have any dealings. If ♀ be in the ascendant, and there be no afflicting aspects, but ♃ cast a △ from ♒, the party, if a female, will be a perfect beauty.

♀ *in* ♏

Denotes a short, stout, well-set, corpulent body, broad face and dusky complexion, and dark or black hair, (unless ♀ be in the terms of ♂ or ♀); one who has nothing very pleasant in the countenance. They are envious, debauched, and vicious; given to contention; and if ♀ be afflicted by ♄ or ♂, to very disgraceful actions; and if both ♄ and ♂ afflict, and there be no assistance by ☉ or ♃, they are possessed of very evil propensities.

♀ *in* ♐

Represents a person rather tall than otherwise, well made, clear or sanguine complexion, fair, oval face, and brown hair. They are generous, spirited, aiming at no mean things, rather proud, passionate, yet, in general, good-tempered, kind, and inoffensive. They delight in innocent recreations, and are, in short, very obliging fortunate persons.

♀ *in* ♑

Describes a small-sized person, short stature, a pale face, thin and sickly; dark hair, (but if ♀ be in her own term, a sad-brown). They are generally persons who love their belly, fond of enjoyment, not fortunate, subject to sudden changes in life and strange catastrophes.

♀ *in* ♒

Gives a handsome, well-formed person, clear complexion, rather corpulent or large body, brown hair, if she be in her own term, flaxen. A good disposition, quiet, affable, courteous, not at all inclined to vicious actions, peaceable, obliging to all, fortunate in his affairs, and respected by his friends and acquaintance in general.

♀ in ♓

Personates a middle stature, a fleshy plump body, a round full face, with a dimple in the chin, good complexion, between pale and ruddy. Good-humoured, just, kind, mild and peaceable, ingenious, but somewhat unstable, yet moderately fortunate in the world.

MERCURY in the Twelve Signs.

☿ in ♈

Gives a mean stature, spare and thin body, oval face, light brown and curling hair, dull complexion. A mind rather ill-disposed, addicted to dispute, to lie, steal, and many tricks and unworthy actions; in short, a mere knave.

☿ in ♉

Gives a middle-sized, corpulent, thick person, strong and well set, swarthy sun-burnt complexion, dark short and thick hair. He is idle, slothful, one who loves ease and gluttony, and who ruins himself among the female sex.

☿ in ♊

Shews a tall, upright, straight body, well formed, brown hair, good complexion, and a very intelligent look. An ingenious pregnant fancy, a good orator, a cunning lawyer, or clever bookseller; one who perfectly understands his own interests, and (if ☿ be not afflicted) one who is a subtle politician, not easily deluded by the most cunning knave he may encounter.

☿ in ♋

Personates a low, short stature, or squab figure, an ill complexion, a thin sharp face, small eyes, sharp nose, dark hair ; one who is given to drink, light-fingered, ill-natured, dishonest, and very deceitful and changeable ; a very mean little wretch, if ☿ be afflicted.

☿ in ♌

Gives a full large body, and good stature, dull, swarthy, sunburnt complexion, light brown hair, round face, full eyes, a broad or high nose. A hasty, proud, conceited, ambitious, boasting, and contentious troublesome character.

☿ in ♍

Denotes a tall, slender, well-proportioned person, dark brown hair, (or if ☿ be in the terms of ♃ or ♄, black hair), not a clear complexion, a long visage, and austere countenance. A very witty, ingenious, talented mind ; and if ☿ be free from affliction, a profound scholar or linguist, and capable of any undertaking which requires great ability.

☿ in ♎

Personates a tall body, well made, but not thin ; light brown, smooth hair, a ruddy or sanguine complexion. A just, virtuous, prudent man, a lover and promoter of learning, and having great natural abilities, and many acquired accomplishments.

☿ in ♏

Gives a short, mean, stature, full and well-set but ill-made body, broad shoulders, swarthy, dark complexion, brown curling hair. Not any way elegant or pleasing, yet ingenious and studious ; very careful of his own interests, fond of the female sex, and partial to company and merry making.

☿ in ♐

Denotes a person of tall stature, well formed, not corpulent,

but rather large boned and spare ; an oval face, a large nose.
and ruddy complexion. A man who is hasty but soon reconciled, rash in many things to his own injury, yet well disposed, striving after honourable things, but seldom attaining
them ; not very fortunate.

☿ *in* ♑

Gives a mean, small stature, often crooked make and bow-
legged, a thin face and figure, dusky complexion, and brown
hair. A very peevish, discontented, dejected, sickly, feeble
person, yet active ; one who is unfortunate to himself and
disagreeable to others, owing to his suspicious nature and ill
temper.

☿ *in* ♒

Shews a person of middle height, rather fleshy and corpulent, a good complexion and clear skin, with brown hair and
full face. An ingenious, obliging character, inclined to study,
fond of arts and sciences, very inventive, and remarkable for
his talent, as well as being a humane, kind, charitable person.

☿ *in* ♓

Gives a short, squab, dumpy figure, though if in his own
term or that of ♄, rather thin, pale face, brown hair, sickly
look, and very hairy body. A very peevish, repining, fop-
pish person, addicted to wine and women ; very effeminate
and contemptible.

The MOON *in the Twelve Signs.*

☽ *in* ♈

Describes a person of indifferent stature, rather fleshy or
plump, round face, tolerably good complexion, light brown
or flaxen hair. The mind is rash, angry, ambitious, and
aspiring, often changing ; and he undergoes various muta·
tions in life ; not often fortunate.

☽ *in* ♉

Gives a strong, corpulent, well-set body, rather short, pretty good complexion, dark brown or black hair. A gentle, obliging, kind, sober, just, and honest man ; one who gains esteem, is much respected, and attains preferment according to his situation in life.

☽ *in* ♊

Describes a tall, well-formed, upright, comely person, brown hair, good complexion, between pale and sanguine. The mind is ingenious, yet crafty and subtle to excess ; not of the best disposition, nor very fortunate, unless other good testimonies by aspects of ♃, ☉, or ♀ concur.

☽ *in* ♋

Represents a middle stature, well proportioned, and fleshy person, a round, full face, pale, dusky complexion, sad-brown hair. The mind is flexible, given to change ; a merry, easy, pleasant, disposition, very harmless and peaceable, fond of good company ; one who is generally well-beloved, and fortunate in most affairs ; unsteady, but free from passion or rash actions.

☽ *in* ♌

Denotes a person above the middle size, well proportioned, strong, and large boned, sanguine complexion, light brown hair, large and prominent eyes, and full face. A lofty, proud, aspiring person, very ambitious, and desirous to bear rule ; one who abhors servitude or dependence, and is generally an unfortunate person.

☽ *in* ♍

Describes a rather tall person, dark brown or black hair, oval face, rather ruddy, but tolerably clear complexion. An ingenious, reserved, covetous, melancho.y, unfortunate person ; not in general very well disposed, and one who seldom performs any very commendable actions.

☽ in ♎

Gives a tall, well-composed body, with smooth, light brown hair, handsome and pleasant cheerful countenance, fine red and white complexion. They are merry, jocund, and pleasant, and much admired by the female sex; very fond of amusement; and, if a female, she is courted by numbers, but yet unfortunate, unless ♀, the dispositor, be very strong and well aspected, &c.

☽ in ♏

Denotes a thick, short, and ill-shaped person, a fleshy obscure complexion, dark hair, often black, (especially if ☽ be in the term of ♃ or ♄). They are sottish and vulgar, malicious, brutish, and treacherous; and if it be a female, she is generally infamous in her desires, and if ☽ be afflicted by the □ or ☍ of ♄ or ♂, she is openly scandalous.

☽ in ♐

Represents a handsome and well-proportioned rather tall person ; oval face, sanguine complexion, rather bronzed, and bright brown or shining chestnut hair. The disposition is good, open and generous, but hasty and passionate, yet forgiving ; one who aims at great things, is fortunate, and much respected by those with whom he associates.

☽ in ♑

Gives a person of low stature, a thin, small, weak body, bad health, and feeble, especially about the knees; the complexion bad, black hair, and small features ; one who is inac-

tive, dull, not ingenious, generally very debauched in his conduct, and held in low esteem by his companions, &c.

☽ *in* ♒

Represents a middle-sized person, well made, and rather
corpulent, brown hair, clear skin, and sanguine complexion.
They are ingenious, affable, courteous, and inoffensive; a
lover of curious and scientific studies, having much invention,
and a person rarely guilty of unworthy actions.

☽ *in* ♓

Describes a person of a mean or low stature, but plump or
fat, pale and bloated face, light brown hair, and sleepy eyes;
one not inclined to action, unless of the worst kind; unfortunate both to himself and others; given to drink.

N.B. If ☽ be well aspected, and in a good house, the disposition is much improved.

EFFECTS OF THE ASPECTS BETWEEN THE SIGNI-
FICATORS.

♄ ☌ ♃.

If ♄ be significator, he gives the querent inheritance of
estates, and profit by means of agriculture; his disposition is
extremely moral and grave; he may gain a fortune by merchandize, or, probably, by preaching.

If ♃ be significator, the disposition is not so good; the
querent seldom meets with much success in the world; he
is very niggardly, and generally acquires property by some
selfish and unusual means; though he seldom enjoys it like
other persons.   He generally lives hated by every one for his
mean and deceitful ways, and dies in obscurity.

If ♂ be in □ to the significator, and in aspect with ☿, the
querent is generally duped of his property, and dies a miserable death.

♄ ☌ ♂.

If ♄ be significator, the querent is of a rast, turbulent disposition, and generally very unfortunate; very often engaged in some public calling of the lowest order, and frequently ends his days in prison.

If ♂ be significator, the disposition is equally bad, but not quite so rash, being more sly and cowardly. Sometimes he gains favour from elderly persons, who assist him with their property, which he generally loses in the end, and becomes very unfortunate; especially if the significators be under the earth.

♄ ☌ ☉

Signifies losses to the querent by fire, (especially if they be in a fiery sign), or by men in power, who persecute him, and confine him within the walls of a prison for some contempt of the law; and he is seldom healthy or of long life.

If ☉ be significator, the querent is generally very disagreeable, deceitful, mistrustful, and unfortunate; always losing his property by some speculation, which in the end often brings him to ruin; particularly if the querent have anything to do with the government, or persons connected with the state.

♄ ☌ ♀

Shews gain to the querent by means of ladies, to a considerable extent; he is much attached to them, greatly addicted to pleasure, and very fortunate where females are concerned. If he be a man of property, he often wastes most of it by gaming or pleasure.

If ♀ be significator, the querent is very artful, sly, unfortunate, destitute of friends, often disappointed by death; and he loses considerably by persons older than himself, especially if he be in trade.

♄ ☌ ☿.

If ♄ be significator, the querent is subtle and crafty, fond of researches into antiquity; one of much gravity and considerable learning; though not always of the most agreeable manners.

If ☿ be significator, he is dull, suspicious, mean, cowardly, calculating, and covetous. Should he turn his attention to literature, he may gain some knowledge, although with great labour; and should he become an author, his writings may bring him into some disgrace.

♄ ☌ ☽.

If ♄ be significator, the person is restless and unsettled in his purposes, and often changes his residence. He is not very fortunate, though he may sometimes benefit by the populace, and by the lower order of females.

If ☽ be significator, he is poor, miserable, and dejected, of unpleasant manners, and sullen disposition; extremely unfortunate, and uncommonly covetous, though possessing scarcely any property. With much suspicious caution, he frequently commits the most unaccountable errors in affairs of the greatest consequence; as, through excess of prudence, he is very likely to doubt and deliberate in the moment of action.

♃ ☌ ♂.

If ♃ be significator, the querent is bold, proud, and ambitious; fond of martial exploits and enterprises; a good soldier or surgeon; though he may lose much by strife and contention, and sometimes receive wounds in quarrels.

If ♂ be significator, he is good, pious, and just; he is eminently successful in the law or the church; and often makes a fortune by those means.

♃ ♂ ☉.

If ♃ be significator, the querent is weak, servile, and credulous; he incurs the displeasure of men in power, by whom he is much oppressed, and often ruined; he has bad health; and is generally a vain, loquacious character, indulging in fanciful speculations about religion, and other matters, for which he is totally unqualified.

If ☉ be significator, the power of ♃ is so much destroyed by the power of ☉, that he has but very little effect; though the party will, in general, be very much given to religion, which, if ♃ be well dignified in other respects, and not ill-aspected, will be sincere, otherwise it is fanatical or hypocritical.

♃ ♂ ♀.

If ♃ be significator, it promises the greatest happiness; the querent is highly favoured by the female sex, by whose means he gains great advancement; he is rich, prosperous, and fortunate; very healthy, and greatly admired and respected. It shews great personal beauty.

If ♀ be significator, it denotes great beauty of person, (unless ♀ be in ♏ or ♑), riches, honours, ecclesiastical preferment; the person so represented is truly virtuous, pious, kind and beneficent to all, with the greatest goodness of heart, and a disposition that will command universal love and esteem.

♃ ☌ ☿.

If ♃ be significator, it denotes a person of great learning, a good lawyer or divine, of excellent abilities and much information.

If ☿ be significator, he is mild, humane, religious, fond of literature; possessing an elegant mind, and a gentle, engaging disposition; he is raised to eminence, and protected by powerful patrons; he accumulates great riches, and is, in general, extremely fortunate.

♃ ☌ ☽.

If ♃ be significator, the person so represented is restless and changeable, and seldom sufficiently settled to procure much wealth; he is, on the whole, very fortunate, often gains considerably by marriage, and is a general favourite with the fair sex; he is a great traveller, and is eminently successful in maritime affairs and among seamen, shipping, &c.

If ☽ be significator, he is fortunate in ecclesiastical affairs; or among mercantile men, magistrates, &c. He obtains great wealth, though he is liable to losses frequently by canting, hypocritical persons, who impose upon his natural kindness and generosity of disposition. He has, however, too much good fortune to be injured by those persons to any serious extent.

♂ ☌ ☉.

If ♂ be significator, the querent is in danger by fire, lightning, or infectious fevers; it has been said in this case, with great truth, "he has the favour of kings and princes," and it may be their frowns too, to his utter undoing; he may rise hastily, but, perhaps, to a precipice.

If ☉ be significator, the querent is brave, but headstrong and violent; he will probably attain some considerable rank in the army or navy; but he will be frequently wounded, and most probably die in battle, or be killed by some accident, or fall a victim to some contagious fever.

♂ ☌ ♀.

If ♂ be significator, the querent is kind and gentle upon the whole, though at times rather hasty; he is moderately fortunate, extremely fond of women, and not always very particular as to their respectability.

If ♀ be significator, he is wicked and debauched, a companion of prostitutes, from whom he generally receives great injury; a drunkard, frequently brawling in taverns or low public-houses; though he may sometimes meet with good fortune, he will quickly dissipate whatever property he may possess in the company of the most worthless of mankind.

♂ ☌ ☿.

If ♂ be significator, it represents the querent as possessed of considerable ability, a skilful mechanic, or a good mathematician; one of an acute sarcastic wit; if he be in the army or navy, for which he is well qualified, he obtains great reputation for his bravery, and is distinguished still more for the policy of his measures. He is never very scrupulous as to the means he employs; and will pay but little respect to the persons or possessions of others, when he can gain any advantage by sacrificing them to his own interest.

If ☿ be significator, he makes a cheat or swindler, a thief, robber, or treacherous miscreant; a frequenter of gaming-houses, rash, furious, and blood-thirsty.

N.B.—Any evil aspect of ♄ increases these evils, and a good aspect of ☉, ♃, or ♀, will much diminish them.

♂ ☌ ☽.

If ♂ be significator, it shews one of an unsettled life and temper, and a favourite of females; he is frequently a wandering adventurer, more remarkable for the variety of his fortune than his success or abilities. He is likely to die in a strange country.

If ☽ be significator, he is a bold, enterprising character; frequently in great danger of a violent death, quarrelsome, and given to duelling, &c. He may be a good surgeon or soldier; and is seldom noted for much humanity. If a female, she is extremely likely to be seduced.

☉ ♂ ♀.

If ☉ be significator, it denotes one of soft and effeminate anners, a pleasing address, a great admirer of the ladies. He is too much given to extravagance and dissipation.

If ♀ be significator, he is of short life, unfortunate, and oppressed; too sickly to make much exertion; very proud and extravagant.

☉ ♂ ☿.

If ☉ be significator, it gives some ingenuity, but not much sound judgment.

If ☿ be significator, he represents a person of mean and shallow abilities; one addicted to fraud and deception; incapable of learning anything which requires memory or judgment, and extremely superstitious. He may succeed well in trade or business, but for study he is wholly unqualified.

☉ ♂ ☽.

If ☉ be significator, it represents a restless and changeable person, who aims at great things, but seldom accomplishes them.

If ☽ be significator, the querent is extremely unfortunate, and generally sickly and unhappy, dejected, and oppressed by men in power. He is rash and violent, subject to burns and scalds, and has frequently some defect in the eyes; and if the ♂ happen near the *Hyades*, *Pleiades*, or *Præspe*, he is likely to be nearly blind. If the ☽ be applying, he is in danger of death, especially if it happen in the 8th house, or ☉ be lord of the 8th; but if ☽ be separating, the danger is not so great.

♀ ♂ ☿

If ♀ be significator, it represents one who is polite, mild, and courteous, fond of the elegant branches of literature; a pleasant companion, a favourite of females ; and cne of an excellent disposition.

If ☿ be significator, he excels in any pursuit that requires taste ; a good painter, an excellent poet or musician, of a very humane disposition, and of the most prepossessing appearance.

N.B. It must be most carefully observed, whether these planets have any other familiarity at the same time; for should ♅, ♄ , or ♂ be in □, it will make a most remarkable difference. Indeed, this must be scrupulously attended to in all cases, but especially, where ♀, ☿, or ☽ may be significator.

♀ ☌ ☽.

If ♀ be significator, it renders a man very mutable and uncertain ; often promising, through goodness of disposition, much more than he is capable of performing.

If ☽ be significator, he is of an easy, happy, disposition, with little care beyond the enjoyment of the present moment; a great proficient in all elegant amusements, and of an easy and genteel address.

☿ ☌ ☽.

If ☿ be significator, the native is possessed of great abilities, though generally very unsteady in his pursuits. He frequently travels in some literary capacity.

If ☽ be significator, the effects are not very different ; his intellectual powers are of the first order ; he is much attached to learning, and gains great reputation by his abilities.

OF THE ⚹ AND △ ASPECTS BETWEEN THE SIGNIFICATORS.

♄ ⚹ or △ ♃.

If ♄ be significator, it gives riches by means of agriculture ; and he is of a sedate and religious disposition.

Y

If ♃ be significator, he is extremely grave, and frequently gains riches by legacies or mining concerns.

♄ ✳ or △ ♂.

If ♄ be significator, it increases the courage of the person so signified, and renders him more open in his resentment.

If ♂ be significator, he is prudent and cautious, bigotted in religion, and, should other aspects befriend ♂, he may gain an estate.

♄ ✳ or △ ☉.

If ♄ be significator, he is generous and noble, though somewhat austere in his behaviour.

If ☉ be significator, he is ostentatious, boastful, and conceited ; he may be expected to gain by legacies, or to be successful as a farmer.

♄ ✳ or △ ♀.

If ♄ be significator, he is prodigal and extravagant, wasting his money among females.

If ♀ be significator, he is modest, shy, and retired in his manners ; he gains the favour cf elderly people, and sometimes inherits their property.

♄ ✳ or △ ☿.

If ♄ be significator, it gives ingenuity and subtilty, though his talents are mostly employed to little purpose.

If ☿ be significator, he is very cautious and prudent, and is addicted to the study of arts and sciences.

♄ ✳ or △ ☽.

If ♄ be significator, the querent is changeable, jealous, and mistrustful.

If ☽ be significator, he is vain and conceited, mean in his actions, though without the excuse of rashness, as he does nothing without much deliberation.

♃ ✳ or △ ♂.

If ♃ be significator, it gives bravery, and the spirit of military adventure ; he is a good soldier, surgeon, or chemist.

If ♂ be significator, he is noble, generous, and ambitious, and will rise rapidly in the army.

♃ ✳ or △ ☉.

If ♃ be significator, it makes one extremely fortunate, and very noble and courageous in his disposition.

If ☉ be significator, he gains money rapidly, is always respected, and possesses a most excellent disposition.

♃ ✳ or △ ♀.

If ♃ be significator, it causes beauty, love, riches, and real goodness of heart : this is the most fortunate aspect that can be formed.

If ♀ be significator, the person is virtuous, amiable, of a noble disposition, incapable of fraud or malice.

♃ ✳ or △ ☿.

If ♃ be significator, it gives great learning, sound judgment, and excellent abilities.

If ☿ be significator, he possesses solid sense, an open, generous disposition, and real good fortune.

♃ ✳ or △ ☽.

If ♃ be significator, it makes a man very fortunate, beloved by females, and much respected by the poorer classes of society.

If ☽ be significator, he is just and charitable, sincere in his friendships, and generous to the full extent of his means.

♂ ✳ or △ ☉.

If ♂ be significator, it gives a very noble disposition, and great mind ; it causes one to rise rapidly in the army ; he is uncommonly successful in war, and will gain much by the patronage of men in power.

If ☉ be significator, it confers great bravery, and a high spirit ; he rises to grandeur by means of his courage and invincible military talents.

♂ ⚹ or △ ♀.

If ♂ be significator, it causes lewdness and dissipation ; his disposition is not radically bad, but he is extremely thoughtless and improvident ; he may gain by females, for he eems to possess a fascinating influence, which he never fails to exert to the utmost with the female sex.

If ♀ be significator, he is handsome, but proud, rash, and inconsiderate ; and neither remarkable for prudence nor principle.

♂ ⚹ or △ ♀.

If ♂ be significator, this aspect gives great acuteness, penetration, and learning ; the querent, however, is crafty, rather hasty, and extremely confident.

If ☿ be significator, he possesses great courage, is very ingenious in any mechanical trade, a good engraver or mathematician, and will succeed in any thing that requires presence of mind, acuteness, and ready wit.

If ☿ receive any aspect of ♅, he is extremely fitted to become a good astrologer, especially if ☽ assist ☿.

♂ ⚹ or △ ☽.

If ♂ be significator, it makes one restless and changeable, servile and talkative ; he travels much, and receives much assistance from females.

If ☽ be significator, he is very passionate and changeable, with a high spirit and good abilities.

☉ ✳ *or* △ ☽.

If ☉ be significator, it confers riches and honour; the querent is fortunate with women, and is much respected by the multitude.

If ☽ be significator, he is proud and aspiring; he is generally successful, but his fortune is not permanent, unless both ☉ and ☽ be in fixed signs.

♀ ✳ *or* △ ☿.

If ♀ be significator, this aspect gives ingenuity subtlety, and good nature.

If ☿ be significator, the querent possesses a refined and accomplished mind; he is neat in his person, and elegant in his manners; a lover of music and the fine arts in general.

♀ ✳ *or* △ ☽.

If ♀ be significator, it is a very fortunate aspect; it shews a person who is much assisted by female friends; and one who, though unstable, often obtains considerable property.

If ☽ be significator, the querent is gentle, obliging, amiable, and genteel in his manners, and is much admired by females; whose condition in life depends on the strength or debility of ♀.

☿ ✳ *or* △ ☽.

If ☿ be significator, the person signified is witty, ingenious, subtle, easily learning any thing to which he applies, and frequently acquiring many sciences without any assistance. He is somewhat reserved, and a little melancholy, but, from his extensive knowledge, he is always a useful and sometimes a pleasant companion.

If ☽ be significator, this is the most favourable aspect for learning or scientific speculation.

THE EFFECTS OF THE □ OR ☍ ASPECTS BETWEEN THE SIGNIFICATORS

♄ □ *or* ☍ ♃.

If ♄ be significator, it shews much trouble oy lawyers or the clergy.

If ♃ be significator, he is always wretched and miserable idle, unfortunate, and beggarly.

♄ □ *or* ☍ ♂.

If ♄ be significator, it is the aspect of cruelty and murder, and the person so signified is extremely unfortunate; he generally lives a most dejected life, and dies a violent death.

If ♂ be significator, the person shewn by him is very malicious, treacherous, and blood-thirsty; one delighting in the most evil deeds, yet very cowardly, sly, and much addicted to suicide and secret revenge; of a cruel complexion: in short, such a character as Don Miguel of Portugal.

♄ □ *or* ☍ ☉.

If ♄ be significator, it is the aspect of infamy and contempt; the person is prodigal, ambitious, overbearing, hating control, very disagreeable in his manners, extremely unfortunate, subject to the frowns of persons in power, and often meets a violent death.

If ☉ be significator, the person is cowardly, spiteful, treacherous, malicious, unfeeling, covetous, repining, always despising any thing of kindness and humanity; one who generally leads a life of wretchedness, and frequently meets with a bad end, and sometimes dies in prison.

♄ □ *or* ☍ ♀.

If ♄ be significator, it shews dissipation, and the person leads a most detestable life, connected with the lowest order of prostitutes, by whom he is eventually brought to ruin and disgrace.

If ♀ be significator, the person is generally of an evil complexion, and not very handsome ; very sly, artful, full of mischief, and much addicted to dissipation, though not suspected ; mostly unfortunate.

♄ □ *or* ☍ ☿ .

If ♄ be significator, it indicates a thief, cheat, or swindler ; a low, cunning fellow, sly, envious, treacherous, and malicious, one who is always planning some scheme to deceive his most intimate friends ; generally forming a bad opinion of every one, and not at all particular as to speaking the truth.

If ☿ be significator, the person is very artful, always involved in strife and contention, and much given to vilify the character of others, by whom he is tormented with lawsuits ; it also indicates pettifogging attornies, who very seldom act honestly towards their clients.

♄ □ *or* ☍ ☽ .

If ♄ be significator, it shews a wandering, unsettled and changeable person, not of a genteel form, but one who is down-looking, and inclined to stoop forward ; always very fretful, and appearing full of trouble ; not a good disposition, nor to be depended on. He seldom attains any high situation, but, if he does, he soon falls into disgrace again.

If ☽ be significator, (*which in some measure she always is of the* QUERENT), the person is extremely unfortunate, always in trouble with the lower order of mankind, from whom he receives many injuries ; he is mean, cowardly, and very dejected ; is rather unhealthy, seldom living a long life, and generally dying a miserable death.

♃ □ or ☍ ♂ .

If ♃ be significator, it denotes violence, ingratitude, a furi
ous temper, and danger of death by malignant fevers.

If ♂ be significator, it shews pride, ingratitude, insolence,
and the hatred of the clergy on account of theological opinions.

♃ □ or ☍ ☉ .

If ♃ be significator, it gives arrogance, prodigality, and
much vanity, with a great desire to be distinguished, which is
but very rarely gratified.

If ☉ be significator, the person represented wastes his property by riotous living and all kinds of extravagance.

♃ □ or ☍ ♀ .

If ♃ be significator, it shews extravagance, dissipation, and
all kinds of debauchery and intemperance.

If ♀ be significator, the person has many enemies among
the clergy, and the legal profession, magistrates, &c., and he
is equally void of virtue and prudence.

♃ □ or ☍ ☿ .

If ♃ be significator, it gives trouble, contention, perplexi-
ties, lawsuits, and, in consequence, indigence.

If ☿ be significator, the person is frequently persecuted for
his singular religious opinions; his understanding is weak,
and he is often involved in strife and contention.

♃ □ or ☍ ☽ .

If ♃ be significator, it shews one of many words, though
of poor abilities; he is weak and foolish, and, if in a public
capacity, is execrated by the multitude.

If the ☽ be significator, he is injured by faithless friends and deceitful relatives : and his property is impoverished by hypocritical fanatics.

♂ □ or ☍ ☉.

If ♂ be significator, it denotes a man of great ambition and violence ; but his fortune is too evil to allow him to succeed.

If the ☉ be significator, he is restrained by no principle of honour or gratitude ; his affairs are always deranged, and he makes use of the most violent means to retrieve them. Such a one frequently becomes a footpad, murderer, or housebreaker, and is either killed in some contest, or falls a victim to the laws of his country.

♂ □ or ☍ ♀.

If ♂ be significator, these aspects cause lust, excess, prodigality, disease, and injury by loose women, and complete waste of fortune.

If ♀ be significator, he is very treacherous, mischievous, base, and inconstant ; or if it be a female, she is a prostitute, or very shameless.

♂ □ or ☍ ☿.

If ♂ be significator, it shews one of some ability, but his talents are applied to the most dishonourable purposes.

If ☿ be significator, it denotes a thief or assassin ; one whose most solemn protestations are not to be believed ; who will desert his benefactors at their utmost need : he is violent, furious, contentious, and despised by every one for his infamous life.

♂ □ or ☍ ☽.

If ♂ be significator, the querent described by him is a fit companion for the lowest and most unprincipled of mankind : ne is very unfortunate, and is probably a wandering vagabond, who travels over the earth without a friend or a home.

If ☽ be significator, he is excessively abusive, malicious, and treacherous. He may travel into foreign countries as a sailor or soldier, amidst innumerable dangers and hardships, and die by pestilence, dysentery, or the sword.

☉ □ or ☍ ☽.

If the ☉ be significator, the person suffers losses, trouble, and much anxiety.

If ☽ be significator, he is obstinate and quarrelsome; he is exceedingly ambitious and prodigal; and is sometimes marked in the face, or his eyes are affected: the latter is especially the case if ☉ be afflicted by ♂, or either ☉ or ☽ are with the *nebulous* stars.

♀ □ or ☍ ☽.

If ♀ be significator, it shews a changeable, unsettled life, great troubles in marriage, and much ill-fortune.

If the ☽ be significator, it shews a dissolute, extravagant life, attended with indigence and poverty, and much trouble from females.

☿ □ or ☍ ☽.

If ☿ be significator, it no doubt gives some abilities, but such persons are too unsettled to apply very closely to any subject; they are continually shifting their situations, (especially if ☿ be in a moveable sign), nor are they very sincere in their professions of friendship, nor very scrupulous in the method by which they may attain their ends.

If ☽ be significator, they have a defect in their utterance, have but little ability, except a kind of low cunning, which they apply to dishonest purposes. But as ☿ is acted on by every planet having an aspect to him, it will be necessary to observe each aspect, and allow for its influence; for if ☿ have a △ of ♃, the □ of ☿ to ☽ will not be near so evil, though the person will be far from sensible, notwithstanding that they are tolerably honest and well-meaning.

OBSERVATION.—The student must always remember, that the true character and condition of the person signified can only be correctly learned by noticing all the aspects the significator may receive, as well as observing the nature of the sign and house it is in, and the degree of strength or weakness it possesses, as well as those planets which aspect it. Thus, if the significator be ♂, and he receive the ☍ of ☉, yet if ☉ be weak, and ♂ have also a △ of ♃, this benefic planet being strong, he may judge that the querent will suffer by the evil influence of ☉, by receiving a severe wound in a duel, or in honourable warfare; whereas if, instead of the △ of ♃, the ☐ of ☿ occurred, there would be little doubt that he would be killed by police officers, or die by the hand of the public executioner · the latter especially, if ☉ was in the 10th house.

A LIST OF FIXED STARS WHICH MAY BE CONSIDERED IN
HORARY QUESTIONS; WITH THEIR APPROXIMATE LON-
GITUDE, JAN. 1, 1835.*

NAMES.	LONGITUDE.		LATITUDE.		NATURE.		MAGNITUDE.
Ram's following Horn .	♉ 5	21	9	57 N.	♄	♂	SECOND.
The Pleiades	♉ 26	55	4	31 N.	♂	☽	FIFTH.
The Brightest of the Seven Stars . . .	♉ 27	50	4	2 N.	♂	☽	THIRD.
Occulus Taurus, or the Bull's North Eye . .	♊ 6	11	2	36 S.	♀		THIRD.
Aldebaran, or the Bull's South Eye . . .	♊ 7	31	5	29 S.	♂		FIRST.
The Bull's North Horn	♊ 20	17	5	22 N.	♂		SECOND.
Bright Foot of Gemini	♋ 6	46	6	48 S.	☿ ♀		SECOND.
Castor	♋ 17	48	10	4 N.	♂ ♀ ♄		FIRST.
Pollux	♋ 20	59	6	40 N.	♂		SECOND.
North Assellus . . .	♌ 4	45	3	10 N.	♂ ☉		FOURTH.
Præspe, or the Claw of the Crab . . .	♌ 5	0	1	14 N.	♂ ☽		NEBULOUS
South Assellus . . .	♌ 6	26	0	4 N.	♂ ☉		FOURTH.
Hydra's Heart . . .	♌ 19	43	7	32 S.	♄ ♀		SECOND.
Cor ♌, the Lion's Heart	♌ 27	33	0	27 N.	♂		FIRST.
Vindemiatrix	♍ 7	38	10	15 S.	♄ ♀ ☿		THIRD.
Arista, the Virgin's Spike	♎ 21	33	2	2 S.	♀ ♂		FIRST.
South Scale	♏ 12	48	0	22 N.	♄ ♀		SECOND.
North Scale	♏ 17	0	8	46 N.	♃ ♂		SECOND.
Frons Scorpio . . .	♐ 0	54	1	2 N.	♄ ♀		SECOND.
Antares, or the Scorpion's Heart . .	♐ 7	29	4	32 S.	☿ ♂		FIRST.
Right Knee of *Ophiucus*	♐ 15	41	7	18 N.	♄ ♀		THIRD.
Capricorn's Tail . . .	♒ 21	15	2	33 S	♄		THIRD.
Scheat Pegasi . . .	♓ 26	29	1	7 N.	♄		SECOND.

* These are the principal fixed stars, near the ecliptic, to which only the planets can approach. If the student require the places of the stars for the purpose of bringing them to the midheaven or ascendant in a nativity, he may learn their right ascension and declination in the Nautical Almanac for each year, and he may readily calculate their longitudes and latitudes therefrom by the rules we have given.

N.B. The longitudes increase about 50" ⅓ each year ; the latitudes do not vary

Rules to find the Zodiacal Latitude and Longitude of a Fixed Star, Comet, Planet, or the ⊕, &c. from the Right Ascension and Declination.

1st. If the right ascension be less than 180°, it is *north;* and if it be more than 180°, it is *south.*

2d. To the logarithm *co-tangent* of the declination add the logarithm *sine* of the right ascension, measured from ♈ or ♎ ; but if measured from ♋ or ♑, the logarithm *co-sine :* the sum (minus 10 in the Index), will be the *log. tangent* of the angle A.

3d. If the right ascension and declination be both *north,* or ooth *south,* add 23° 28′ to angle A, and it will give angle B.

4th. If the right ascension and declination be one *nortn* and the other *south,* the difference between 23° 28′ and angle A will give angle B.

Note.—If angle B exceed 90°, the latitude will be of the contrary name to the declination ; but if angle B be less than 90°, the latitude will be of the same name as the declination.

To find the Longitude.

To the arithmetical comp. of the log. *sine* of angle A, and the log. *sine* of angle B, add the log. *tang.* of R.A. from ♈ or ♎, (or the log. *co-tang* of R.A. from ♋ or ♑). The sum will be the log. *tang.* of the longitude from ♈ or ♎, or the og. *co-tang.* of the longitude from ♋ or ♑.

To find the Latitude.

To the arithmetical comp. of the log. *co-sine* of angle A, and the log. *co-sine* of angle B, add the log. *sine* of the declination. The sum will be the log. *sine* of the latitude.

N.B. The arithmetical complement of a logarithm is found by subtracting it from . . . 10.00000

Example. The log. sine of 13° 10′ is . 9.35752

——————

0.64248

or it may be found with equal ease, by taking each figure (beginning at the *left* hand or index), from 9, except the last or right-hand figure, which must be taken from 10.

Thus : if from	.	.	.	.	9.99990
we take	.	.	.	.	9.35752
It gives	.	.	.	.	0.64248

the object of this being to perform each problem by addition, in lieu of the lengthy process otherwise required.

EXAMPLE.—Required the zodiacal longitude and latitude of Halley's comet, at noon, on the 18th October, 1835, Greenwich mean time?

Comet's right ascension, 16^h 25.31 equal in degrees to 246° 19', which, being more than 180°, is *south*. The declination is 0° 35' *north*.

Co-tangent dec.	.	0° 35	= 11.99219
Sine R.A. from ♎	.	66 19	= 9.96179
Tang. angle A	=	89 22	— 11.95398
From angle A take	.	23 28	
It gives angle B	.	65 54	

Then for the Longitude.

To the *sine* angle A (arith. comp.)	.	.	0.00003
Add the *sine* angle B	.	.	9.96039
And Tang. R. A. from ♎	66° 19'	=	10.35791
Tang. longitude from ♎	64 20	=	10.31833
Take the long. of ♎ and ⟩ m from this . . ⟨	60 0		
It leaves . . . ♐ 4 20, the longitude.			

Then for the Latitude.

To the log. co-sine angle A (arith. comp.) .	1.95650
Add the log. co-sine angle B . . .	9.61101
And log. sine of the dec.	8.00779
It gives the log. sine of the latitude 22° 6′ =	9.57530

As angle B is less than 90°, the latitude is of the same name as the declination; which being north, the latitude is north also.

Hence the comet will be, at mean noon, Greenwich time, on the 18th of October, 1835, in ♐ 4° 20′, with 22° 6 north latitude.

EXPLANATION OF TERMS USED IN THIS WORK.

Abscission.—See " Frustration."

Affliction.—A planet, or the cusp of a house, being in evil aspect to any planet, or ♂ to a malefic.

Angles.—The four houses which commence at the points where the ☉ rises, culminates, sets, and arrives at midnight ; viz. the east, south, west, and north.

Application.—The approaching of one planet to another, or to the cusp of any house, either by ♂ or any aspect.

Ascendant.—The eastern horizon, or the cusp of that house which represents the party ; as the cusp of the 5th is the ascendant for a child of the querent.

Aspect.—The being placed at certain distances from a planet, or the cusp of a house : as, if ♃ be 60 degrees from ☽ then they are both said to be in *sextile* aspect to each other. They are found to agree exactly with *the angles of regular polygons which may be inscribed in a circle.* An elucidation of this property of all astrological aspects may be seen in the " *Grammar of Astrology.*"

Barren Signs.—♊, ♌, and ♍.

Benefics.—The two planets ♃ and ♀.

Bestial Signs.— ♈, ♉, ♌, ♐ (the first half excepted), and ♑.

Besieged.—A planet being enclosed between two others.

Bicorporeal.—See " Double Bodied."

Cadent.—Falling from an angle : these are the 3d, 6th, 9th, and 12th houses.

Cazimi.—The heart of ☉, or being within 17 minutes of the

exact longitude of ⊙ ; which is considered a **strong** position, but, we think, erroneously.

Collection of Light.—When a planet receives the aspects of any two others which are not themselves in aspect. It denotes that the affair will be forwarded by a third person, described by that planet ; but not unless they both receive him in some of their dignities.

Combustion.—The being within 8° 30′ of the ⊙, which is said to burn up those planets near him, so that they lose their power. It is always an evil testimony.

Common Signs.— Ⅱ, ♍, ♐, and ♓.

Conjunction.—Two planets being in the same longitude. If they be exactly in the same degree and minute, it is a partile conjunction, and very powerful ; if within the half of the sum of their two orbs, it is a platic conjunction, and less powerful.

Culminate.—To arrive at the midheaven.

Cusp.—The beginning of any house.

Day House.—That house ruled by any planet by day ; as ♒ is the day-house of ♄ ; ♐ of ♃, &c. If the question be asked by day, or while ⊙ is above the horizon, and it be required to know what house ♄ rules, look for ♒ ; and wherever it may be found, that is the house of ♄.

Debilities.—See "Dignities."

Declination.—The distance any heavenly body is from the equator.

Decreasing in Light.—When any planet is past the ☍ of ⊙, it decreases in light ; it is a testimony of weakness.

Decumbiture. — A lying down ; the figure erected for the time of any person being first taken ill, and taking to their bed.

Degree.—The 30th part of a sign in the zodiac ; or the 360th part of any circle.

Z

Descendant. — The western horizon ; or cusp of the 7th house.

Detriment.—The sign opposite the house of any planet ; as ♂ in ♎ is in his detriment. It is a sign of weakness, distress, &c.

Dignities.—These are either essential or accidental. The former are when any planet is in its own house, exaltation, triplicity, term or face ; the latter are, when any planet is in an angle, and well aspected, not afflicted, swift in motion, increasing in light, &c. The reverse of dignities are debilities.

Direct.—When any planet moves on in the regular order of the signs, from ♈ towards ♉, &c.

Direction.—The calculating the arc between two heavenly bodies, &c. It is a term chiefly used in nativities.

Dispose, Dispositor.—A planet disposes of any other which may be found in its essential dignities. Thus, if ☉ be in ♈, the house of ♂, then ♂ disposes of ☉, and is said to rule, receive, or govern him. When the dispositor of the planet signifying the thing asked after is himself disposed by the lord of the ascendant, it is a good sign. To dispose by house is the most powerful testimony ; then by exaltation, then triplicity, then term, and lastly, face, which is a very weak reception.

Double-bodied Signs.—♊, ♐, ♓.

Dragon's Head.—It is thus marked, ☊, and is the north node of ☽, or where she crosses the ecliptic into north latitude. It is always a good symbol, denoting success, a good disposition, &c.

Dragon's Tail.—It is thus marked, ☋, and is where the ☽ crosses the ecliptic into south latitude, or her south node. It is very evil, and in all things the reverse of ☊ ; it diminishes the power of good, and increases that of evil planets.

Earthy Signs.—♉, ♍, and ♑, which form the earthy triplicity.

Ephemeris.—An almanack of the planets' places. The best is White's, until the year 1834, when it ceased to give the longitudes for each day. For horary questions, the best now published is Partridge's Almanack.

Exaltation.—An essential dignity, next in power to that of house.

Face.—The weakest of all the essential dignities.

Fall.—A planet is in its fall when in the sign opposite to its exaltation. It shews a person in a weak and hopeless state, unless the planet be well aspected.

Familiarity.—Any kind of aspect or reception.

Feminine Signs.—These are all the even signs, reckoning from Aries ; as the 2d, 4th, 6th, 8th, &c.

Fiery Signs, or *Fiery Triplicity.*—♈, ♌, ♐.

Figure.—The diagram which represents the heavens at any time : it is also called a scheme or horoscope.

Fortunes.—♃ and ♀; and the ☉, ☽, and ☿, if aspecting them, and not afflicted, are considered fortunate planets.

Fruitful Signs.—♋, ♏, and ♓.

Frustration.—The cutting off or preventing any thing shewn by one aspect by means of another. Thus, if ♀, lady of the ascendant, were hastening to the △ of ♂, lord of the 7th, in a question of marriage, it might denote that the match would take place; but if ☿ were to form an ☍ of ♂ before ♀ reached her △ of that planet, it would be a frustration ; and would shew that the hopes of the querent would be cut off; and if ☿ were lord of the 12th, it might denote that it would be done by a private enemy.

Horary Questions.—So named from the Latin word *hora,* an

hour, because the time of their being asked is noted, and the figure of the heavens for that time is taken to judge the result. The word *hora* appears to be derived from the Egyptian name for the Sun, which Herodotus informs us was *Horus* or *Orus*; the Hebrew *or*, lux, light, or day, and *oriens*, eastern, all appear to have had the same origin. The Budhists call the Sun *Hiru*, which, with its Braminical name also, appears equally to have been derived from Egypt, the first cradle of astrology.

Horoscope.—The ascendant is sometimes so called; but it is more generally a term for the figure of the heavens used by astrologers for predicting by nativities, mundane astrology, and horary questions.

Houses.—The Twelve divisions or compartments into which the circle of the heavens is divided; also the signs in which any planet is said to have most influence.

Human Signs.— ♊, ♍, ♒, and the first half of ♐. Any person's significator therein, shews them to be of a humane disposition.

Impedited.—This signifies being afflicted by evil stars. The ☽ is impedited in the highest degree when in ♂ with ☉.

Joined to.—Being in any aspect.

Increasing in Light.—When any planet is leaving ☉, and is not yet arrived at the ☍; after which it decreases in light. The former is a good, the latter an evil testimony, especially as regards the ☽.

Increasing in Motion.—When any planet moves faster than it did on the preceding day.

Inferior Planets.— ♀, ☿, and ☽; so called because their orbit is inferior to that of the earth.

Infortunes.—♅, ♄, and ♂; also ☿ when he is much afflicted.

Intercepted.—A sign which is found between the cusps of two houses, and not on either of them.

Latitude.—The distance any star, &c., is north or south of the ecliptic. The ☉ never has any latitude. Latitude on the earth is the distance any place is north or south of the equator.

Lights.—The ☉ and ☽.

Light of Time.—The ☉ by day and the ☽ by night.

Longitude.—The distance any star, &c., is from the first point of ♈, or beginning of the zodiac.

Lord.—That planet whose house is occupied by any other, is said to be the lord or ruler of that other; and if his sign be on the cusp of any house, he is called the lord of that house. Thus, if ♈ ascend in any figure, ♂, who rules that sign, is the lord of the ascendant.

Masculine Signs.—They are the odd signs, viz. the 1st, 3d, 5th, &c.

Medium Cœli.—The midheaven.

Meridian.—The midheaven, or place where ☉ is at noon. The opposite point, or where ☉ is at midnight, the cusp of the 4th house, is the meridian under the earth.

Moveable Signs.—♈, ♋, ♎, and ♑.

Night Houses.—Those signs in which the planets are stronger by night than by day. See "Day Houses."

Nodes.—The points where any planet crosses the ecliptic in its path of latitude.

Occidental.—See "Oriental."

Order of the Houses.—They rank in power as follows:—1st, 10th, 7th, 4th, 11th, 5th, 9th, 3d, 2d, 8th, 6th, 12th.

Orb.—That distance round a planet to which its influence more particularly extends. The orb of the cusp of any house, a fixed star, or ⊕, is five degrees.

Oriental.—Planets found between the fourth house and the midheaven, rising, are in the eastern half of the figure, and said to be oriental. When they have passed the midheaven, and until they reach the 4th again, they are occidental. In nativities, the ☉ and ☽ are oriental from the 1st to the 10th, and from the 7th to the 4th, and occidental in the opposite quarters.

Peregrine.—Having no essential dignity whatever. A planet is not reckoned peregrine that is in mutual reception with any other.

Platic.—Any aspect which is not partile or exact, but only within orbs, or rather within the moiety of the two planets' orbs. As if ♄ be in ♈ 10°, and ☽ in ♎ 20°, the ☽ is still in ☍ to ♄ ; because the half of their joint orbs being 10° 30′, she still wants 30′ of being clear of his ☍.

Querent.—The person who queries or inquires.

Quesited.—The person or thing inquired about.

Radical.—That which belongs to the radix, or root; fit to be judged.

Reception.—The being received by any planet is being in that planet's essential dignities ; it is a good testimony when mutual. See "Dispose."

Refranation.—When two planets are coming to any aspect, and one falls retrograde before the aspect is complete, it denotes that the matter will wholly fail.

Retrograde.—When any planet is decreasing in longitude. It is a very great debility.

Separation.—When any aspect is past, but is yet within orbs, the planets are said to separate from each other. It denotes that the influence is passing away.

Significator.—The planet which is lord of the house which rules the matter inquired after, is the significator of the

quesited ; the lord ♐ the ascendant is the general significator of the querent. The ☽ is in general his consignificator.

Signs of Long Ascension.—♋, ♌, ♍, ♎, ♏, ♐.   A ✶ in
them is said to have the effect of a ☐, and a ☐ that of
a △.

Signs of Short Ascension.—♑, ♒, ♓, ♈, ♉, ♊.   A △ is
said to have the effect of a ☐, and a ☐ that of a ✶.

Swift in Motion.—When a planet moves faster than its mean
motion.

Table of Houses.—These are necessary to erect a figure of the
heavens.*

Term.—An essential dignity.   (See page 72.)

Testimony.—Having any aspect or dignity, &c., or being in
any way in operation in the figure as regards the question
asked.

Translation of Light.—The conveying the influence of one
planet to another, by separating from the aspect of one
and going to the aspect of the other.   It is a very powerful
testimony.

Triplicity.—An essential dignity.   The zodiac is divided into
four trigons, or triplicities; the fiery, ♈, ♌, ♐; the
earthy, ♉, ♍, ♑; the airy, ♊, ♎, ♒; and the watery,
♋, ♏, and ♓; agreeing with the four elements into which
the ancients divided the whole of the natural world.

Void of Course.—Forming no aspect in the sign it is in.
When ☽ is so, it denotes in general no success in the question.

Watery Signs.—♋, ♏, and ♓.

* A complete set for London and Liverpool, answering for all the
kingdom, follows the *Grammar of Astrology.*

Watery Triplicity.— ♋, ♏, and ♓.

Zodiac.—A belt which surrounds the earth, about eighteen degrees broad, in which the Sun and Planets continually move.

THE END OF INTRODUCTION TO ASTROLOGY.

other quality paperbacks
by NEWCASTLE

Self-Enrichment Books

S-2   LOVE, HATE, FEAR, ANGER
          and the other lively emotions   *By June Callwood* $2.45
G-6   IMPORTANCE OF FEELING INFERIOR
                                              By Marie Beynon Ray $2.95
P-10 FORTUNATE STRANGERS
                            By Cornelius Beukenkamp, Jr., M.D. $2.95
G-9   THE CONQUEST OF FEAR   *By Basil King* $2.95
H-4   YOU ARE WHAT YOU EAT   *By Victor H. Lindlahr* $2.25
D-11 VITAMIN COOKBOOK   *By Victor H. Lindlahr* $2.95
H-15 EAT AND REDUCE   *By Victor H. Lindlahr* $2.45
H-16 ROMANY REMEDIES AND RECIPES
                                    By Gipsy Petulengro $1.95

Occult Books

W-1   RITUAL MAGIC   *By E. M. Butler* $3.45
P-3   MAGIC, WHITE AND BLACK   *By Franz Hartmann, M.D.* $3.45
P-5   GHOSTS I HAVE MET   *By John Kendrick Bangs* $2.45
P-10 BOOK OF DREAMS AND GHOSTS   *By Andrew Lang* $2.95
P-8   THE DEVIL IN BRITAIN AND AMERICA *By John Ashton* $3.75
P-14 AN INTRODUCTION TO ASTROLOGY *By William R. Lilly* $3.75
T-7   FORTUNE TELLING FOR FUN   *By Paul Showers* $2.95
W-13 ORIGINS OF POPULAR SUPERSTITIONS AND CUSTOMS
                                  By T. Sharper Knowlson $2.95

Please check with your favorite Bookseller for any of the books listed
on this page or order directly from:
NEWCASTLE PUBLISHING COMPANY, INC.
1521 North Vine St., Hollywood California 90028

.NEWCASTLE PUBLISHING COMPANY, INC.